PICTURING
LOS ANGELES

PICTURING
LOS ANGELES

Jon and Nancy Wilkman

GIBBS SMITH
TO ENRICH AND INSPIRE HUMANKIND

Paperback Edition

15 14 13   5 4 3 2

Published by
Gibbs Smith
P.O. Box 667
Layton, Utah 84041

1.800.835.4993 orders
www.gibbs-smith.com

Designed by Steve Rachwal
Printed and bound in China

Gibbs Smith books are printed on either recycled, 100% post-consumer
waste, FSC-certified papers or on paper produced from sustainable PEFC-
certified forest/controlled wood source. Learn more at www.pefc.org.

Library of Congress Cataloging-in-Publication Data
Wilkman, Jon.
    Picturing Los Angeles/Jon and Nancy Wilkman.–1st ed.
        p. cm.
ISBN 978-1-58685-733-2 (hardcover)
ISBN 978-1-4236-2343-4 (paperback)
1. Los Angeles (Calif.)–History–Pictorial works.
I. Wilkman, Nancy. II. Title.
F869.L857W55 2006
979.4'94050222–dc22

                                    2006010132

CONTENTS

PREFACE

*"The problem with writing anything about Los Angeles is
that by the time it sees print it is no longer quite accurate."*

MIKE JACKSON, Columnist for the [now-defunct] Los Angeles Herald Examiner

Compared to Cairo, Beijing, London or New York, the history of Los Angeles may be relatively short, undervalued and often misunderstood, but to find it you only need to look. There is no more evocative way to begin than with a photograph.

Life in America's second-largest city can seem to defy the widest lens and fastest shutter speed, but decades of individual photographs, like frames of motion picture film, offer glimpses of an evolving portrait. Drawing upon more than two hundred years of images and human experience, the pages of *Picturing Los Angeles* offer a private screening of L.A.'s past.

The City of Angels, as it is sometimes proudly, and often ironically known, is perhaps the most photographed in the world, especially including images from the movies. One hundred years of movie-making have turned the streets, neighborhoods and landscape of Los Angeles — both the city and the region it represents — into an international image of America. But L.A. is much more than a product of Hollywood. The approximately 466 square miles within the city's borders could comfortably contain seven of America's most important metropolises, with a small strip left for the Island of Manhattan. Far from a superficial "Tinseltown," L.A. is one of the world's most complex and diverse urban environments, with an economy that ranks with nations, not just other cities.

So, how did this happen? The obvious answer is history.

Most of the images found in this book were first seen in newspapers. They include historical snapshots of the movie industry and the world of entertainment, sports, politics, industry, social change, crime, disasters, the arts and "features" from everyday life. Yet, even with millions of

Cathedral of Our Lady of the Angels, 2005.

Mission San Gabriel, 1875.

photographs to choose from, creating a historical portrait of Los Angeles also requires a search for images that have been ignored or overlooked. The lives of many Angelenos never made it to the pages of local newspapers, and not all pictures were considered fit to print. From the earliest days, L.A. was out to sell itself, and the sales pitch was illustrated with appealing glimpses of the good life and fun in the sun. Less flattering photographs were, if possible, left in the photographer's darkroom.

Outsiders also influenced the assembled portrait of Los Angeles. With the rise of the movies, life in the City of Angels was often characterized by glamour, scandal and shallow make believe. Representative or not, these were the pictures people wanted to see. Years of hyperbole and oversimplification left L.A. as a sitting duck for cynics. Even after the city grew into a major metropolis, many arbiters of greatness—mostly from the East Coast—glanced at what they saw as a hastily constructed urban improvisation and left appalled.

Despite this, there was always more to Los Angeles than the wittiest one-liner or superficial snapshot. In 1950, journalist Hamilton Basso wrote: "... [Los Angeles's] belief in newness and bigness, its addiction to fads, its hope for the future, its willingness to try anything once, its idealistic pragmatism, its cultural gropings and materialistic grain... [are] our national character writ large." To Basso and other less parochial evaluators, Los Angeles appeared to be alien and unformed because it was, for better or worse, a laboratory for America's future—a place that demanded to be measured by new standards, not defined by older urban ideals. In fact, as Los Angeles grew and changed, its identity wasn't formed by imitating the rest of the United States as much as it was a product of millions of newcomers—Americans, and others from around the world—arriving in Los Angeles to reimagine themselves and their lives, and in the process creating something new—a uniquely American city.

Whatever boosters may wish, L.A.'s history isn't solely a saga of glorious achievement. Along with innovation and hope, the pages of this book offer ample evidence of ignorance, injustice and unfulfilled promises. Los Angeles shares the ambitions, challenges and failures of other great world capitals, but unlike older cities, L.A.'s past isn't a stately procession, formed from ranks of tradition. More often it is as *L.A. Times* columnist Jack Smith described it: "A series of booms, punctuated with explosions."

A true portrait of Los Angeles can seem like a hyperactive kaleidoscope. *Picturing Los Angeles* is inspired and informed by that ever-shifting landscape. Given the scale and complexity of our subject, we can only touch highlights. Even so, we hope L.A. buffs enjoy perusing their favorite city's past, and we'd be pleased if academic historians find a few unexpected tidbits. But ultimately this book is not only meant for enthusiasts or specialists, but for anyone who has encountered the enormity and ambiguities of Los Angeles and wondered: What is this place, how did it get the way it is and what in the world does it mean? The answers are part of a story as Angeleno as enchiladas, automobiles and Walt Disney Concert Hall, and as American as diversity, struggle and change. With each new photograph, decades pass, and image by image, the City of Angels is transformed from an isolated Mexican outpost to the quintessential American city.

ACKNOWLEDGMENTS

We wish to thank our many friends and fellow Los Angeles enthusiasts and historians for their invaluable camaraderie, support and expertise. Special thanks go to editor/writer/bookseller Davis Dutton for suggesting us as writers for this book, as well as acting as a knowledgeable early reader of our text. Many people and institutions assisted with gathering photos, especially Carolyn Kozo Cole, Curator of the Los Angeles Public Library Photo Collection, and Dace Taube of the University of Southern California Regional History Collection. Distinguished California historian Leonard Pitt read drafts of the text, as did writer/editor Lee Dembart. If there remain any errors or ill-conceived ideas, it is because we failed to follow their sage advice.

— JON AND NANCY WILKMAN

FROM OUTPOST TO UPSTART

"To my mind, this spot can be given the preference
in everything, in soil, water, and trees…
It has all the requisites for a large settlement."

FRAY JUAN CRESPÍ, Diaries, August 1769

The United States of America and the City of Los Angeles were conceived about the same time, but separated at birth. In the 1760s, while English colonists were grumbling about taxes, across the continent the empire of Spain was securing holdings in Alta California. Russians were probing southward from Alaska and there was little time to lose.

In 1769, a party of Spanish explorers, led by military officer Gaspar de Portolá, headed north from Loreto in Baja California. On August 2, after almost five months and more than 800 miles, the expedition arrived in a basin of gently rolling grassland, surrounded by low-lying hills. In the distance, farther north and east, a range of rugged mountains rose steeply into an overcast sky. Nearby, a meandering river snaked lazily past, heading south toward the ocean, roughly twenty-five miles away. Portolá and his men set up camp beside the shallow tree-lined stream. In celebration of an annual Franciscan feast day, they named the river and the surrounding area Nuestra Señora de los Angeles de la Porciúncula (Our Lady of the Angels of the Porciúncula). Porciúncula is the name of a chapel in Italy known as the cradle of the Franciscan order.

During their travels in the area, the Spaniards already had been introduced to a local hazard—

L.A.'S FIRST PHOTO. This is believed to be the first photograph of Los Angeles, taken in the late 1850s or early 1860s. Agricultural fields and the L.A. River are in the distance. In the foreground, the plaza looks deserted. If any Angelenos were around and moving, the camera's long exposure reduced them to invisible blurs. The square building in the lower left is a brick reservoir, evidence of the importance of water.

CONTEMPORARY PHOTO OF EAGLE ROCK. Tongva Indians, the first Angelenos, harvested acorns near this natural landmark named for the shape of an eagle in flight apparent on the face of the rock.

earthquakes, including one that "lasted about half as long as an Ave Maria." This didn't dissuade Fray Juan Crespí, a priest and diarist with the expedition. He wrote enthusiastically that the campsite near the Rio de Porciúncula "had all the requisites for a large settlement." The friendly Tongva villagers who greeted them had known that for hundreds, if not thousands, of years.

The Portolá expedition was part of a first step in an ambitious effort initiated by Spanish King Carlos III, at the urging of his representative in Mexico, José de Gálvez. The ultimate plan for Alta California included missions, military forts or presidios, as well as agricultural pueblos. To smooth the way, fifty-five-year-old Franciscan Father Junípero Serra began establishing a string of twenty-one missions to provide way stations, "civilize" the Indians and extend Christianity. The first of these was Mission San Diego de Alcalá. The fourth was San Gabriel Arcángel, consecrated by Serra subordinates in 1771. A short distance away, a few years later, as part of an extensive settlement program, the region's governor, Felipe de Neve, chose a site for a pueblo.

Los Angeles was founded in a manner that modern commentators might characterize as "laid back." During the summer of 1781, small groups of settlers recruited from the Mexican provinces of Sinaloa and Sonora left Mission San Gabriel and trekked nine miles to a site near the Tongva village of Yabit and the Rio de Porciúncula. Here would be the Mexican

RIO DE PORCIÚNCULA. Essential to the survival of the pueblo and city, the Los Angeles River met all domestic and agricultural water needs until the early twentieth century.

immigrants' new home. Although the last of the original forty-four *pobladores,* or settlers, wouldn't arrive until later, the new community was formally established on September 4, 1781. It was called El Pueblo de la Reyna de los Angeles: The town of the Queen of Angels.

While the *pobladores* were settling in, rebel English colonists celebrated at Yorktown, Virginia, marking a turning point in their war for independence. Despite these shared landmarks, with little in common, neither side of the continent took much notice of the other. It would be a while before they did, and even longer before they acknowledged a shared heritage.

Infant L.A. was far from impressive. Established on twenty-eight square miles, the settlement—little more than a cluster of huts—had ample water and a pleasant climate. Although there were a number of nearby Native American villages, as well as Mission San Gabriel, the pueblo was as isolated as a colony on the moon. The first citizens were a multi-ethnic gathering, with African, Indian and Spanish bloodlines. They were granted plots of land, and by 1788, the settlement had its first *alcalde,* or mayor, José Venegas, a shoemaker.

By 1790, New York was already the largest city in the new United States of America with a population of 33,131. In the Spanish outpost of Los Angeles the head count (excluding Indians) was 139. By the early 1800s, the West Coast settlement had more cows than people. Grassy hills provided ideal grazing land, supporting an economy based on hides, tallow and beef. While Boston, New York and Philadelphia were bursting with mercantile ambition, Angelenos (presumably the men) were described by one morally outraged missionary as "a set of idlers, addicted to cards, song, and the seduction of Indian women."

Initially, Alta California may not have appeared promising, but it wasn't long before other countries were eyeing northern New Spain's untapped potential. Shortly after dropping anchor in San Diego harbor on March 17, 1803, the crew of an American fur-trading ship, *Lelia Byrd,* commanded by Captain William Shaler, attempted to commandeer a cache of otter hides. Caught in the act, the Yankees were forced to fire their shipboard cannons to escape—the first armed conflict between Mexicans and Americans. That didn't stop others from coming. On the way home from trading in Hawaii and Asia, ships from England and the United States stealthily sized up the California coast, and whenever possible, indulged in a little smuggling.

In 1818, Joseph Chapman became the first English-speaking newcomer to settle in El Pueblo de Los Angeles. A carpenter and

blacksmith from Maine, Chapman was a crew member on a pirate ship when he was cap- tured during an attack on the Alta California port of Monterey. Later pardoned, he came to the Los Angeles area where he joined the set- tlement's roughly 650 residents. His skills proved useful in the construction of a dam and gristmill for the prosperous Mission San Gabriel as well as the church that still stands beside L.A.'s old plaza.

In 1821, Mexico won a war of independ- ence from Spain, marking the beginning of the end of the Spanish mission system. Mission life had been hard on Native Americans. Secularization left them worse, and defense- less against disease and starvation. As the Mexican government struggled to stabilize newly won freedoms, foreigners continued to close in. In 1826, an American fur trader, Jedediah Smith, blazed a trail to Los Angeles. When the *extranjero,* or foreigner, showed up

at Mission San Gabriel, alarmed and annoyed Californios told him to go back to where he came from. He did, but not before surrepti- tiously scouting central and northern California.

Another American arrival, Abel Stearns, was allowed to stay. Before settling in Los Angeles around 1832, he'd already converted to Catholicism and become a naturalized Mexican citizen. With income from his accu- mulation of expanses of land and great herds of cattle, supplemented by occasional smug- gling, "Don Abel" was soon one of California's richest men. Also helpful was his marriage, at age forty, to fourteen-year-old Arcadia Bandini, the beautiful daughter of a wealthy and power- ful Mexican landowner, Don Juan Bandini.

After escaping angry Mexican officials in the southwest trading town of Taos, the first overland party of American immigrants arrived in Los Angeles in 1841. Their leaders were Englishman William Workman and Missourian

John Rowland. Life-long friends, Rowland and Workman became prominent Anglo dons. So did Benjamin "Don Benito" Wilson. After arriving with the Rowland-Workman Party, Wilson married heiress Ramona Yorba and acquired acres of rancho lands, including the present site of the University of California at Los Angeles. His vineyards produced some of the area's finest wines.

L.A.'s pioneer vintner was Frenchman Jean Louis Vignes. In 1831, Vignes planted vines imported from France, eventually making Los Angeles a center for early American wine production. Southern California's most famous agricultural product, oranges, got a start in 1804 when a small grove was planted at Mission San Gabriel. Beginning in 1841, former Kentucky fur trapper William Wolfskill cultivated 2,500 orange trees, creating what would become the largest grove in the United States.

For most of the world, the earliest impressions of the Pueblo of Los Angeles came from *Two Years Before the Mast,* reminiscences of the 1835 to 1836 adventures of a novice seaman and future reformer from Boston, Richard Henry Dana Jr. In the San Pedro mudflats that

ABEL STEARNS, an early Yankee immigrant and one of the richest men in California during Mexican rule, served as a member of the state's first American constitutional convention.

ARCADIA BANDINI, probably in her forties in this portrait, was one of the early pueblo's great beauties when she became the wife of Abel Stearns. After his death, she married Robert Baker, cofounder of Santa Monica. When she died, an elegant heiress in 1912, she left $8 million, one of early L.A.'s largest estates.

RICHARD HENRY DANA JR., a Bostonian, visited the California coast as a common seaman aboard the brig *Pilgrim* in the 1830s. His descriptions of the Pueblo of Los Angeles were vivid but far from flattering.

DON PÍO PICO was born in San Gabriel in 1801. A revolutionary as a young man, Pico attempted to adapt to the influx of Yankees after the American conquest, but the last Mexican governor of California died powerless and poor in 1894.

passed as a port for Los Angeles, Dana was miserable loading dried hides, now valuable enough to be known as "California bank notes." With Yankee indignation he described the pueblo as primitive and lawless, and considered the town's citizens to be susceptible to a laziness known as "California Fever." Dana was impressed by the prosperous Anglo dons, including Stearns and Wilson, but left with little hope for the City of Angels.

That didn't stop the United States from looking for an opportunity to extend its domain from coast to coast. In 1846, with dreams of "Manifest Destiny," President James K. Polk declared war on Mexico and rallied the United States to claim North America as a divinely determined birthright. An old and overextended Spanish empire, and internal squabbles among the Mexicans, resulted in a relatively easy American victory in 1848. The conflict in California had ended the year before. On

January 13, 1847, in an adobe at the northern end of Cahuenga Pass in Los Angeles, across from today's Universal Studios, American Lieutenant Colonel John C. Fremont and Mexican Commander Andrés Pico agreed to terms for local Mexican capitulation. In the end, the United States government paid Mexico $15 million for conquered southwestern land, and in 1850, California joined the Union as the thirty-first state.

That same year, the County and City of Los Angeles were defined and declared officially American. The first federal census reported a county population of 3,530, including 344 Indians, twelve free African Americans, eight Jewish settlers and two Chinese. But the action was in San Francisco. Near there, in 1848, gold had been discovered, attracting a sudden rush of new arrivals from across America and around the world. Los Angeles was quickly left

THE VICENTE LUGO FAMILY, Californio pioneers, pose at their rancho home around 1892. Vicente's father, Antonio Maria Lugo, typified the aristocratic horseman of the 1850s and '60s. His saddle, bridle and spurs were made of silver and worth $1,500, a small fortune at the time.

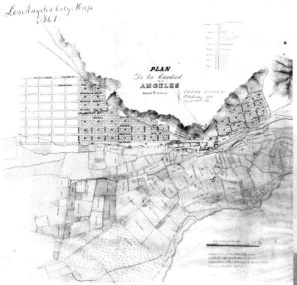

AMERICAN L.A.'S FIRST MAP. **After the U.S. conquest of California, Los Angeles hired Army Lieutenant Edward Ord to survey the city as it existed in 1849.**

EARLY VIEW OF L.A. **One of the first images of Los Angeles, a sketch by William Hutton in 1849.**

behind, and in time, so was nearly a century of Hispanic California.

During the early 1800s, much of Southern California was divided into enormous ranchos. These great tracts were granted mostly to soldiers and citizens for services to Mexico and the Spanish government. They provided their owners, such as the Domínguez, Lugo and Sepúlveda families, with sizable fortunes. Upper-class Californios, as they were called, lived with as much elegance and grandeur as isolated Los Angeles allowed. Foreign ships brought furniture and fashions. Horse races, fights between bears and bulls, and all-night fandangos provided the pueblo with entertainment. Mexican vaqueros set the standards

for the cowboys of the American West, and the hospitality of the dons was gracious and generous. As romantic as this sounds, much of the relatively comfortable existence of the Californio elite was supported, as it was during Mission days, by the near-slave labor of local Native Americans.

When the Americans took over, this atmosphere of feudal gentility quickly changed. Eyeing the pueblo and surrounding ranchos, the Yankees' first thoughts were to organize open land into marketable real estate. During the summer of 1849, U.S. Army Lieutenant Edward O. C. Ord created the city's first map. Assisting him was artist William Rich Hutton. As the pair staked off plots, numbered lots

TIBURCIO VÁSQUEZ. During the unsettled times after the American conquest, Tiburcio Vásquez was considered a bandit by some, a revolutionary by others. He once had a double bounty on his head—$8,000 alive, $6,000 dead. Vásquez was finally captured on May 14, 1874, near the corner of Santa Monica Boulevard and Kings Road in present-day West Hollywood.

and labeled streets in both Spanish and English, Hutton sketched the pueblo's first portraits. In the summer of 1857, a traveler from Hungary provided words that pictured the city further: "The streets of Los Angeles are not elegant. The houses are low, long and of a single story, without exception. They have dark, prison-like exteriors, endless covered porches, and small windows screened by iron or wooden bars through which the female population peeps from dawn to sunset."

The ink on the Ord survey was hardly dry before American Angelenos held their first real estate auction. In rancho days, boundaries were usually defined by a prominent tree or other natural landmark. In 1851, the U.S. government issued the Land Act. The Americans demanded that the Mexican dons prove their ownership with maps and legal paperwork. To the Californios, the process was alien, time-consuming and costly. It wasn't long before most of the old Mexican ranchos passed into the hands of Yankees and their lawyers. When

the last of the original *pobladores* of El Pueblo de la Reyna de los Angeles, Maria Guadalupe Gertrudis Pérez (Nieto), died in 1860, L.A.'s Mexican identity was being rapidly overrun.

In the 1850s and '60s, the pueblo was the wildest of Wild West towns. William Brewer, an 1860 traveler, wrote: "Fifty or sixty murders per year have been so common here in Los Angeles . . . As I write this there are at least six heavy loaded revolvers in the tent, besides bowie knives and other arms." Vigilante committees were formed to keep the peace and mete out instant justice. Some displaced Californios had turned to banditry. One of the most famous was Tiburcio Vásquez. "I believe we were unjustly deprived of the social rights that belonged to us," he said. For nearly twenty years, Vásquez and his gang roamed California, raiding towns and robbing stagecoaches. A favorite hideout was an unusual formation of rocky ledges north of Los Angeles. A century later, Vásquez Rocks would become famous as a location for westerns and science fiction movies. Vásquez was finally captured in what is today West Hollywood. Facing his fate with dignity that even Anglos admired, the wily bandit was hanged in 1875. Reportedly, he had only one last word: *"pronto."*

In the chaos and violence of the 1850s, Los Angeles struggled to build a community. Not all new arrivals were lawless. "This City of Angels," painter John W. Audubon commented as early as 1849, "is anything else, unless the angels are fallen ones, but Americans are pouring in, and in a few years will make a beautiful place of it."

It took courage to immigrate across the Atlantic to the American East Coast. It took even more bravery and initiative to venture to the far reaches of Los Angeles. Getting there involved a hazardous and exhausting cross-continental trek, or a journey by ship to the malaria-infested Isthmus of Panama, with its shortcut to the Pacific, or an even lengthier voyage around the southern tip of South America. Those who arrived safely and stayed were tough, determined and enterprising.

Nineteen-year-old Harris Newmark emigrated from Prussia in 1853. His Uncle Joseph, a lay rabbi, had come to San Francisco a year before. In Los Angeles, the younger Newmark joined a small but ambitious immigrant community that included settlers from France, Germany, Italy and other parts of Europe. Jewish pioneers like the Newmarks were already establishing themselves in the American West. In L.A., Joseph Newmark helped form the Hebrew Benevolent Society in 1854, the city's first charitable institution. By 1873, Congregation

HARRIS NEWMARK AND HIS WIFE, SARAH, were pioneers in Los Angeles's nineteenth-century Jewish community. Newmark's *Sixty Years in Southern California: 1853–1913* is a classic of early Los Angeles history.

ST. VINCENT'S HOSPITAL. The humble Aguilar adobe provided space for the first hospital in Los Angeles, established by the Catholic Daughters of Charity in 1858.

L.A. LAW IN 1870. On December 17, 1870, a crowd, including children, gathers to watch vigilantes hang an accused murderer. Ironically, the hill in the background would later be the site of the county courthouse.

WATER WHEEL. From 1858 until it collapsed in 1861, this forty-foot-tall wheel lifted precious water from a spring near modern-day Chinatown. Carried by flume to a reservoir in the plaza, the water was distributed to users through wooden pipes.

B'nai B'rith was established enough to build an impressive synagogue. Harris Newmark eventually became a successful businessman; however, he is known best for his detailed and invaluable 1916 memoir of sixty years in early Los Angeles.

In 1856, the Daughters of Charity, an organization of fearless Catholic Sisters, traveled across the continent and set up an orphanage, a private school for girls and L.A.'s first hospital. Other 1850's landmarks include the first house made of brick, built on Wine (later Olvera) Street; two new school-houses; a public library; the first Spanish-language newspaper, *El Clamor Público;* a new brick reservoir to supply the pueblo with water; an informal bank; and the earliest availability of oysters and ice cream—consumed separately, of course.

In 1858, the first Butterfield Stagecoach arrived with mail and passengers. Originating in St. Louis, it made the trip to San Francisco via Los Angeles in twenty-four days and twenty-three hours. By that same year, Phineas Banning, an entrepreneurial young man from Wilmington, Delaware, had visions of turning the unimpressive tidal mudflats of San Pedro into an important West Coast port. Like generations of Angelenos to come, Banning's dream, and his fortunes, would greatly benefit from government contracts.

FIRST SYNAGOGUE. **In 1873, L.A.'s first Jewish synagogue was constructed between Second and Third streets. This photo was taken around 1880.**

Some of the first resulted from a deepening national debate over slavery that would erupt into civil war.

California had joined the United States as a "free" state, where slavery was illegal, but with many immigrants from the South, in the election of 1860, Angelenos voted two to one

BRIDGET "BIDDY" MASON was a slave brought to Los Angeles in 1851. She won her freedom in a landmark 1856 court case and went on to become wealthy by investing in real estate.

THE PRIMITIVE PORT OF SAN PEDRO, as it appeared in the 1860s, gives little indication of the major transformations to come. They would be hastened by the Civil War.

against Abraham Lincoln. Despite this, there were citizens determined to uphold the Union and the law. African American slave Bridget "Biddy" Mason was brought to Los Angeles by her master in 1851. In 1856, when her owner threatened to leave California and return her to bondage, Robert Owens, a prominent free African American Angeleno, came to her aid and the issue was brought before local district judge Benjamin Hayes, a Southern sympathizer. In defiance of pro-slavery Angelenos, Hayes followed the law at the time and ruled in favor of Mason's right to freedom.

Biddy Mason stayed in Los Angeles as a midwife and raised a family. Just as entrepreneurial and socially involved as any of her fellow Angelenos, she invested wisely in downtown real estate and became a founding member of the First African Methodist Episcopal Church, still a religious heart of the African American community in Los Angeles. When Biddy Mason died in 1891, she was well known and respected, mourned in both the city's black and white communities.

During the 1860s, Phineas Banning's wagon transportation and trading businesses

PHINEAS BANNING. **Ever the entrepreneur, after his arrival in Los Angeles in 1851, Banning opened wagon trading routes, built harbor facilities and, in partnership with Benjamin Wilson, brought Los Angeles its first local railroad in 1869.**

prospered. In the early years of the decade, an older segment of the local economy was hit hard. Nature regularly reasserted itself as the citizens of the city attempted to tame their surroundings. Beginning in 1861, heavy rains and flooding, followed by a long period of drought, left cattle with little food and weak and diseased. It wasn't long before 80 percent of Southern California's extensive herds were dead, marking the end of the region's cattle-based economy.

About this time, the pueblo was pictured for the first time in a photograph. It is a lonely and even forlorn image, but the City of Angels was preparing to make a more active impression.

In 1860, a transcontinental telegraph line was completed to San Francisco, and from there south to Los Angeles, where it connected the city to most of America. In 1869, gas lamps appeared on L.A.'s unpaved streets. That same year, Billy Buffum, owner of a local saloon, led a move to establish the city's first volunteer fire department. Also in that year, Phineas Banning unveiled his latest entrepreneurial endeavor — a little locomotive named San Gabriel, delivered from San Francisco. It was

CAMELS IN LOS ANGELES. **During the Civil War, camels were used for transportation in the Southwest. Here, one is parked at Camp Drum in Wilmington. The imported beasts were often uncooperative, and after eight years the scheme was abandoned.**

a proud moment. Later, a second steam engine was shipped around Cape Horn from the Schenectady Locomotive Works in New York. This time L.A. boosters got a humbling reminder that their frontier hometown was less than world famous. They had specified that the new locomotive proudly display the city's name. When the engine arrived a name was there, but the sign painter in far away Schenectady had misspelled it — Los Angel*os*.

Despite this minor humiliation, the trains of the Los Angeles & San Pedro Railroad provided modern technology to move cargo to and from a still-primitive port. Horse-drawn buses, a more conventional means of getting around, began to appear on city streets in the early 1870s and were soon conveying visitors to the elegant, three-story Pico House Hotel, opened in 1870, owned by California's last Mexican governor, Don Pío Pico. Not to be outdone, the nearby Bella Union declared that it was "the best hotel south of San Francisco."

In 1870, the population of Los Angeles had grown to 5,728, and the city celebrated with a new theater, the Merced. Adobes were being rapidly replaced by wood-framed homes, and multistory commercial buildings rose from streets that were often dust-blown or mired in mud. Contrary to these new signs of "civilization," L.A. still had rough and

ST. VIBIANA'S CATHEDRAL was dedicated in 1876 and completed four years later. It was severely damaged in the 1994 earthquake. Replaced by the Cathedral of Our Lady of the Angels, St. Vibiana's was renovated and reopened as an arts center in 2005.

THE LOS ANGELES PLAZA IN 1876. The old Spanish-style Plaza church, left, has been fitted with a Victorian-style cupola, evidence of a new Anglo identity superimposed over a Hispanic past.

L.A.'S FIRST HOTEL. Competing for the title of early L.A.'s luxury hotel was the Bella Union, seen here in 1871.

THE LAPD IN 1876. By the end of the 1870s, L.A. was slowly becoming civilized. There was even an official police force.

LAFAYETTE HOTEL STAGE. Around 1875, a stagecoach owned by the Lafayette Hotel poses with the one-story Coronel Adobe in the background beside the Calle de los Negros. The brick building, left, housed a general store and corner saloon selling five-cent beer.

L.A.'S FIRST RAILROAD. Around 1880, four Los Angeles & San Pedro Railroad cars are parked at the Los Angeles Depot at Alameda and Commercial streets.

CHINESE RAILROAD WORKERS in 1876, photographed near where the Southern Pacific Railroad finished the last section connecting San Francisco and Los Angeles, linking L.A. to the rest of America by rail.

sometimes brutal edges. The Gold Rush and the building of the Western railroads had brought thousands of Chinese to California. Nearly all men, they settled throughout the state, keeping mostly to themselves, and working hard. Because of this, many Americans viewed them as inscrutable, and worse, a threat to their jobs.

In Los Angeles on October 24, 1871, long-seething anti-Chinese hostility turned violent. When police attempted to intervene in a Chinese community dispute, Robert Thompson, a "respected citizen," was shot and killed. In angry response, a mob of Angelenos took justice into their own hands. In five hours of lawless fury, the mob murdered nineteen Chinese men and boys, hanging fifteen of

them in front of a local shoe store and on the gate of a nearby lumberyard. The few law-abiding Angelenos who tried to restore order were ignored. After an investigation and lengthy trials, seven rioters were convicted and shipped off to San Quentin State Prison, only to be later exonerated and released on appeal.

The Chinese Massacre, as it was known, put Los Angeles in East Coast headlines for the first time. Those who read the news in the *New York Times* pictured the City of Angels as backward and brutal. Eastern clergymen wondered if missionaries should be sent to Christianize the town. However, in 1876, this grim first impression began to change. In that year, Los Angeles welcomed the first Southern Pacific trains from San Francisco, providing a transcontinental link to the rest of the nation. L.A.'s insignificance and distant isolation were coming to an end.

To encourage travelers, and increase revenues, the railroad heavily promoted Southern California as a sunny paradise. For its part, L.A. was pleased to picture itself as a Garden of Eden, with a climate that was a boon to good health and long life. The weather was certainly pleasant, but most of the city's more colorful and luxurious landscape was imported. Transplanted citrus flourished, eucalyptus trees from Australia were first used as wind-breaks and immigrant palm trees contributed to an environment that suggested a Biblical oasis. Surrounded by a semi-desert, newcomers didn't care where the greenery came from, they viewed it as a sign of fertility and great promise.

Since the 1860s, the L.A. area had been pictured as a natural sanitarium for sufferers of tuberculosis and other debilitating diseases. If the gold seekers of the 1850s transformed San Francisco, in the 1870s and '80s, Southern California experienced a "Sick Rush" that had even greater impact on

SONORA TOWN. Around 1885, a view of the Mexican community north of the Plaza Church. In the decades to come, railroad facilities and industrial development would encroach in this old neighborhood, forcing poor families to move.

PORT OF SAN PEDRO. Lumber shipped from the Northwest was vital for the growth of relatively treeless Los Angeles. In the background is Dead Man's Island, named for invading U.S. soldiers buried there after they were killed by Mexican Angelenos defending their city in 1846.

CENTRAL PARK. Around 1880, looking down at L.A.'s oldest park. It was later named Pershing Square after the U.S. WWI general, John J. Pershing.

1878. An American town emerges. Looking north on Main Street. The "skyscraper" in the distance is the Baker Block, built on the site of El Palacio, Abel Stearns' one-story adobe home, considered lavish in its day.

THE FIRST ELECTRIC LIGHT POLE was installed on Main Street, a little north of Commercial. Eight stories high, the light was turned on for the first time on December 31, 1882.

CALLE DE LOS NEGROS. Looking north on Calle de los Negros around 1882. As evidence of "civilization" and the impact of new technology, multilayered utility poles tower over the site of the 1871 Chinese Massacre.

REAL ESTATE OFFICE. Once the city hall and later a jail, in 1882, this old adobe was a combination rail, real estate and insurance office—just in time for the "Boom of the '80s."

BARREN LOS ANGELES, looking toward foothills above the agricultural community that would become Hollywood. In 1886, there's not much in between, but the size of scattered homes indicates that many L.A. residents are well off.

Los Angeles. Every week trainloads of new arrivals, weak and coughing, staggered into local health resorts and boarding houses. In 1875, the city of Pasadena was founded by health-conscious colonists from Indiana. That same year, Santa Monica became a primitive but popular seaside retreat.

Not all visitors were sickly. Some simply came to avoid Midwest and East Coast winters. The wealthier sun seekers could afford the comforts of grand new hotels. Some decided to stay and built mansions on Bunker Hill overlooking downtown Los Angeles or along thoroughfares such as Pasadena's Orange Grove Avenue. Like European immigrants arriving on the East Coast, American new-comers in Los Angeles were "yearning to breathe free," but they were far from "huddled masses." Many arrived with profits from a successful business or the sale of the family farm, and not all new arrivals were immediately impressed. An immigrant from Keokuk, Iowa, wrote home in 1877: "We have been walking around . . . the narrow streets full of strange

HERE COME THE TOURISTS. In 1887, at the height of the "Boom of the '80s," newcomers arrive on opening day at the Hotel Wilmore in Long Beach.

A FLORAL PARADISE. Near Lake Avenue in Altadena, travelers stop close to the end of the Red Car line to gather and admire poppies, just the kind of photograph that encouraged thousands more to come to Los Angeles.

Spanish and Chinese faces, passing low adobe houses swarming with dusky children and reeking with foreign odors.... The eastern element here is not of the highest order; the streets seem full of reckless hard-looking cases." The Iowan stayed but she and her husband decided to settle in more sedate Pasadena.

A sedate life was not the goal of Helen Hunt Jackson. The successful New England writer was passionate about America's cruel and unjust treatment of Native Americans. In 1852, there were fifteen thousand former Southern California Mission Indians. When Jackson visited Los Angeles in 1882, thirty years later, there were only four thousand. Death and disease had a heavy hand. Jackson's 1881 book, *A Century of Dishonor,* was a searing indictment of U.S. government policies toward Native Americans, but it had little impact. She decided to try to attract a wider audience with a novel. The result, in 1884, was *Ramona,* a book that changed the course of Southern California history. But not as Jackson hoped.

HELEN HUNT JACKSON. Writer and activist for Native Americans, Jackson, author of the novel *Ramona,* makes an appropriately imposing impression in this 1884 photograph.

MYTH AND REALITY MIX. Ramona Lubo, a Cahuilla woman, photographed as the "real" Ramona, the heroine of Helen Hunt Jackson's influential novel, poses beside the grave of her murdered husband Juan Diego, called Alessandro in the book.

ANTONIO CORONEL, Helen Hunt Jackson's friend, serenades his wife, Mariana, at their Los Angeles adobe around 1886. At the time one of the city's most famous Californios, Coronel held many city and county positions. His personal collection became the basis of L.A.'s first museum.

Ramona was inspired in part by the author's conversations with Don Antonio Coronel, a wise and kindly former mayor and Californio survivor from the 1830s. In 1883, the old don was a founding member of the Historical Society of Southern California. Although Jackson's book is infused with his nostalgic memories of rancho life, her plot was driven by Yankee cruelty and injustice. Despite this, most readers glossed over the writer's outrage, preferring idyllic images of gentle padres and bright-eyed senoritas, and L.A. boosters made her more romantic imagery an essential part of their sales pitch. In books, pamphlets and advertising, promoters promised newcomers the "real" land of Ramona. It wasn't long before Helen Hunt Jackson's misunderstood work of fiction was transformed into a romanticized history that was as colorful and reassuring as it was a powerful tool for tourism.

The timing couldn't have been better. In

VILLE DE PARIS. A 1931 newspaper photo editor cropped this 1880s photo of a fancy dry goods store on Broadway, leaving some of the proud staff out of the picture, as well as the future historical record.

IMPORTING EDEN, 1889. **A palm tree is moved into place to impress arrivals at the Southern Pacific's new Arcade Depot at Fifth Street and Central Avenue.**

1885, with the arrival of the Santa Fe Railroad, Los Angeles welcomed a second transcontinental link. A heated rate war followed, bringing a new rush of tourists and hopeful transplants. For one day in 1886, the cost of a ticket from Kansas City was reduced to $1. During the next two years, Los Angeles experienced a real estate boom that was unprecedented in American history. In 1883, the editorial pages of the *Times* proudly invited all comers to the new paradise on the Pacific: "Los Angeles people do not carry arms. Indians are a curiosity, the gee string is not a common article of apparel here, and Los Angeles has three good hotels, twenty-seven churches, and 350 telephone subscribers."

Urged by enthusiastic promoters and a cacophony of railroad advertising, land prices spiraled as property was bought and sold, sometimes more than once in a single day. A lot that was considered worthless in 1885 was snapped up for $40,000 two years later. In 1886, money changed hands at the rate of $3 million a month, a staggering figure in the 1880s. Los Angeles was overrun with new

PETE JOHNSON. **Most of the new arrivals of the 1880s were white, but L.A. already had a small African American community, including street preacher Pete Johnson, seen here in Chinatown, offering a lively sermon.**

DIRECT FROM SUNNY L.A. In 1886, this train rushed fresh California fruit to Midwest and East Coast markets, another lure to what was advertised as the cornucopia of Los Angeles.

HAZARD'S PAVILION, built in 1887 at the corner of Fifth and Olive, was a major arts and entertainment center in nineteenth-century Los Angeles. It was torn down in 1906 to make way for Temple Auditorium, the first home of the Los Angeles Philharmonic.

arrivals seeking a place in the heavily promoted American paradise. Some bought ready-to-build kits from mail-order catalogs and camped in tents as their new homes were built. Of course, it couldn't last. By 1888, the fever passed, but by the end of the decade, Los Angeles was no longer a small town. In 1880, the census counted 11,183 Angelenos. Ten years later, there were 50,395, more than four times as many.

As a result of this growth, the 1880s was a decade of new beginnings. In 1877, the city changed the name of the dirt passageway where the Chinese Massacre occurred. From then on Calle de los Negros (sometimes crudely known as "Nigger Alley") would be Los Angeles Street. In 1880, stretches of Main Street were paved, and the Methodist Episcopal Church founded the University of Southern California. In 1882, Los Angeles became one of the first American cities to illuminate its streets with electricity. That same year, telephones were installed. Child's Grand Opera House opened in 1884, presenting plays and musicals "direct from New York City." The most impressive cultural center was Hazard's Pavilion, which opened in 1887 with four thousand seats, a restaurant, art salon and grand entrance with fifty-foot-high ceilings.

ELIAS "LUCKY" BALDWIN shows a winning hand in a game with local reporters. When asked about L.A. real estate, he said, "Hell, we're giving away the land. We're selling the climate."

LUCKY BALDWIN'S COTTAGE. The Queen Anne–style home still stands in the Los Angeles County Arboretum. Modern readers may recognize it from the 1970s and '80s television series *Fantasy Island*.

Los Angeles theaters may have been impressive, but for many, the great showplace of Southern California in the 1870s and '80s was east of Pasadena—the Santa Anita Ranch, owned by Elias "Lucky" Baldwin. Seeing the area for the first time, Baldwin was said to have declared: "By gad, this is paradise! I'm going to buy it!" He soon assembled great herds of cattle and maintained vineyards that produced four hundred thousand gallons of wine a year. He was most famous for a stable of thoroughbred horses, including three Kentucky Derby winners. Lucky acquired his nickname as a result of more than one gift of good fortune.

An early source of his wealth came from the Comstock silver mine. As the story goes, before leaving on a world tour he instructed his broker to sell his shares in another of his mining interests if the price fell. It did, but Baldwin had forgotten to leave the key to the safe where the share certificates were kept.

CABLE CAR OPENING.
Angelenos celebrate the inauguration of a double-track electric
cable car line, June 8, 1889.
Replacing horse cars, new rail
systems proved especially
advantageous for real estate
developers with land to sell on
the outskirts of the city.

BUGGIES ON SUNSET. Cruising Sunset Boulevard in the 1890s. L.A. was already on the move.

GETTING AROUND IN 1892. A Southern Pacific Depot horse-drawn trolley pauses for a portrait with the Los Angeles Post Office in the background.

FIRE! A subject that would become a news photo staple. At 10 a.m. on December 16, 1887, pistol shots called firemen to a major blaze at the elegant Belmont resort hotel on Bunker Hill. As the building burned down, staff and guests saved what they could and gathered their belongings outside.

MAKING WAY FOR PROGRESS. In 1888, the first Los Angeles high school is lifted up and over a cable car route. It was moved from a prominent hilltop site to make way for a new county courthouse.

Because of this, his broker was unable to follow his orders. That didn't stop other panicky investors who sold and lost heavily. Then, unexpectedly, the mine produced another strike and was soon worth even more than before. Baldwin returned from his trip to find himself wealthier than when he left. If his broker had been able to sell, his fortunate client would have been wiped out.

Along with good fortune, Lucky Baldwin enjoyed the good life. Married at least four times, he preferred very young mistresses. When he was fifty-six, a sixteen-year-old former lover won $75,000 after he broke his promise to marry her. When he was sixty he faced a paternity suit. In his defense he claimed that his reputation as a ladies' man was so well known that any woman who met him had to have been forewarned.

Finally, in his eighties, Baldwin's luck seemed to run out. When his flamboyant life came to an end in 1909, he was deeply in debt. But the old rake turned out to be as lucky after his death as he was when he was alive. Shortly after he died, oil was discovered on

RACING TO A FIRE. Pecheron horses pull a turn-of-the-century Los Angeles Fire Department hook and ladder wagon. Since action news-style photos were virtually impossible in the 1890s, the crew was probably showing off for the camera.

CHARLES E. MILES became the first foreman of the Los Angeles volunteer fire company in 1876. He poses proudly with a megaphone, a symbol of his command.

property he owned. Due to his irreversible circumstances, Baldwin was unable to cash in on this last gift of good fortune.

Entrepreneurial Los Angeles wasn't about to bet its future on good luck. To promote its virtues, the city established a Chamber of Commerce in 1888. By the turn of the century, the enterprising organization occupied a six-story downtown building with two floors of exhibit space mostly touting agricultural products. Boosters spread the good news about Los Angeles with traveling shows to fairs and expositions. With items collected and preserved by Don Antonio Coronel, the Chamber offices also were an informal historical museum.

By the 1890s, the city was "wide awake" and full of vigor. One of the community's biggest boosters was bellicose Harrison Gray Otis, publisher of the *Los Angeles Times.* Historians Leonard and Dale Pitt describe his overbearing influence: "Otis shaped the young city of Los Angeles much as a mature schoolmaster shapes an impressionable child..." An arrival from Ohio in 1881, Otis detested those who doubted L.A.'s great destiny, meddling reformers and, most of all, labor unions. Describing his first impression of the city, he later wrote: "It is the fattest land I ever was in...." Otis went on to dedicate his life and the pages of his newspaper to

BICYCLE CLUB. Before the age of the automobile, Los Angeles bicycle champions pose for the camera around 1888.

WALNUT ELEPHANT. An elephant made of locally grown walnuts was just one of the eye-catching exhibits created by the energetic and entrepreneurial Los Angeles Chamber of Commerce, which tirelessly sold the city's wonders to the rest of America.

PLAZA GALLERY. Art and culture have arrived in L.A. Earnest photographers, writers and artists gather at a local gallery around 1890.

BASEBALL IN LOS ANGELES. By the turn of the century, the sport was already a popular pastime.

THE SANTA FE RAILROAD'S LA GRANDE DEPOT was a Los Angeles showplace. Pictured here in 1908, the station greeted arrivals with an exotic mix of Moorish and Turkish architecture, palm trees and an aura of *The Arabian Nights*.

L.A.'S FIRST TELEPHONE PAY STATION on Spring Street in 1899. Newly inaugurated long distance service to San Francisco cost fifty cents a minute.

promote a Los Angeles where private enterprise was unfettered and free to prosper.

Ironically, one of America's biggest and most successful businesses stood in the way. The tracks of the Southern Pacific Railroad were a lifeline for Los Angeles and the state of California. With control of schedules and freight rates, the Southern Pacific maintained a potential stranglehold on the local economy. In the 1870s, railroad President Charles H. Crocker considered bypassing Los Angeles unless the city turned over $600,000 and the rights to Phineas Banning's Los Angeles & San Pedro Railroad. If local leaders failed to capitulate, Crocker threatened, "I will make grass grow in the streets of your city!" Los Angeles had no choice. The power of the Southern Pacific was assured by its influence at all levels of government. The railroad could buy and sell politicians, and many elected officials were eager to join the marketplace.

During the 1890s, however, activist Angelenos gave birth to a daring new movement that spread to the rest of the state. Anticipating the "trust-busting" policies of President Theodore Roosevelt, a group of mostly Republican business and civic leaders, soon to be known as the California Progressives, took on the Southern Pacific. Harrison Gray Otis wasn't normally comfortable with reformers, but he found common ground with the Progressives' demand to turn San Pedro into a "free port," controlled by local interests, not the railroad.

Collis P. Huntington, one of the owners of the Southern Pacific, was determined that if

BUNKER HILL was a posh Los Angeles address in 1898. The imposing Crocker mansion dominated the summit. Later, at the end of the street, the Hill Street tunnel and Angels Flight funicular cable railway would be built in 1901.

Los Angeles had a port, it would be in Santa Monica, where the Southern Pacific already controlled rail access. With a mix of public spirit and old-fashioned self-interest, prominent Angelenos fought back and took their case to Congress. With the help of federal government studies favoring San Pedro over Santa Monica, and the effective oratory of California Senator Stephen M. White, they overcame the Southern Pacific's formidable financial resources and political influence and won.

On April 26 and 27, 1899, the city celebrated with a Free Harbor Jubilee, and work began on a new stone breakwater. San Diego and San Francisco had impressive natural harbors. Los Angeles, with help from the federal government, met the competition with a mostly man-made port. It was an early example of how the city would continue to be shaped and empowered by effective politics and modern technology.

The San Pedro harbor fight was a landmark for a new era in American political and economic life. As the twentieth century was about to begin, a spirit of progressivism was spreading, and the citizens of the United States were politically reasserting themselves. Since its humble origins as a Spanish outpost one hundred eighteen years before, Los Angeles had emerged from obscurity with an unprecedented last-minute surge. The picture of this energetic new city was certainly appealing and showed promise, but it remained unfocused and far from clearly framed.

EARLY BEACH HOUSES. By 1898, more permanent structures replaced tents on Santa Monica beach.

BATHERS AT SANTA MONICA playfully expose a few inches of black-stockinged calves and ankles.

SAN FERNANDO VALLEY. In the 1890s, Mission San Fernando is the only structure in sight in a barren landscape. Water brought from 233 miles away would change that picture.

A NEW HARBOR. Stones from Catalina Island and the northwest San Fernando Valley are dropped into place by a giant rail-guided crane during the construction of a breakwater for the new harbor at San Pedro in April 1899.

STRANGERS IN PARADISE

"Southern California is man–made, a gigantic improvisation."

CAREY MCWILLIAMS, Southern California Country, *1946*

From the day when Fray Juan Crespí imagined a large settlement beside the Rio de Porciúncula, the fate of Los Angeles has been inextricably tied to water. Early Spanish settlers created reservoirs with dams made from mud and brush, and later dug *zanjas,* or ditches, to direct the river's flow to where it was needed. Sometimes the stream disappeared into a sandy bed or surged into a devastating flood, but for nearly a century the Los Angeles River (few Yankees could pronounce Porciúncula) kept the pueblo alive. The demands of newcomers who arrived in the 1870s "Sick Rush" provided the first evidence that this might not always be the case. The explosive population boom of the 1880s seemed to confirm it.

In 1877, a twenty-one-year-old Irishman and former sailor rode into town on a trail-weary horse. His name was William Mulholland. For more than fifty years, water and the future of Los Angeles would be his life. Mulholland's efforts would transform the city. He started, literally, at the bottom, as a laborer for the town's privately owned water system. His job was clearing mud and debris, including the occasional dead animal, from the *zanjas*. When he wasn't shoveling muck, Mulholland enjoyed reading. His hard work and self-taught expertise in hydraulic engineering impressed his bosses. At age thirty-one, the ambitious and dedicated young man had risen to become superintendent of the company. One of his most influential early decisions was

A PACIFIC ELECTRIC RED CAR makes a stop at Bliss station—an ideal destination for tourists

seeking heaven on earth in 1909 Los Angeles.

VISIONARIES OR VILLAINS? Three men who helped make modern Los Angeles possible, from left: J. B. Lippincott, Fred Eaton and William Mulholland.

to install meters to keep an accurate record of water use. The result assured the company full payment from its customers. It also encouraged conservation and facilitated planning for future needs.

The future was always on the minds of L.A.'s business and civic leaders. They knew that without an adequate supply of water their ambitions for Los Angeles, and the profits future growth would bring, would, it could be said, simply dry up. Just as they determined to create a port in San Pedro under municipal control, rather than trust their fate to the private ownership of the Southern Pacific Railroad, the voters of Los Angeles decided to buy the city's private water system. In 1902, with a payment of $2 million, it was theirs. Already known as "the Chief," William Mulholland's proven service

THE LOS ANGELES TIMES, established on December 4, 1881, was, and continues to be, a significant force in defining and developing Los Angeles. In this turn-of-the-century ad, the paper touts its "modern" facilities. The *Times* played a major role in "selling" the Owens Valley Aqueduct.

to the city, and his knowledge of virtually every pipe and valve, made him the unquestioned choice to continue as superintendent.

Mulholland's involvement with water was a professional responsibility. But in the decades that followed, his commitment would become deeply personal. This all-consuming dedication and the power and authority it brought were the source of his greatest achievements. They also contributed to his ultimate undoing.

In 1904, Fred Eaton, Mulholland's former boss at the private water department, and a former mayor and city engineer, came to the Chief with an ambitious idea. Both men were concerned that the Los Angeles River could no longer supply a city whose population was capable of doubling with unprecedented regularity. Eaton had a solution — an aqueduct that would transport water from the snow-fed Owens Valley, 233 miles to the north. With a downhill grade, gravity alone could carry the flow. After taking a firsthand look, a doubtful Mulholland was sold. So were a select group of business leaders and members of the city's water commission. For the time being, however, the people of Los Angeles and, most importantly, the farmers and ranchers of the Owens Valley were kept in the dark.

Progressive President Theodore Roosevelt was eager to develop the resources of the American West, and the newly established United States Reclamation Service was already interested in the Owens Valley. Considering a major irrigation project for the area, the Service dispatched a respected engineer, Joseph B. Lippincott, to evaluate the possibilities. Lippincott was well known and liked in Los Angeles and William Mulholland and Fred Eaton were among his friends. He was soon more enthusiastic about supplying water to the growing southern metropolis than developing an irrigation system for the sparsely populated Owens Valley. Without telling his bosses in Washington, D.C., Lippincott signed on as a consultant to Los Angeles.

Meanwhile, Fred Eaton began quietly buying up land, implying to Owens Valley residents that he was working with the Reclamation Service, or simply thinking about becoming a local rancher. In mid-1905, with potential federal support and enough land and water rights, aqueduct planners were preparing to go public. On July 29, the *Los Angeles Times* broke the news embargo with a front-page story and banner headline: "Titanic Project to Give City a River." The citizens of Los Angeles were surprised and thrilled. The farmers of the Owens Valley felt deceived and betrayed. There was little they could do. Key parcels of land and associated water rights had been bought and paid for. They were now the legal property of a thirsty city more than two hundred miles away.

Fred Eaton envisioned the L.A. water scheme as a public-private partnership, with himself as the private beneficiary. However, the support of the U.S. government was essential if the aqueduct was to be completed. In the end, with the belief that bringing water to Los Angeles provided "the greatest good to the greatest number," the government sided with the city. It was stipulated, however, that the project had to be solely a public venture. Eaton was disappointed to be forced out as a partner in the ambitious plan, although he later collected $450,000 from selling land and water rights to the city, plus an additional $100,000 in commissions on sales of other properties he'd handled. He also kept control of a key parcel that would be ideal for a large reservoir.

In the 1930s, East Coast journalist Morrow Mayo called the story of the aqueduct "the Rape of the Owens Valley." L.A. apologists pointed out that, for the most part, Owens Valley residents were paid what they asked for their land, and that secrecy was necessary to avoid unfairly inflated prices. In 1906, President Theodore Roosevelt added his substantial influence to the controversy. The interests of "the few settlers" of the Owens Valley, he declared, "must unfortunately be disregarded in view of the infinitely

HARRY CHANDLER married into the most powerful family in Los Angeles, but he quickly matched his father-in-law, Harrison Gray Otis, in influence and surpassed the old man in entrepreneurial ambitions.

greater interest to be served by putting the water in Los Angeles...." An additional incentive for Roosevelt's decision was news that private utility companies were eyeing the hydroelectric potentials of the Owens Valley watershed. As he wooed political support in the big cities of California, the Progressive-minded president also wanted to encourage public-sponsored water and power development. The leaders of Los Angeles couldn't agree more. Their aqueduct plans included city-owned hydroelectric plants.

The story of the Owens Valley Aqueduct

remains one of the most bitter and controversial episodes in L.A. history. The debate became even more heated when it was revealed that, while aqueduct plans were being made in secret, ten insiders, including *Los Angeles Times* publisher Harrison Gray Otis, were positioned to benefit from land they had acquired in the aqueduct's planned terminus, the sandy and windblown northern San Fernando Valley. Whether Otis and his associates took unfair advantage of inside information was never proved. Certainly, with no guarantees that the ambitious waterway would ever be built, the investment had risks. However, at a minimum, the members of the syndicate, especially Otis, also had the power to influence public opinion, enhancing the odds in their favor.

Whether the insiders' motivations were personal profit, civic improvement or a mix of both, property in the San Fernando Valley was soon worth millions. By 1909, with work on the aqueduct under way, Otis's son-in-law Harry Chandler joined another land-development scheme, the Los Angeles Suburban Homes Company. The company's holdings included almost the entire southern half of the valley. Chandler's opportune investment became the foundation for one of L.A.'s largest family fortunes.

For nearly half of the twentieth century,

Harry Chandler was perhaps the single most powerful man in Los Angeles. He'd come to the city as a health seeker in 1883. His "weak lungs" benefited, as did his personal fortunes. He started delivering newspapers and soon built a citywide distribution system that challenged and impressed Harrison Gray Otis. In 1894, the enterprising young man married one of Otis's three daughters, and became business manager for the *Times.* The social and political power of journalism was Otis's passion. Chandler was driven by real estate and business deals. With a mix of economic self-interest and civic pride, like his father-in-law, Harry Chandler was fiercely dedicated to the growth and prosperity of the City of Angels.

On September 7, 1905, after an ardent and, some claimed, exaggerated lobbying campaign in local newspapers, the citizens of Los Angeles approved a $1.5 million bond issue to acquire Owens Valley land and water rights. In 1908, even with alleged insider scandals and bitter complaints from Valley residents, a $24.5 million construction bond issue also passed. Work began later that year. Declared well conceived and feasible by an independent board of engineering consultants, the project was so extensive that it was compared to the size and significance of turn-of-the-century America's other great

THE FIRST AUTO IN LOS ANGELES was hand built by the driver, J. Philip Erie, in 1897. In the rear seat is L.A. Mayor William Workman Jr., son of a leader of the first American immigrant party to travel overland to Los Angeles in 1841.

WESTLAKE PARK. Trains allowed L.A. to spread to places like rustic Westlake Park on the western outskirts of the city. In the distance, a few "country homes" line the shoreline.

engineering venture, the Panama Canal. Like the aqueduct, the canal would be a boon for Los Angeles.

An early indication of L.A.'s emerging importance was the arrival of the "Great White Fleet" of U.S. warships, sent around the world by President Roosevelt to display American military might and the nation's potential for imperial power. The fleet's recognition of Los Angeles as a western port reaffirmed the city's position on the American political and military map. And the promise of water from the aqueduct seemed to assure an ability to grow. Not to do so was, well, un-American.

In 1900, the population of Los Angeles was 102,479. The former "Queen of the Cow Counties" was home to a significant new metropolis. Downtown L.A. was bustling with electric trolleys, horse-drawn carriages and even automobiles. In 1897, the first car was reported sputtering on city streets. In 1900, the Automobile Club of Southern California was formed. Four years later, the police blotter reported the first grand theft auto. In 1907, a citation was issued to a lead-footed motorist, caught speeding at twenty-three miles per hour.

Setting a slower pace, bicycling had been the rage since the 1890s. And there were other means to move Angelenos around. In 1901, a 304-foot-long funicular, the Los Angeles Incline Railway, better known as Angels Flight,

ARRIVAL OF THE GREAT WHITE FLEET. As evidence of L.A.'s emerging international prominence and military strategic importance, the Great White Fleet arrives in San Pedro Harbor in 1908.

FIESTA DE LOS ANGELES PARADE. In 1906, a Miss Clark leads the "auto section" of the annual event, begun during the 1890s to reinvigorate a decline in tourism. The fiesta celebrated the city's Hispanic heritage, but involved few Hispanics.

SPRING STREET AND TH **AT THE TURN OF THE CE** Los Angeles is still a hors town, but a new automob into view at lower left.

ANGELS FLIGHT IN 1903 carried passengers to the top of Bunker Hill. A staircase with one hundred twenty-three steps was built for those who preferred to walk.

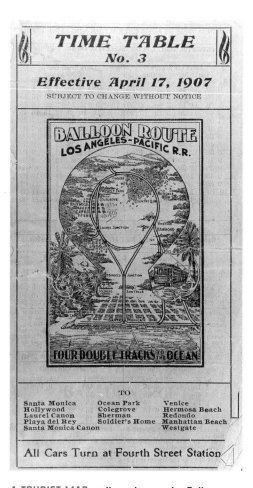

DR. MARGARET J. CHUNG, a graduate of USC and the first Chinese American physician in Southern California, finds an archetypical Angeleno setting for a 1909 portrait.

A TOURIST MAP outlines the popular Balloon Route, a round trip that featured the highlights of the Los Angeles area—from the ocean to the mountains.

HENRY HUNTINGTON, nephew of Collis Huntington, one of the "Big Four" who owned the Southern Pacific Railroad, made a fortune by selling and developing land adjacent to his Pacific Electric lines. This portrait was taken in the 1920s.

conveyed prosperous residents from the great mansions on Bunker Hill to the city's shopping and entertainment districts.

Along with agriculture and light manufacturing, tourism continued to be an important component of the Southern California economy. Henry Huntington, nephew of Southern Pacific partner Collis Huntington, provided the transportation. His Pacific Electric Railway opened in 1901. During the summer and winter tourist seasons, as many as 10,000 people a month bought tickets for the "Balloon Route," a grand loop that took them from downtown L.A. to Hollywood, Santa Monica, and ten beaches along the bay, passing by, not coincidently, undeveloped home sites that Huntington just happened to have for sale.

L.A. RAILWAY, 1909. By connecting Los Angeles with Pasadena in 1894, the Los Angeles Railway Company became the first interurban line to serve Angelenos. Henry Huntington gained control of the company in 1898.

TROLLEY TOWER WAGONS. Special horse-drawn wagons were built with wooden towers to allow workers to maintain the overhead power lines of L.A.'s 1900s electric trolley system.

More famous was the trip from Los Angeles to Altadena, ending with a hair-raising ascent on the Great Cable Incline Railway to Echo Mountain and on to the summit of Mount Lowe, named for the respected Pasadena citizen and Civil War balloonist and aeronautics pioneer Thaddeus Lowe. The railway was Lowe's idea. Clinging to narrow ledges, the cars climbed 1,400 feet in less than 3,000 feet of track. At the top was Ye Alpine Tavern, featuring spectacular pre-smog views of Pasadena, and the still mostly agricultural Los Angeles basin.

In 1904, pioneering American astronomer George Ellery Hale also took advantage of the city's clean air and the proximity of the sheer San Gabriel Mountains. He decided to build an observatory on Mount Wilson, a 5,715-foot-high peak named for Anglo pioneer "Don Benito" Wilson. With the support of the Carnegie Institution, the Mount Wilson Observatory eventually housed a 100-inch telescope, the most powerful in the world.

From Mount Wilson, astronomers learned that the sun wasn't in the center of the Milky Way, and that the universe was strewn with galaxies as plentiful as stars, in the process of speeding away from the source of "The Big Bang" that started it all. For more than thirty

ECHO RAILWAY. A thrill ride of its day, the Cable Incline Railway took Southern California visitors on a precipitous climb to the top of Echo Mountain overlooking Pasadena.

A MOUNT LOWE RAILWAY train winds from Echo Mountain toward its final destination, Ye Alpine Tavern. At 5,000 feet above sea level, the trip offered impressive views.

THE SIXTY-INCH REFLECTING TELESCOPE INSIDE THE MOUNT WILSON OBSERVATORY. Named for George Ellery Hale, it was the largest in the world when it began photographing stars and other space objects in 1908.

THE FUTURE THAT NEVER CAME. J. W. Fawkes built this propeller-driven monorail around 1908, the first in the United States. On board, a band welcomes riders. The inventor called his new transportation system "The Aerial Swallow." To others it was "Fawkes Folly."

THE HOME AND GARDEN OF ARTIST PAUL DE LONGPRE was the prime Hollywood tourist stop on the Balloon Route before the movie studios arrived.

years, until it was eclipsed in 1949 by the 200-inch telescope on Mount Palomar north of San Diego, Mount Wilson was a world center for the study of the solar system and the secrets of the stars.

Henry Huntington's ambitions were more down-to-earth. Always looking for a way to lure visitors to his trains and tracts of land, he came up with an attraction that became another landmark in L.A. history. His inspiration was a 1907 magazine article written by author/adventurer Jack London. In the article London introduced American readers to an exhilarating activity he'd encountered during a visit to the Hawaiian Islands — the sport of surfing.

L.A.'S FIRST SURFER DUDE, George Freeth with young 1900s acolytes. Freeth not only introduced surfing to Los Angeles, he made important contributions to increased awareness and improvements in water safety.

Polynesians had been surfing for centuries, but London's inspiration was twenty-three-year-old George Freeth. As described by London, Freeth—part English and part Polynesian—was a "brown Mercury" riding an eight-foot-long board across the waves at Waikiki. That summer the brown Mercury came to California to promote Hawaiian tourism, displaying his aquatic prowess in the surf at Venice Beach. Within months, Henry Huntington hired him to ride the waves twice a day in front of the railroad magnate's tourist hotel at Redondo Beach. People came by the hundreds to watch the handsome young man "walk on the water." For the first time, images of surfing were added to the evolving picture of Los Angeles.

More than just a surfing pioneer, Freeth's passion was water safety. In 1910, he was awarded a Congressional Gold Medal for single-handedly saving the lives of seven local Japanese fishermen caught in a sudden winter storm in Santa Monica Bay.

Despite occasional dangers, Southern California's beaches had been tourist attractions since the 1870s. During the early 1900s, a major new destination for tourists and Angelenos was Venice of America. Opened on July 4, 1905, Venice featured an amusement pier, Italianate colonnades and canals with costumed gondoliers. This

ABBOT KINNEY, one of many Easterners who came to Los Angeles for his health, is best known as the founder of Venice of America.

imaginative environment was the creation of Abbot Kinney.

A native of New Jersey, Kinney studied law and medicine and traveled the world in search of adventure and good health. In 1880, he decided to build a home in the foothills west of Sierra Madre. Ironically, his fortune came from a cigarette-manufacturing business, but he dedicated his life to cultural pursuits and healthy living. Also imbued with a social conscience, he assisted Helen Hunt Jackson in her effort to increase awareness of the conditions of California's Native Americans.

VENICE OF AMERICA. Crowds gather for the grand opening on July 4, 1905. On the left, the colonnades

Venice was a result of Kinney's entrepreneurial enthusiasm for the promise of a better life in Los Angeles. First envisioned as both a seaside resort and a cultural center that would offer orchestral concerts, operas and lectures, culture soon gave way to amusements, and Venice of America became known as the Coney Island of the Pacific. Attractions included a grand bathhouse, a skating rink, a dance hall, an aquarium and a 2,500-seat auditorium. Even with repeated fires, Kinney's beachside extravaganza attracted and delighted visitors until the Depression of the 1930s began a period of decay.

Venice represented an ambitious attempt to combine European imagery with American popular culture — and make money in the process. Early Los Angeles writers exhibited an equal mix of rough-hewn ambition, overblown hyperbole and a serious search for

A VENETIAN GONDOLA carries tourists down the Aldebaran Canal around 1910. The canal would be filled in later and become Market Street.

something new. In 1881, an immigrant from Indiana, Colonel Horace Bell, published *Reminiscences of a Ranger,* a theatrical retelling of L.A.'s Wild West days in the 1850s. "During the years '52 and '53," he wrote, "it was a common and usual query at the bar or breakfast table, 'well, how many were killed last night?' then 'who was it?' and 'who killed him?'" As editor of a satirical tabloid, *The Porcupine,* Bell defended the city's Mexican and Indian minorities and enjoyed taking verbal potshots at L.A.'s Yankee elite, calling them *bárbaros del Norte* (northern barbarians).

JOURNALIST/GADFLY HORACE BELL nurtured the legends of Wild West Los Angeles and never shied from controversy with L.A.'s elite.

LUMMIS AND ROOSEVELT. Ebullient Harvard chums Charles Lummis, left, and President Theodore Roosevelt share enthusiasms for the West during a 1912 meeting at Occidental College.

In 1884, twenty-five-year-old Charles Fletcher Lummis, a Harvard dropout, was curious about the American West. With a flair for the dramatic and a determination to be unconventional, Lummis decided to make a trip from his home in Chillicothe, Ohio, to Los Angeles, on foot. During a more than 2,000-mile trek, he chronicled his adventures in letters to the *Los Angeles Times* and his hometown newspaper. When he showed up in San Gabriel, Harrison Gray Otis, publisher of the *Times,* was there to offer him a job.

Twelve hours after his arrival, with energy, enthusiasm and an outsized personality, Lummis was hard at work as a local journalist. His cross-country travels had excited him about the cultures and landscape of the Southwest. Expressing his passion as a writer, activist, amateur anthropologist and photographer, one of his earliest causes was the crumbling California missions. In 1895, in a successful effort to save and restore the old Spanish outposts, he founded the Landmarks Club.

That same year, Lummis became the editor of *Land of Sunshine,* a magazine sponsored by the Los Angeles Chamber of Commerce. From the beginning, he was committed to making the publication more than a promotional pamphlet for L.A. tourism. "God made Southern California—and made it on purpose," he wrote.

EL ALISAL, the mostly self-built home of Charles Fletcher Lummis, the colorful writer, editor, activist and founder of the Southwest Museum.

With ambitious enthusiasm, Lummis eventually changed the name to *Out West* and solicited submissions from new Western writers and artists, including Mary Austin, author of *Land of Little Rain,* and other independent women. Lummis's interest in the oppostie sex went beyond literature. Married three times, he kept a diary where he recorded his extramarital conquests in a special code.

In 1898, doing much of the labor himself, Lummis started construction on El Alisal, his stone home beside the Arroyo Seco, east of downtown, an area that served as a rustic retreat for individualists and artisans. In 1901, with the support of President Theodore Roosevelt, a friend from Harvard, the indefatigable and sometimes overbearing activist established the Sequoya League to support the cause of Indian rights and welfare. Two years later, he was leading efforts to create the Southwest Museum, L.A.'s first curatorial institution. Dedicated to the art and culture of Native Americans, with many artifacts from Lummis's personal collection, the museum opened on August 1, 1914.

Even a taste for strong drink didn't keep Lummis from filling seemingly endless pages, working in his study known as "the Lion's Den." For six years, starting in 1905, he even stirred up things as an energetic and controversial city librarian. Until he died in 1928, "the Old Lion," as he was called, turned out sixteen books about his beloved Southwest. His legacy is grandiose and controversial. And,

like Los Angeles, it was as unconventional as it was undeniable.

While the bohemian lifestyle and outspoken advocacy of Charles Lummis made him a larger-than-life figure in 1900s Los Angeles, there was plenty of room for others. Flamboyant Colonel Griffith Jenkins Griffith settled in the city in 1885 after making a fortune in San Francisco. Two years later, he married Mary Agnes Christina "Tina" Messmer, the daughter of the wealthy owner of a local hotel. The 1891 City Directory describes him as "a capitalist and proprietor, Los Feliz Rancho and Briswalter Tract." Griffith had purchased the 4,071–acre rancho in 1882. Consisting mostly of rugged, hilly terrain, it was a real estate developer's nightmare. In 1896, Griffith decided to donate to the city two-thirds of his Los Feliz holding — five square miles — for use solely as a public park. His gift gave Los Angeles the possibility for an enormous new urban amenity and, of course, helped Griffith lighten the burden of his property taxes.

GRIFFITH J. GRIFFITH, the man who gave Los Angeles Griffith Park, looks proper and dignified in this portrait, but he was at the center of one of L.A.'s early scandals and spent time in San Quentin State Prison.

As the twentieth century began, the city didn't know quite what to do with its windfall. Colonel James Eddy, creator of Angels Flight, suggested a funicular railroad to the tract's tallest peak. There he envisioned a great observatory. The funicular would never happen, but Griffith was intrigued by the observatory idea. In 1913, he made another donation to build an outdoor Greek theater. Like the observatory, it would be years before the theater was built.

Griffith Park — the name required as part of Griffith's gift — was the Colonel's longest-lasting legacy. It would become America's largest municipal park, but a great scandal made him far more famous in 1903. A secret drinker, Griffith could turn abusive. His wife, Tina, knew this well.

One afternoon, as the couple was visiting in Santa Monica at the luxurious Arcadia Hotel, named for heiress Arcadia Bandini, he suddenly produced a revolver and accused his spouse of trying to poison him. Her denials only enraged him more and he pulled the trigger. At the last moment Mrs. Griffith turned away, but the bullet penetrated her temple and fragments cut through her right eye, leaving her partially blind. Alive but hysterical, she jumped out the hotel window, safely landing on a roof directly below.

Griffith J. Griffith had the money to hire the best lawyer in Los Angeles, and he did. Earl Rogers was a brilliant defense attorney, who also knew first-hand the demons of drink. Rogers's defense, based on "alcoholic insanity," was inventive but didn't work. Still, Griffith got off with a relatively light conviction for assault with a deadly weapon. He was sentenced to a $5,000 fine and two years in San Quentin State Prison. A model prisoner, the colonel was released in December 1906, eight months after the great San Francisco earthquake and fire.

Los Angeles was physically unaffected by the 1906 San Francisco earthquake. However, the tragedy changed the city in other ways.

JAPANESE ABALONE FISHERMEN at White's Point in San Pedro in 1905.

Thousands of Japanese immigrants, left home-less by the disaster, decided to move south. In L.A. they couldn't escape a long American tra-dition of anti-Asian prejudice, yet they found a new home in the downtown community of Little Tokyo, first established in 1885. In 1901, Japanese fishermen began harvesting abalone along the Palos Verdes Peninsula, and by 1907, several hun-dred had settled on Terminal Island in L.A.'s har-bor. That year was a landmark for Japanese immi-gration. More than 10,000 newcomers from Japan settled in Southern California. The Japanese-language newspaper *Rafu Shimpu* (translated as "Los Angeles"), founded in 1903, served the close-knit community.

In 1909, Japanese, Chinese, Russian and American produce growers opened the City Market of Los Angeles. In a short time, Japanese were providing 75 percent of all fresh vegetables consumed in Los Angeles. Two years earlier, the mostly Anglo California Fruit Growers Exchange, a cooperative of citrus concerns, together with the Southern Pacific Railroad, promoted Southern California agriculture with fast, refrigerated trains filled with oranges. The destination was Midwestern states such as Iowa. When the trains arrived, the car doors were pulled open to reveal cargo so unexpected and delicious that it seemed to originate from paradise itself. "Oranges for Health — California for Wealth," the growers boasted. Soon fresh orange juice was a common way to start the day, and thousands of Iowans were off to find a sunny future in the City of Angels.

THE LOS ANGELES PRODUCE MARKET near Central and Third was a center for Asian agricultural enterprise from the turn of the century.

OTIS RESIDENCE. Seen in 1900, Harrison Gray Otis's home, known as "the Bivouac," far right, was next door to his publishing competitor, Edwin T. Earl. The Otis home was donated to the Otis Art Institute in 1918.

Pictures of open-air and healthy Los Angeles not only added to the city's fame and population growth, they also inspired new ways to live. In 1893, two brothers from Cincinnati, Ohio, Charles and Henry Greene, moved to Pasadena. The Greenes were young architects who would turn a modest style of architecture, the bungalow, into impressive art. Sharing the traditions of the European Arts and Crafts movement, with influences from Japan, the great Greene and Greene homes, such as the Gamble House, built for Ohio transplant David B. Gamble, an heir to the Procter & Gamble fortune, feature broad roofs, projecting beams and open porches.

The wood interiors exhibit hand craftsmanship at its finest, and the open relationship between inside and outside expresses a sense of freedom and closeness to nature that characterized California life. In time, these ideas would travel east and influence architecture across America.

Only the very wealthy could own homes designed by Greene and Greene, but more affordable "high" art and culture were making their way to Los Angeles. In 1897, the city welcomed a new opera from composer Giacomo Puccini. It was the American premiere of *La Bohème*. In 1901, tenor Enrico Caruso was in town performing Bizet's *Carmen*.

While art and culture found roots, civic leaders such as Harrison Gray Otis were convinced that unfettered capitalism was critical to the city's survival and growth. He was supported by a powerful local business

THE GAMBLE HOUSE, designed by brothers Charles and Henry Greene for heirs of the Procter & Gamble soap fortune, is an Arts and Crafts masterpiece that redefined the idea of home, just as Los Angeles was redefining the concept of city.

G. W. BRIGHT
Driver Chem Eng. Co. No 1
Appointed callman Oct. 2d.
1897. Promoted to hoseman
Nov. 1st, 1897. Promoted to
driver, third class, Jan 31st,
1900.

organization, the Merchants and Manufacturers Association. At the same time, across America, unionism was on the rise. Like military officers defending their motherland, Otis and L.A.'s business leadership were prepared for war. There was no mistaking the position of the *Times* publisher. His home was called "the Bivouac," and he once mounted a small cannon on his limousine.

In the 1900s, the civic-minded Progressive movement, which had resulted in a government-sponsored port at San Pedro, was gaining strength. If the *Times* was a powerful voice for entrenched interests, it was far from unop-

posed. Harrison Gray Otis's nemesis was Edwin T. Earl, publisher of the *Evening Express.* Unlike Otis, Earl wanted reform. He was joined by William Randolph Hearst, a San Franciscan who had bought the competing Los Angeles *Examiner* in 1903. Finally, farther to the left was the Socialist-leaning *Record,* always alert for injustice and misdeeds among L.A.'s high and mighty.

Dr. John Randolph Haynes was a wealthy man, and Harrison Gray Otis's personal physician. He also was a Christian Socialist committed to an open, honest and effective city government. In the 1906 municipal elections, Haynes and local reformers, including Meyer

HOLLYWOOD, 1905. Without modern landmarks, it's hard to tell precisely where these young rural Angelenos are standing, but it's somewhere on Sunset Boulevard near Vine Street or Gower, in the heart of Hollywood.

BREWERY WORKERS, 1900. The population of Los Angeles was more than prosperous and middle class. Working-class Angelenos, like these 1900 brewery employees, provided an important economic foundation. Many like them were looking for better working conditions in anti-union L.A.

Lissner, an L.A. lawyer and major Progressive political strategist, declared their determination to "clean up Los Angeles." They wanted voters to have the right to recall elected leaders, to submit legislative initiatives and to put legislation to a public referendum. In 1909, under the threat of a recall, the Progressives forced Los Angeles mayor Arthur Harper to resign after it was learned that, among other things, he was especially solicitous to constituents from a local brothel, who had in return offered him occasional personal concessions.

American Progressivism was on the move and Los Angeles was an energetic source of ideas and support. As the first decade of the twentieth century came to a close, Progressives and reformers rallied behind Hiram Johnson as their candidate for governor. In Los Angeles, even though some Progressives stopped short of endorsing unions and godless Socialism, Job Harriman, a Socialist and charismatic labor lawyer, was emerging as a strong candidate for mayor.

While many citizens of Los Angeles were conservative Midwesterners, an often-ignored and increasingly restive working class provided the foundations for the well-publicized California lifestyle. At the same time, a large percentage of middle-class Angelenos had come west to escape eastern political corruption. They wanted their adopted city to be something new — and better. Pressures for change were building. The Progressives demanded good and honest government and the unions were determined to topple Harrison Gray Otis's open-shop fortress.

Anarchist Emma Goldman anticipated victory. "Los Angeles," she wrote, "was a health resort for parasites and cranks, a city that consisted almost entirely of tourists, without any personality of its own. . . . The eternal spirit of revolution and the solidarity of labor have transformed the sickly hot-house flower into a rugged wild plant with its branches reaching out for more light and freedom."

As the 1900s came to a close, the developing picture of Los Angeles, a city built on sunshine and tourism, was shadowed by growing tensions and the potential of social and political upheaval.

DYNAMITE, WATERWORKS AND PICTURE SHOWS

"There it is. Take it."
WILLIAM MULHOLLAND, 1913

October 1, 1910, began as a typically quiet Los Angeles night—until shortly after 1 a.m. An enormous explosion shattered the stillness. The blast was heard as far as ten miles away. In minutes, the downtown headquarters of the *Los Angeles Times* was engulfed in smoke and flames. Horse-drawn fire equipment rushed to the scene. Despite heroic efforts, when dawn arrived, the fortress-like stone building was a smoldering shell. High on a surviving wall, the newspaper's militant symbol, an eagle, still spread its wings, but twenty-one *Times* employees were dead and many more injured. The next day, unexploded bombs were found at the home of the secretary of the anti-union Merchants and Manufacturers Association and at the residence of *Times* publisher Harrison Gray Otis. Los Angeles appeared to be a city under siege.

With General Otis in Mexico, his son-in-law Harry Chandler quickly took charge. Tears streaming down his cheeks, the *Times*'s business manager was determined to get in print as soon as possible. Only hours later, the paper was on newsstands with a banner headline: "Unionist Bombs Wreck The Times; Many Seriously Hurt." Despite the front-page certainty, no one knew who had planted the bombs, or whether in fact the tragedy was simply an accident.

OPENING OF THE AQUEDUCT. Los Angeles celebrates the opening of the Owens Valley Aqueduct in November 1913. Only two years later, L.A. annexed 168 square miles of dusty valley lands, more than doubling the city's size overnight.

HARRISON GRAY OTIS. Ever the "general," although lieutenant colonel was his highest Union army rank, *Times* publisher Harrison Gray Otis battled progressivism and organized labor until his death in 1917.

THE TIMES IN RUBBLE. Firemen survey what remains of the *Los Angeles Times* headquarters at First and Broadway the morning after an explosion started a deadly and destructive fire.

Since the summer, Los Angeles had been embroiled in a walkout led by the Structural Iron Workers Union. Strikebreakers were brought in and there had been violence, but nothing like this. On the defensive, union leaders claimed the tragedy was the result of a gas leak and that barrels of ink had fueled the fire. As for the unexploded bombs that were found, unionists charged that they had been planted to falsely incriminate labor supporters. But Otis and Chandler weren't entertaining alternatives.

The city attorney hired legendary detective William J. Burns to track down the perpetrators. Nearly seven months later, on April 12, 1911, just as Otis and L.A. law-enforcement officials were losing their patience, Burns operatives arrested James B. "Jim" McNamara and Ortie McManigal. Both were members of the Structural Iron Workers Union. Even more incriminating to investigators, their luggage was reported to contain material for making bombs.

McManigal quickly confessed, naming Jim McNamara and his brother John Joseph

("J. J."), the secretary of the International Association of Bridge and Iron Workers, as the men behind the bombings. Picked up in Detroit, Jim was thin and disheveled. In contrast, J. J., arrested on April 22, was well dressed, even-tempered, religious and upstanding. Burns didn't care what they looked like. Under heavy guard, all three—McManigal and the McNamara brothers—were separately secreted aboard a fast train headed west to Los Angeles.

When the news broke of the McNamaras' arrest, union sympathizers were certain it was a frame-up. Convinced of the brothers' innocence, American Federation of Labor President Samuel Gompers turned to the country's greatest defense lawyer, Clarence Darrow. At first Darrow resisted, but he couldn't say no. He made a good living as a corporate lawyer. His reputation, however, rested on his success as a defender of the poor and labor causes, and as a staunch opponent of the death penalty. Put in total charge of the case, and with a generous budget and fee, Darrow held in his hands the lives of the McNamaras and the reputation and future of the labor movement in America.

In May 1911, fifty-year-old Job Harriman was nominated as the Socialist candidate for mayor of Los Angeles. Like Harry Chandler, Harriman had come to Los Angeles for his health. Now he was one of the most vigorous defenders of progressive reform and unionism, and a member of the McNamara defense team. In the mayoral primary on October 31, Harriman easily won a place in the runoff election, attracting more votes than his opponent, the incumbent, George Alexander. A final vote was scheduled for December, and Socialist hopes were high. It looked as if the iron-fisted anti-unionism of Harrison Gray Otis was finally coming to an end.

To reformers like Harriman and Hiram Johnson, the Progressive Republican candidate for governor, Otis was an insidious obstacle to progress. Before the bombing, Johnson responded to an especially vicious *Times* attack with invective of his own: "Harrison Gray Otis," he said, is "a creature who is vile, infamous, degraded, and putrescent. Here he sits in senile dementia, with gangrened heart and rotting brain, grimacing at every reform and chattering in impotent rage against decency and morality, while he is going down into his grave in snarling infamy." In June 1911, former president Theodore Roosevelt added his disapproval, calling Otis "a consistent enemy of every movement for social and economic betterment," and "a consistent enemy of men in California who have dared resolutely to stand against corruption and in favor of honesty . . . ." Despite influential enemies,

HANDSOME EARL ROGERS opposed Clarence Darrow in the *Times* bombing trial, but came to his defense when Darrow was charged with bribery.

THE COURTHOUSE AND HALL OF RECORDS, about 1917. Two L.A. buildings that played a role in the *Times* bombing drama are only memories today. The ornate 1888 county courthouse is on the right.

Harrison Gray Otis had his own powerful allies among L.A.'s wealthy and conservative business community.

During the arraignment in July, the McNamara brothers pleaded not guilty, and the politically sensitive jury-selection process began. Both sides maneuvered for advantage and used spies to gather information. It was a hardball competition where prosecution and defense stretched the limits of the law, and sometimes went beyond. After six weeks, there still was no jury. Then, on December 1, 1911, Darrow made an astonishing announcement. There would be no trial. The McNamaras had changed their plea to guilty. In return, the Los Angeles district attorney had agreed not to demand the death penalty. Otis and the anti-labor forces had won.

McNamara supporters and Darrow admirers felt devastated and betrayed. Job Harriman's hopes to be the next mayor of Los Angeles came to an abrupt end. In the city election four days later, he was soundly defeated. If that weren't enough, the district attorney charged that, in his zeal for acquittal, Darrow had bribed potential jurors. Otis and his allies wanted more than a verdict; they wanted to destroy the reputation of unionism and with it Clarence Darrow's credibility.

For the lawyer known as the "defender of the defenseless," the bribery trial was an agonizing experience. L.A.'s ablest attorney, Earl Rogers, an opponent of unionism, agreed to act in Darrow's defense. Even though there was strong evidence of guilt, the jury voted for acquittal. Angry and humiliated, Darrow headed home to Chicago. In the years to come, he would try and win many famous cases, but he never again worked for American labor. How could he have done it, unionists asked? The answer was hard to take. The case against the McNamaras was insurmountable. Although it was claimed that the brothers only wanted to put a scare into anti-union forces, and certainly not to kill anyone, Darrow believed that the only hope to save his clients from the death penalty was to cut a deal.

For reformers, the McNamara case was a shocking setback. But not all the news was bad. While Socialism and unionism may have suffered a major defeat, the Progressive movement was still strong. Harrison Gray Otis and his allies were victorious in Los Angeles, but Progressive Republican Hiram Johnson was elected governor of California.

In Los Angeles, 1910 would be remembered for the bombing of the *Times*. However, the year started with a far more uplifting event. Between January 10 and 20, a bean field northwest of Long Beach was strewn with rickety contraptions. They were "aeroplanes,"

gathered for the first successful American aviation show and competition. New York had put together a similar event in 1908, but none of the planes got off the ground.

As hot-air balloons and dirigibles drifted overhead, aviator Glenn Curtiss lifted airborne in a self-made flying machine. Seven years after the Wright brothers, it was the Pacific Coast's first powered flight. Curtiss would later barnstorm the country as "the Flying Dude." In the years during and after World War I, he pioneered the design of seaplanes and created the "Jenny" trainer, the world's first mass-produced aircraft. Glenn Martin, another aviation pioneer, was also there in his own handmade flier.

At the bean farm, christened Dominguez Field for the air show, an audience of 50,000

THE FIRST AIR SHOW was an indication of L.A.'s future role in aviation. The 1910 air meet was the first successful event of its kind in America. In this composite photo, the product of an overly enthusiastic news photographer, the craft look more like winged insects than airplanes.

GLENN CURTISS. Shown at the wheel of his handmade biplane, Curtiss won $6,500 in two speed events at the 1910 Los Angeles air meet. During WWI, his company made more airplanes than any other in the world.

FRENCH AVIATOR LOUIS PAULHAN set new altitude and distance records at the Dominguez Hills air meet. Here, in a Henry Farman biplane, Paulhan passes a balloon advertising the *Examiner* newspaper. In the basket below, an intrepid photographer snaps a close-up.

cheered French daredevil Louis Paulhan when he set a new record, making a forty-five-minute round-trip flight to Arcadia in the San Gabriel Valley. On the last day of the meet, Paulhan soared to an altitude record of 4,164 feet. Enjoying ideal weather, thousands of enthusiastic spectators left thrilled and inspired. Aviation had been added to the picture of twentieth-century Los Angeles.

While Harrison Gray Otis and the Merchants and Manufacturers Association were ridding Los Angeles of unionism, and aviators were soaring over the city for the first time, William Mulholland was assuring L.A.'s long-term future. Work was underway on one of the world's most impressive new technological wonders: the 233-mile-long Los Angeles–Owens Valley Aqueduct. Famous for his gruff realism, "the Chief" once told growth-minded civic leaders, "If you don't get the water, you won't need it." Now the water was on the way.

New York City was proud of its thirty-eight-mile Croton Aqueduct, but if Mulholland had past examples in mind, they were the great gravity-fed waterways of classical Rome, some extending as far as sixty miles. Even the ancient Romans couldn't match the engineering ambitions of America's new imperial city. As preparations were made to create an intake to divert the flow of the Owens River, construction began on a five-mile tunnel at the end of San Francisquito Canyon, forty-five miles north of the city. In the process, workers set a world record, digging through 604 feet of hard rock in a single month. As the project moved toward completion, 215 miles of road, and 230 miles of pipeline and electrical power lines were threaded across a barren landscape. Fifty-seven work camps housed as many as 3,900 laborers, with tents, food, animals and machinery, and telegraph, telephone and rail lines to support them. Like a general in command of a military campaign, Mulholland kept the effort on time and on budget, sometimes supervising on horseback, or rattling over recently graded roads in a steam-powered staff car.

The aqueduct used gravity to carry water from the Owens Valley at 4,000 feet to near sea-level Los Angeles. When obstacles such as valleys or canyons were encountered, pipes carried the water down one side with enough force to push it over the other. The most impressive dip in the aqueduct was at Jawbone Canyon, an 8,095-foot-long elbow of riveted steel.

To manage and maintain the flow along the route, Mulholland had his crews build three reservoirs. The largest, Haiwee, held enough water to keep the system at full capacity for eighty days. The aqueduct's initial

visionary, former mayor Fred Eaton, tried to get the city to buy a portion of his remaining Owens Valley land for another reservoir. An angry Mulholland considered the offer profiteering and refused. It would be seventeen years before a deal was struck. By then Eaton was hopelessly in debt and seriously ill.

On November 5, 1913, as many as 40,000 people assembled at the northeast edge of the sandy San Fernando Valley. In front of them, a curving concrete trough emerged from a hillside. Speeches were made, a local soprano sang and a band played "America." Finally, William Mulholland rose to speak. "This rude platform," he said, "is an altar, and on it we are here consecrating this water supply and dedicating the Aqueduct to you and your children and your children's children for all time." With that, cannons fired a salute, an American flag was unfurled, and the gates at the top of the hill were opened. Water from 233 miles away began to tumble down the concrete trough, as the crowd cheered and surged toward the torrent. The Chief held out his arms. "There it is. Take it," he said. Mulholland was hailed as "California's

WILLIAM MULHOLLAND. Looking trim and handsome in this publicity photo, the Chief had firsthand knowledge of the route of the city's first aqueduct, as well as the later one bringing water from the Colorado River.

MULE TEAMS pull large metal pipe sections across the desert from locations along a Southern Pacific track as the Owens Valley Aqueduct takes shape.

ELIZABETH TUNNEL. After three years and four months of drilling through hard rock, workers complete the most difficult challenge during the building of the aqueduct.

JAWBONE CANYON. More than 8,000 feet of steel piping were laid here, in a desolate expanse 120 miles north of Los Angeles.

THE CASCADES. Men turn two huge wheels, releasing the first flow of Owens Valley water down a stair-stepped concrete channel known as the Cascades.

VAN NUYS, 1911. Hardly any trees or grass greeted dignitaries and prospective residents brought by a special Southern Pacific train for the dedication of the new town of Van Nuys.

Greatest Man." Reformers even urged him to run for mayor. The self-educated Irishman was honored but always impatient with politics; he bluntly declined. "Gentlemen," he said, "I would rather give birth to a porcupine backwards than be mayor of Los Angeles."

Even though Mulholland refused to run for office, he knew that water was not only sustenance; it represented political and economic power. In 1913, "greater Los Angeles" encompassed a handful of independent communities, many of which wanted a share of L.A.'s new man-made river. But the city had financed and built this river, and considered the bounty its own. The Chief argued that to sell or lease water could leave towns high and dry if Los Angeles needed more for itself. To receive a share, landowners had to agree to be annexed. In 1915, the largest single annexation was 168 square miles of the San Fernando Valley, more than doubling the size of the city almost overnight.

Before it became a part of Los Angeles, the Valley was a dusty semi-agricultural expanse. Pioneers such as Charles Maclay, George K. Porter, Isaac Lankershim and his son-in-law Isaac Newton Van Nuys were farmers and ranchers who left their names on towns, local streets and real estate developments.

With water came residential subdivisions and new communities, such as Marian (named after Harrison Gray Otis's daughter and later renamed Reseda) and Owensmouth (named with a direct reference to the aqueduct, and later called Canoga Park). A new thoroughfare, Sherman Way, spanned the valley from east to west. Initially envisioned as a local version of

SAN FERNANDO VALLEY LAND SALES OFFICE. In 1912, the first Van Nuys tract office advertises lots from $350 and up. Literature and electric car service to downtown L.A. was provided free.

BEVERLY HILLS HOTEL.
When it opened in 1912, the 325-room Beverly Hills Hotel was an oasis in the middle of farmland.

Mexico City's grand Paseo de la Reforma, the broad roadway was named after streetcar magnate Moses Sherman, a commissioner with the city's water board and an investor with Harrison Gray Otis and other insiders in the first Valley land syndicate.

As the San Fernando Valley, and other independent communities, joined newly watered Los Angeles, the former pueblo grew into an urban giant. In 1900, L.A.'s boundaries embraced about forty-three square miles. By 1920, they contained more than eight times that — nearly 364 square miles.

Scattered within the city's boundaries were unincorporated towns with water resources of their own, allowing them to resist the lure of L.A. annexation. They included Burbank, Glendale, Santa Monica and, perhaps the most famous, Beverly Hills, incorporated in 1914.

The construction of the Beverly Hills Hotel in 1912 attracted visitors looking for an escape into the country. After 1919, when film star Douglas Fairbanks built Pickfair Mansion for his new bride, actress Mary Pickford, other wealthy Hollywood personalities were drawn to the area. During the '20s and '30s,

PICKFAIR. With what would now be considered a very modest Beverly Hills home in the background, Mary Pickford and Douglas Fairbanks canoe in the swimming pool on their new estate.

humorist Will Rogers was Beverly Hills' honorary mayor, mixing his homespun style with an enthusiasm for polo.

While Beverly Hills was built as a retreat from urban Los Angeles, the city was expanding a transportation system to keep everything connected. In 1911, Henry Huntington and Southern Pacific magnate Edward J. Harriman joined their Los Angeles streetcar and interurban rail lines to create the largest urban train system in the world. At the same time, many Angelenos were abandoning the rails in favor of increasingly affordable autos. By 1915, Los Angeles streets were filled with more than 55,000 private automobiles, more than in any other city.

In 1912, the initial San Pedro breakwater was completed, and two years later the first ship arrived after passing through the Panama Canal. L.A.'s man-made port and the local economy were eager to benefit from their proximity to the new Central American shortcut. Now they were also better positioned to take advantage of trade from Asia. Even San

SAN PEDRO, 1913. Steam-powered freighters and rows of rail cars testify to the rising importance of L.A.'s port after the opening of the Panama Canal.

FIRST ELECTRIC TROLLEY. The first trackless electric trolley line in North America operated in unincorporated areas near Hollywood from 1910 to 1915.

MISSION TROLLEY STOP. From downtown Los Angeles, Pacific Electric Red Car riders could reach nearly every attraction in the area, including Mission San Gabriel, shown here in 1910.

TRAFFIC CONGESTION, 1910S. For a time, horse-drawn wagons competed for space on public streets with gasoline-powered autos and electric trolleys.

AN AUTO AND BIPLANE RACE, AROUND 1913. Pitting two of L.A.'s most influential new technologies, Barney Oldfield races his front-drive Christie machine against a Curtiss biplane at the Ascot track at Central and Florence avenues.

Francisco, with its impressive natural harbor, began to feel competition from the south.

With the promise of increased foreign trade, Los Angeles could picture itself as an important international metropolis, even though the city's population was mostly American-born and overwhelmingly white. But changes were underway. Although the size of the black community doubled between 1910 and 1920, it was only 2.7 percent of the total. That didn't stop black Angelenos from supporting one of the oldest African American newspapers in the West, the *California Eagle,* founded in 1879.

Between 1912 and 1951, the managing editor and publisher of the *Eagle* was Charlotta Spears Bass. Beginning as a reform-minded Republican, Bass became an outspoken activist, editorializing on behalf of equal justice and direct action for civil rights. In 1918, she helped elect Watts resident Frederick Roberts as California's first African American assemblyman. Roberts, later revealed to be a third-generation descendent of Thomas Jefferson and his slave mistress Sally Hemmings, was also the first African American graduate of Los Angeles High School. In the assembly election, he faced a

CHARLOTTA SPEARS BASS, pictured here as a young woman, arrived in Los Angeles in 1910. An activist for African Americans, she protested the portrayal of blacks in *The Birth of a Nation* and edited the Black-owned *California Eagle* newspaper from 1912–51.

BLACK FIREMEN. By 1918, L.A.'s African American firefighters were few and would be assigned to segregated stations for decades to come. But they still served with evident pride.

white candidate who attempted to win votes with cards that bluntly read: "My opponent is a nigger." Despite this not-so-subtle tactic, Roberts won.

Black Angelenos such as Frederick Roberts, Charlotta Spears Bass, and her husband, Joseph, were not easily dissuaded in their pursuit of equality. In 1952, anticipating the modern civil rights movement, Bass ran an energetic but unsuccessful campaign as the vice presidential candidate of the United States on the Progressive Party ticket.

The struggle for an equal place in American life involved more than African Americans. In 1913, California passed the Alien Land Act, legislation that made it illegal for Asian immigrants to own land. In Los Angeles the response was a strengthening of community bonds in places such as Little Tokyo and the creation of Japanese American schools, churches and fraternal and philanthropic organizations. The same had happened long before in the city's Chinatown. As for Mexicans, most continued to work in the fields or as laborers, always subject to the whims of changing American economic needs and immigration policies.

If the Los Angeles population was mostly white and American-born, it was also older. In L.A., even death was given an innovative and upbeat treatment with the transformation of a Glendale cemetery. The father of Forest Lawn

FIRE ALARM. It's time to race for the pole and down to the horse-drawn wagons.

WAITING FOR THE ALARM. Two views of the life of 1900s L.A. firemen. In between fires there was time to relax with a little music and perhaps a game of chance.

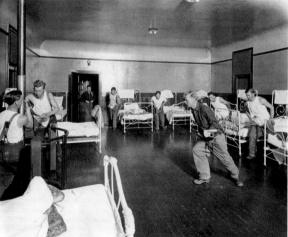

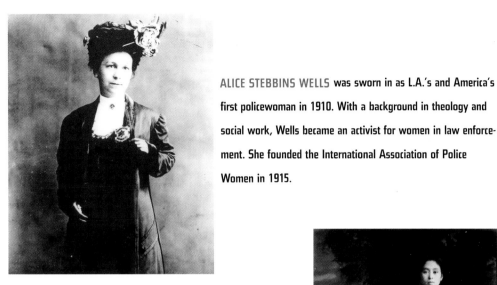

was sworn in as L.A.'s and America's first policewoman in 1910. With a background in theology and social work, Wells became an activist for women in law enforcement. She founded the International Association of Police Women in 1915.

A 1915 PORTRAIT OF THE SHIMODA FAMILY, Japanese Angelenos. Clockwise from top: Masue (mother), Toshiko, Ayako and Moritaro (father).

GATEWAY TO HEAVEN. The entrance to Forest Lawn Memorial Park in Glendale. Founder Hubert Eaton's goal was to change dreary cemeteries into places of art, beauty and profit.

was Hubert Eaton, a deeply religious former metallurgical chemist and businessman from Liberty, Missouri. Instead of grim and crumbling tombstones, Eaton envisioned "a great park, devoid of misshapen monuments, filled with towering trees, sweeping lawns, splashing fountains, singing birds, beautiful statuary, cheerful flowers, noble memorial architecture with interiors full of light and color, and redolent of the world's best history and romances."

An unexpected yet perfect fit with L.A.'s boomtown heritage, Forest Lawn was a real

THE ENTRANCE TO AGRICULTURAL PARK led to an oval track where horses, bicycles and automobiles raced. In 1909, a racy reputation led L.A. reformers, many from adjacent USC, to transform the facility into a more wholesome environment renamed Exposition Park.

estate development for the afterlife. Opening in 1917, Eaton's creation was a hugely successful heaven on earth, just as Los Angeles had pictured itself since the 1870s.

While Forest Lawn would eventually feature replicas of the world's great art, Los Angeles supported the real thing too. In the early 1900s, with a growing population of educated and wealthy residents and newcomers, the city began building cultural institutions as counterparts to those in major Midwest and East Coast cities.

On November 6, 1913, the day after William Mulholland christened the Owens Valley Aqueduct, a new County Museum of History, Science and Art opened near the campus of the University of Southern California. The

THE LOS ANGELES COUNTY MUSEUM OF HISTORY, SCIENCE AND ART. Soon after it opened, the science department received a special gift — the La Brea Tar Pits and all their ice age fossils.

ANCIENT HISTORY. **A proud paleontologist shows off a recent discovery in the La Brea Tar Pits.**

museum was on the former site of Agricultural Park, developed for farm and produce shows in 1876. By the 1890s, the public park had deteriorated into a well-known hangout for gamblers and other riffraff who gathered for horse races and further good times in the surrounding bars and bordellos. In 1910, reformers moved in, claiming the land as a more proper place, and renaming it Exposition Park.

A major holding of the new Museum of History, Science and Art was the world's largest collection of Ice Age fossil bones, found only a few miles away in one of Los Angeles's oldest landmarks, the La Brea Tar Pits. Fray Juan Crespí took note of the bubbling pools of pitch in 1769, and as early as 1875, amateur paleontologists had uncovered prehistoric remains. Great saber-toothed cats and long-tusked mammoths were among the most unusual animal finds. The oldest artifact was a 40,000-year-old fragment of wood.

THE SOUTHWEST MUSEUM. **A Pacific Electric interurban car passes on its way to Pasadena. The MTA Gold Line light rail follows the same route today.**

The Tar Pits also produced possible evidence of L.A.'s first-known murder. The bones of a Native American woman, estimated between eighteen and twenty-four years old, were uncovered in 1914. She had died 9,000 years before, and her fractured skull suggested that a blow to the head might have killed her. Nearby were the remains of a domesticated

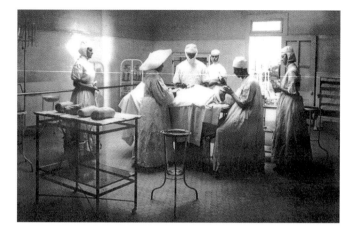

DAUGHTERS OF CHARITY nurses working with surgeons at the Los Angeles Infirmary. In 1913, the infirmary was the first hospital in California accredited by the American College of Surgeons.

dog. Was it a pet? In respect for her Native American ancestors, "La Brea Woman's" bones are no longer on display. How and why she died remains a mystery fit for a prehistoric detective story.

In 1914, the same year as the discovery of La Brea Woman, the Southwest Museum, one of Charles Lummis's causes, moved to an impressive new building on a hill overlooking the outspoken activist's Arroyo Seco home. Two years later, the three-hundredth anniversary of the death of William Shakespeare was commemorated in Beachwood Canyon with an outdoor performance of *Julius Caesar,* including a cast of 3,000 and an overflow audience estimated at 40,000. In 1918, the Otis College of Art and Design, established in the former home of Harrison Gray Otis, and named in his honor, became L.A.'s first school for fine art.

In 1919, Henry Huntington established a formal Library and Art Gallery on his San Marino estate. It was opened to the public in 1928.

Musical ensembles had been popular in Los Angeles since the days of the Mexican dons. In 1919, philanthropist and music lover William Andrews Clark Jr. endowed the Los Angeles Philharmonic, the city's first professional symphony orchestra. Los Angeles joined New York, Boston, Chicago, Cincinnati and St. Louis as one of the few American cities with a professional classical orchestra. The inaugural concert included, appropriately for L.A.'s self-image, Antonin Dvorak's New World Symphony and Emmanuel Chabrier's España.

The most famous Los Angeles site for concerts, opera, theater and just about anything else on a grand scale was located on the corner of Fifth and Olive downtown. The

THE NINETY-FOUR-MEMBER LOS ANGELES PHILHARMONIC poses before its first concert in Trinity Auditorium in October 1919. At the podium: benefactor William Andrews Clark Jr., left, and conductor Walter Rothwell.

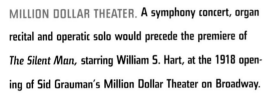

MILLION DOLLAR THEATER. A symphony concert, organ recital and operatic solo would precede the premiere of *The Silent Man,* starring William S. Hart, at the 1918 opening of Sid Grauman's Million Dollar Theater on Broadway.

THE ORPHEUM THEATRE. Describing the interior as "a symphony in rose, ivory and gold," and its shallow depth as a "down-to-date" design, the *Times* welcomed the Orpheum to L.A.'s Broadway theater district in January 1911.

building began in 1886 as a barn-like structure called Hazard's Pavilion. It was replaced by a new auditorium and office complex owned by the city and Temple Baptist Church. The performance space was christened Clune's Auditorium in 1915, and renamed Philharmonic Hall in 1920 when the city's new orchestra adopted it as their concert hall.

In 1915, Clune's hosted the world-famous dancer Vaslaw Nijinsky, performing with an ensemble from Sergei Diaghilev's Ballet Russes. But the greatest attraction that year was not a ballet company, concert, play, opera or even a traveling circus. It was the world premiere of a movie—

THE INTERIOR OF TALLEY'S KINETOSCOPE THEATER at 311 South Spring Street in 1897, the first to show motion pictures in Los Angeles. "Peep show" machines line each wall, showing a round-by-round "reproduction" of the Corbett-Fitzsimmons boxing match.

The Birth of a Nation. D.W. Griffith's controversial masterpiece, with battle scenes shot in the San Fernando Valley, played to packed houses for two years. A twenty-piece orchestra supplied the live soundtrack, and song and dance programs provided preludes for each screening.

Although it offered a racist interpretation of the Civil War, *The Birth of a Nation* set a powerful new standard for motion picture storytelling. Invented in the 1890s, the movies had come a long way in a very short time. They arrived in Los Angeles as early as 1897 when entertainment entrepreneur Thomas Talley proudly exhibited "wholesome" films in his downtown "peep show." Fondly called

"flickers," these early movies only lasted a few minutes. Tickets sold for ten cents.

In the beginning, the American motion picture business was controlled by inventor and entrepreneur Thomas A. Edison. If there was a movie capital, it was in and around Edison's headquarters in New Jersey or New York City, with an outpost in Chicago. To be a legal producer in the 1900s it was necessary to join the Motion Picture Patents Company and pay Edison royalties. Those who wanted to avoid this monopoly set up illegal cameras as far away from the East Coast as possible. In America, there were few places farther than Los Angeles.

The first California movie location was the

THE FIRST HOLLYWOOD MOVIE STUDIO. Famous for westerns and comedies, in 1911, Nestor Studios was the first movie production company to establish headquarters in Hollywood. Five years later the studio was bought by Universal Pictures.

beach at Santa Monica. In 1907, exteriors were shot for *The Count of Monte Cristo,* produced by "Colonel" William Selig, a former magician and minstrel show operator based in Chicago. Impressed by the weather and a variety of possible Southern California environments, Selig built a studio in an old Chinese laundry in downtown Los Angeles, and later in the suburb of Edendale. In 1917, to supply animals for his adventure films, Selig established his own zoo. At the time, it was called the largest collection of wild animals in the world.

The first "Hollywood" producers were two brothers, David and William Horsley. In 1911, they opened Nestor Studios in an old tavern near the corner of Sunset and Gower. Hollywood then was a teetotalist, semi-agricultural village with a population of 500. Typical of Southern California, many of Hollywood's prosperous settlers were from the Midwest. They lived in stately homes surrounded by orchards and farmland.

A local celebrity was painter Paul DeLongpre. Tourists on the Pacific Electric "Balloon Route" stopped at DeLongpre's house to visit his flower gardens and studio. During the next few years, new arrivals began renting land, buying old barns and building studios of their own. They weren't painting flowers like DeLongpre. They were making movies.

After 1910, a remarkable generation of

UNIVERSAL STUDIOS. **A welcoming banner across the entrance to the new Universal Pictures Company in 1915 boasts the studio's founder, Carl Laemmle, as "King of the Movies."**

UNIVERSAL TOURS, 1915. **Tourists watch movie making from an observation platform, part of a popular studio tour.**

DIRECTOR CECIL B. DEMILLE, second from right, on December 29, 1913, the first day of filming *The Squaw Man* for the Lasky Feature Play Company.

cultural entrepreneurs moved to Los Angeles. Among the first was Carl Laemmle, born in Laupheim, Germany, the tenth of thirteen children. In 1884, at age thirteen, Laemmle joined a brother in Chicago, working in the garment business as a bookkeeper and store manager. In 1906, he opened a nickelodeon that led to a small chain of movie theaters. In 1909, he decided to take on Thomas Edison's powerful patent monopoly and established the forerunner of what would become the Universal Company in 1912.

In 1915, after a move to California, Laemmle built a studio in his own town, Universal City, in the San Fernando Valley. To help with Universal's bottom line, the movie pioneer set up bleachers so visitors could watch filmmakers at work. A box lunch was available for twenty-five cents. Later, the advent of movies with sound meant that noisy spectators were no longer welcome, so the Universal Tours were discontinued. In 1964, with specially designed studios and exhibits, they were reestablished to become one of Southern California's most popular tourist attractions.

Samuel Goldwyn (born Goldfish) came to America from Warsaw, Poland, in 1899, when

A TRUCKLOAD OF TALENT for the film *The Squaw Man*. During Hollywood's early days, studios often picked up day extras at a corner of Sunset and Gower, known then and now as Gower Gulch.

he was nineteen. He established a successful glove-making factory in New York. In 1913, he joined with his brother-in-law Jesse L. Lasky, a former musician and vaudeville manager, and Cecil B. DeMille, once a touring actor and theater manager, as a partner in a movie-production company. A few months later, the team merged with Adolph Zukor, a former boxer, furrier and theater owner, to create Famous Players-Lasky Company, which would eventually evolve into Paramount Pictures. A tough negotiator with vision, Zukor was attracted to the idea of translating great plays into movies. In 1916, Samuel Goldwyn moved to Hollywood and two years later formed his own company, Goldwyn Pictures. He became one of Hollywood's longest-lasting and most successful independent producers.

Goldwyn and Lasky's early partner, Cecil B. DeMille, started as an actor and manager of his mother's touring theater company. In 1913, he became a movie director, using a converted Hollywood barn as a studio to create a full-length feature film, *The Squaw Man*. Famous later for his biblical epics, DeMille included enough passion and sex appeal to make his movies hugely successful. His signature puttees and megaphone made him the popular image of a movie director.

The greatest of the early directors was David Wark Griffith. Born in rural Kentucky ten

D.W. GRIFFITH, right, worked closely with innovative cameraman G.W. "Billy" Bitzer for sixteen years. Among their most important collaborations was *The Birth of a Nation*, released in 1915.

years after the end of the Civil War, Griffith began his career as an unsuccessful actor. As with many like him, he was forced to turn to the lowly movies to make a living. It wasn't long before he was directing short films that would expand his skills as an innovative moviemaker. After 450 one- and two-reelers, he was in Hollywood and ready for a major leap ahead — an ambitious project based on a popular novel titled *The Clansmen*. The full-length feature film was *The Birth of a Nation*. After its premiere in Los Angeles in 1915, the

INTOLERANCE SET. The enormous Babylonian set for D. W. Griffith's 1916 film, a masterpiece of the silent era, stood near the present site of public television station KCET.

movies and American art and entertainment would never be the same, and the moviemakers kept coming.

In 1912, Jack L. Warner arrived in Los Angeles. With his brothers Sam, Harry and Albert, he owned a movie distribution business and small theater chain in Ohio. Previously, the brothers had tried various jobs, including work as cobblers, butchers, ice cream salesmen, carnival barkers and soap dealers, before sharing ownership of a bicycle shop. They made their first successful film in 1919.

Louis B. Mayer once worked in his father's scrap and junk business. He launched his own career in 1907 when he bought a run-down Boston movie theater. From there the young entrepreneur built one of the largest theater chains in New England. Moving to Los Angeles in 1918, the former junk dealer eventually reigned over Hollywood's classiest studio, MGM. "I want to make beautiful pictures about beautiful people," he said. During the 1930s, Mayer was America's highest-paid business executive, with an annual salary of $1 million. With the other "moguls" of his generation, many of them once-poor Jewish immigrants, Louis B. Mayer imagined the American Dream and pictured it in the movies. As historian Robert Sklar wrote: "The movies did not describe or explore America, they invented it...and persuaded us to share the dream."

The backdrop for much of this re-imagined America was the City of Los Angeles.

The Hollywood moguls were in charge, and they had financial counterparts in New York who held the production purse strings, but the people movie fans knew and loved best were those whose images they saw on theater screens. Charlie Chaplin, Buster Keaton, Harold Lloyd, Mary Pickford and Douglas Fairbanks were almost as famous around the world as they were in America.

Born into a British family of traveling performers, Charlie Chaplin was six years old when the death of his father left him mostly on his own. With his brother Sidney, Chaplin made his way as a street performer. By fourteen he was playing small theater parts. In 1910, Chaplin's success as a vaudeville comedian resulted in a trip to the United States and a contract with the movies. By 1917, his ten-minute one-reelers were popular enough to allow him to become his own producer. His "little tramp" character had elements of his English music hall days mixed with American action and sentimentality. Together they had universal appeal.

Chaplin's primary rival was Buster Keaton, also a product of vaudeville and knockabout comedy. Keaton's stoic expression, as the world whirled around him, delighted audiences, and the mechanical ingenuity of his humor was a source of laughter and awe. Chaplin and Keaton created their own gags. Harold Lloyd was a comic actor who skillfully followed a script. As physically adept as his two comic colleagues, Lloyd's early persona was "Lonesome Luke," a put-upon everyman. In the '20s, he adopted the character of an eager young man who, when he stumbled into dangerous situations, survived with luck and unexpected skill. Not unlike the City of Los Angeles.

Mary Pickford was "America's Sweetheart," and one of the most powerful figures in Hollywood — male or female. Born in Canada as Gladys Smith, Pickford's father was an alcoholic who died young. To make ends meet, her mother put her children to work on stage. Gladys thrived. By 1907, she was appearing on Broadway in New York with a new name: Mary Pickford.

In 1910, Pickford auditioned for movie director D. W. Griffith and moved with his company to Hollywood to begin a career in motion pictures. By 1915, working for Adolph Zukor, she was the first Hollywood "star," a performer who audiences loved and came to see again and again. In 1920, when Pickford married Douglas Fairbanks, it was the American equivalent of a royal match.

With no dialogue, the movies engaged audiences with action and grand emotions. The acrobatic heroism of Douglas Fairbanks transported viewers to worlds filled with sword fights and flying carpets. Slapstick comedies featuring popular characters such as Max Sennett's Keystone Kops turned city streets into crazy racecourses. The comedy team of Stan Laurel and Oliver Hardy were children in the bodies of adults, fumbling their way through early-twentieth-century life. As the influence of Hollywood movies spread, the environment of Los Angeles became synonymous with America. To the rest of the world, the process of picturing L.A. produced an image of life in the United States.

If Hollywood was an image factory for America, Los Angeles remained a distant appendage to the traditional United States economy. The economic success of turn-of-the-century L.A. rested on a limited foundation. Many of the people who came to the city were more interested in finding a comfortable life than building factories and businesses. Agriculture was as important as ever, and so was tourism, but industrialization as it was known in the East remained relatively underdeveloped. World War I made this clear. With the exception of some shipbuilding, Los Angeles made few industrial contributions in the great conflict. As one local banker said, "The most conspicuous fact about Los Angeles lies in its being a residential and not an industrial community." Another summed up

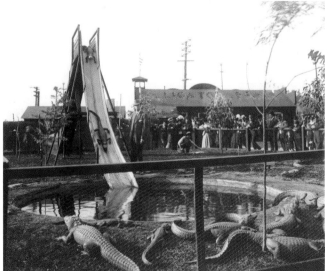

THE CALIFORNIA ALLIGATOR FARM. If Florida could do it, why not L.A.? Located on Mission Road in Lincoln Heights, the California alligator farm was conveniently next door to an ostrich farm. The Selig Zoo was also just down the road.

THE SELIG ZOO was established in 1915 by film producer William Selig to house animals for his movies. It was sold and renamed Luna Park ten years later.

1913—14 FLOODS. If L.A. was a man-made city, nature was always ready to show who was boss. The Arroyo Seco is shown here near its confluence with the Los Angeles River during the 1913—14 winter floods, the most destructive in L.A. history.

the local economy as a process of "swapping jackknives back and forth among ourselves."

In 1918, a worldwide epidemic of Spanish flu claimed twenty million lives. In Los Angeles there were 3,000 victims, including pioneer surfer George Freeth. Tourism fell and the local economy suddenly seemed vulnerable. Even though there was an ever-growing population, a new source of water, an infant

international port and continuing riches from agriculture, real estate and the emerging power of the movies, many Angelenos still wondered whether there was enough to assure future survival and, even more important to an entrepreneurial business community, growth. By 1919, Los Angeles was a place of great promise. The question remained: Could the promise be kept?

THE GREAT AMERICAN BOOMTOWN

"Los Angeles, the optimistic, the positive, the vociferous — Jazz Baby of the Golden West, I greet you!"

DON RYAN, Angels Flight, *1927*

"If New York is the melting pot for Europe," a writer once declared, "Los Angeles is the melting pot for America." In the 1920s, Eurocentric East Coast tastemakers and intellectuals proudly accepted the first half of that equation. They laughed at any thought of the last.

After decades of self-promotion and hyperbole, the '20s accelerated a long tradition of journalists and commentators arriving in Los Angeles from the East, looking around for a few days, and returning to write about a place they concluded was eccentric, uncultured and irredeemably irrelevant. Baltimore journalist and wit H. L. Mencken had a one-word description: "Moronia." "The whole place stank of orange blossoms," he added grumpily. English novelist and poet D. H. Lawrence was more ambivalent, "I don't want to live here, but a stay here rather amuses me. It's a sort of crazy-sensible." Journalist Paul Jordan-Smith sensed there was more. After a catalog of inadequacies, he added: "...the place is alive with illusions, and illusions are the stuff of art."

Name-calling aside, in the 1920s, along with the rest of the nation, energetic Los Angeles had mixed feelings about the arid constraints of Prohibition. The city had many dry enthusiasts, but as it was in New York and Chicago, the result was more high jinks than sobriety. In the end, if the

CITY HALL was the symbol of modern Los Angeles. Completed in 1928, it was designed by a team that included John Parkinson, Albert C. Martin Sr. and John Austin.

rest of America in the 1920s was, as the song said, "Runnin' Wild," Los Angeles was racing ahead. No city in the nation was growing faster. When the decade opened, nearly one million people lived in L.A. County, making it America's most populous. In 1920, with 575,000 people living within city limits, Los Angeles surpassed San Francisco as California's biggest city. As it had in the two previous decades, during the 1920s, the population of the city and county would double again.

As before, most newcomers were transplants from the Midwest. Los Angeles boosters liked to picture their city as a "white spot" on the map of America. That had never been true. During the 1920s, restrictive immigration policies halted new arrivals from Asia, yet Los Angeles had a Chinatown that dated to the

nineteenth century, and in 1925, a Japanese community of 21,000 was made more visible by the opening of the Nishi Hongwanji Buddhist temple, the largest in the United States. With 39,000 African Americans and 97,000 of Mexican descent, non-whites made up 14 percent of the population, mostly confined in segregated neighborhoods.

By the end of the decade, Los Angeles was no longer an industrial fledgling. Along with agriculture, real estate, manufacturing and the movies, underlying the Los Angeles economy, in more ways than one, was oil. The city sprawled across one of the largest oil fields in the world. By 1923, at least 270 wells were pumping crude on Signal Hill, near Long Beach Harbor. This field of derricks would prove to be one of the most productive on

TIME PASSES.
In 1923, three different views
of Los Angeles celebrate the
growth of the city.

the planet. With other wells in communities such as Wilmington, Venice and Baldwin Hills, during the 1920s, the Los Angeles area provided one-fifth of the world's petroleum.

Given this, it is not surprising that one of the greatest scandals of the era involved oil and that it took place in booming, fast-and-loose Los Angeles. Smooth-talking Chauncey C. Julian, "C. C." to his friends and victims, arrived in 1922 and started selling $100 shares in two well sites he had leased in nearby Santa Fe Springs. Advertising on radio and in newspapers, Julian promised an opportunity for "the little guy" to cash in on the oil boom. It wasn't long before he'd collected nearly $700,000.

The first well turned a profit. The second, on the same site, was a dry hole. Undeterred, Julian kept selling stock until he had more investors than shares. His Julian Petroleum Company, nicknamed "Julian Pete," was eventually oversold by $2 million. The dapper

CABRILLO BEACH, seen in this 1923 postcard, was a popular seaside retreat adjacent to the harbor at San Pedro. It was named for Spanish explorer Juan Rodriguez Cabrillo, who anchored off the Los Angeles coast in 1542.

CATALINA ISLAND was formerly owned by chewing gum magnate William Wrigley Jr. Seen here in 1929, it was already a popular offshore playground.

salesman reassured investors that all was well by spending lavishly, buying a gold-plated bathtub and once tipping a cab driver $1,500.

By 1925, the FBI was suspicious. C. C. slipped the noose by selling his company to two new owners with connections in the highest circles of L.A.'s elite. The two, S. C. Lewis and Jacob Berman, were even more unscrupulous than C. C. To inflate share prices, they issued $5 million in fraudulent certificates. In the financial feeding frenzy that followed, the con men attracted the interest and investments of movie moguls Louis B. Mayer and Cecil B. DeMille, and even Harry Chandler, publisher of the powerful *L.A. Times,* as well as other respected businessmen, some of whom were willing to look the other way about details in return for sizable returns on their investment.

CHAUNCEY C. JULIAN. Would you buy an oil well from this man? In 1920s Los Angeles, everyday folks, eager to profit from the oil boom, sent hundreds of thousands of dollars to the founder of the "Julian Pete" oil company. Most lost it all.

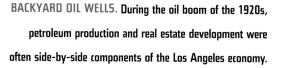

BACKYARD OIL WELLS. During the oil boom of the 1920s, petroleum production and real estate development were often side-by-side components of the Los Angeles economy.

It was a classic pyramid scheme. With little in reserve, Lewis and Berman used new money to pay old investors. They had created a tower of teetering cards held up by greed. The cards came crashing down on May 5, 1927. When the con was finally discovered, 42,000 investors were left empty-handed, and a phantom $40 million vanished from the local economy.

Along with Lewis and Berman, fifty-three others, including some of L.A.'s most prominent citizens, were on the indictment list. But the trial was a fiasco. Undermined by political pressures and bribes, an inept prosecution resulted in an astonishing not-guilty verdict in favor of the schemers. In a later trial, after bribery claims were proven, S.C. Lewis and Jacob Berman finally served jail time. Tellingly, so did their former prosecutor, Los Angeles District Attorney Asa Keyes.

After his release, Keyes bounced back to become a successful automobile dealer, while Lewis and Berman faded from view. As for C.C. Julian who started it all, he railed against bankers as the real culprits and continued to

promote quick money schemes, keeping one step ahead of the law. On March 23, 1934, he was still putting up a lavish front in Shanghai, China. In fact, he was broke. That night he took an overdose of drugs after a twenty-year-old secretary and confidante turned down his last joint venture — marriage.

In increasingly fast-paced Los Angeles, Angelenos and tourists traveled between new communities that kept popping up near 1,000 miles of Pacific Electric interurban train tracks. The '20s were busy years for the Pacific Electric, with 2,400 trains scheduled every day. Nearly 110 million passengers rode the rails in 1924, a peak year. Even so, automobile owners were honking their horns. They wanted trains and trolleys out of the way. In 1920, more than 100,000 cars were cruising

DOWNTOWN PEDESTRIANS. In a picture that could have been taken in New York, the old urban core of Los Angeles is the heart of the city, but suburban expansion, already underway, would change that.

HISTORY LEFT BEHIND. By 1927, the center of Anglo Angeleno life moved south and west, leaving the old plaza and its church to mostly Mexican and Chinese residents, as it had been in the 1860s.

MIRACLE MILE. Wilshire doesn't look much like a miracle in this 1930 photo, but those large lots will soon be filled with new stores, apartments and office buildings.

OIL FIELDS EVERYWHERE. Evidence of a powerful addition to L.A.'s multifaceted economy, A. F. Gilmore employees pose at one of the company's oil-drilling sites in today's Fairfax district.

Los Angeles County streets, and billboards and gas stations were sprouting like weeds.

Automobiles were transforming Los Angeles in other ways. While downtown L.A.'s north-south thoroughfare, Broadway, was burgeoning, a western section of Wilshire Boulevard attracted so many fancy new stores and office buildings that by 1928 it was already known as "the Miracle Mile." Author Reyner Banham called it "the first real monument to the Motor Age." Two years later, the opening of the art deco Bullocks Wilshire department store was a sign that shopping in Los Angeles wouldn't remain solely in the traditional heart of the city. Indicating even more about auto-inspired influences to come, Bullocks' main entrance faced a rear parking lot, catering to shoppers arriving by car.

L.A.'s fancy thoroughfare was the name-sake of Gaylord Wilshire, an Angeleno who perfectly fit East Coast perceptions. Born to a wealthy Ohio family, Wilshire was a real estate entrepreneur and outspoken utopian Socialist who made a fortune selling an "electric belt" he claimed could cure virtually any ailment. As wild-eyed as Wilshire appeared to Easterners in the early twentieth century, more than a few of the social causes he and others advocated, including the dream of a national pension plan, would become American realities in the decades to come. At the time though, they were

DOWNTOWN NORTH HOLLYWOOD. During the 1920s, once-agricultural communities like the San Fernando Valley town of Lankershim, later named North Hollywood, began to establish independent identities.

COLLISION COURSE. By the 1920s, traffic was already a problem in downtown Los Angeles. With more people choosing cars over trolleys, Angelenos began complaining about traffic snarls. It was the beginning of the end for the trains that gave the early city its extended shape.

BEVERLY HILLS. Looking south over the Beverly Hills Hotel and Sunset Boulevard about 1920. In the far background, swampy lands known as *cienegas* are yet to be drained and developed.

AN L.A. FIRST. Building the tunnel for L.A.'s first subway in 1926. Relatively short, it led to the downtown Hill Street station of the Pacific Electric Railway.

BUSTLING BROADWAY welcomes a 1925 Shriners' Convention.

A NEW THOROUGHFARE. In 1922, plans were being made for Santa Monica Boulevard in the developing community of Westwood.

MOTORCYCLE MODELS. A friendly warning for a 1927 Convention of the Association of Highway Patrolmen. L.A. wasn't ready for women with badges on bikes; the pert riders are department secretaries and office workers.

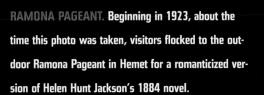

RAMONA PAGEANT. Beginning in 1923, about the time this photo was taken, visitors flocked to the outdoor Ramona Pageant in Hemet for a romanticized version of Helen Hunt Jackson's 1884 novel.

GO SLOW and see our town
GO FAST and see our jail

lumped in with Wilshire's electric belt as just another example of eccentric, starry-eyed L.A.

With more cars and people came new institutions and landmarks. In 1921, the Hollywood Bowl, a natural amphitheater in the hills between Hollywood and the San Fernando Valley, was inaugurated with its first Easter Sunrise service. The following year, the Los Angeles Philharmonic opened a yearly summer series of "Concerts Under the Stars." In 1923, visitors got a new world-class downtown hotel, the Biltmore, and college sports fans gathered in the Pasadena Rose Bowl for the first time. That same year, with city plans to host the 1932 Olympic Games, a new sports arena, the Los Angeles Memorial Coliseum, was finished. Nearby, the world's largest auditorium, the rebuilt 6,000-seat Shrine, was completed in 1926. Two years later, the city leased land for a municipal airport, Mines Field, which would evolve from isolated farmland into Los Angeles International Airport, one of the busiest in the world.

It may have missed critics and casual

THE HOLLYWOOD BOWL in 1929 had permanent seats in an arrangement designed by architect Myron Hunt. A new shell had replaced one designed by Frank Lloyd Wright's son Lloyd.

HOLLYWOOD BOWL UNDER CONSTRUCTION. A natural amphitheater at the south end of Cahuenga Pass was the location chosen by private funders for the Hollywood Bowl. During the early years, audience members sat on the grassy hillside.

observers, but Los Angeles had serious, and even intellectual, aspirations. A beautiful new downtown public library was dedicated in 1926, and in 1927, the University of California at Los Angeles broke ground for a campus on the gently rolling hills of Westwood.

While UCLA was being born, the University of Southern California was making a name for itself in football. In 1926, the Trojans took on Knute Rockne's Notre Dame, drawing a sell-out crowd of 76,000 to the Coliseum and launching a rivalry that would last for decades between the Midwest and a city filled with former Midwesterners. The first score was 13-12 in favor of the "Fighting Irish." Over the years, Southern California grew to dominate the matchup, adding athletic prowess to a growing East-to-West power shift. Two years later, in 1928, USC's

UCLA CAMPUS. In 1930, a tour bus passes a lake where Pauley Pavilion, home of UCLA basketball, would be built decades later. Royce Hall and the College Library can be seen in the far right distance.

USC FOOTBALL PLAYERS. Staged or not, this isn't the kind of photo to strike fear into USC football opponents. In 1920, Trojan players pretend to work out on the beach at Santa Monica, but when game time came, they were more than ready.

NEWLY COMPLETED COLISEUM. In 1924, with the campus of the University of Southern California in the foreground, the Los Angeles Memorial Coliseum is ready for the 1932 Olympics.

L.A.'S NEW CITY HALL, completed in 1928 between Spring and Main streets, was the city's tallest building until the 1950s.

"Thundering Herd" earned the first of eight twentieth-century national championships.

In 1928, Los Angeles celebrated another source of civic pride. A striking new thirty-two-story City Hall dominated the low-rise downtown skyline. The gleaming white tower ignored the city's Spanish-influenced past, and looked to the ancient days of Biblical Assyria and Babylon, as if to suggest that a new cradle of civilization was emerging on the American West Coast. City Hall was an exception to a height limit on downtown

buildings, set in the city charter after the 1906 San Francisco earthquake. It was topped by a beacon dedicated to aviator Charles Lindbergh—a celebration of a rapidly emerging aviation age already at home in Southern California.

Despite a decade of serious institution building, what often attracted the attention of visiting observers was a more playful and eccentric style of architecture. If East Coast photo editors wanted to picture oddball Los Angeles, the city obliged with more buildings that looked like animals and other overgrown objects than anywhere in the world. The most famous was the first Brown Derby restaurant, built on Wilshire Boulevard in 1926.

The most visible unconventional Los Angeles landmark started as a real estate advertisement. In 1924, a group of investors, which included the ubiquitous Harry Chandler, developed a community in Beachwood Canyon just north of Hollywood. They marked their turf with a sign constructed of fifty-foot letters that spelled "Hollywoodland." High on a hillside, the Hollywood sign, outlined with electric lights, could be seen for miles, but the Depression of the 1930s dampened enthusiasm for Beachwood Canyon's stately stone castles and Mediterranean villas. By the 1950s, the "land" had fallen down, leaving

SPHINX REAL ESTATE. Such fanciful constructions led many East Coast visitors to conclude that life in L.A. was out of control, if not mad. Crazy or not, it attracted attention to a new housing development near Fairfax Boulevard.

HOLLYWOODLAND. A huge hillside sign draws prospective buyers to the Hollywoodland development. After the "land" part of the sign fell off, the remainder was restored to become one of L.A.'s most famous landmarks.

MOTHER GOOSE PANTRY. In 1925, the Mother Goose Pantry on Colorado Boulevard in Pasadena offered dining in a shoe.

THE BROWN DERBY. The world-famous restaurant on Wilshire Boulevard, seen during the 1930s.

LOS ANGELES JUNIOR ORCHESTRA. In an unusual example of racial integration in 1920, the Los Angeles Junior Orchestra included two young African American musicians, at upper right.

BEHIND THE SCENES in 1928 Los Angeles, Mexican women make handmade tortillas.

AGRICULTURE WAS A FAMILY AFFAIR FOR JAPANESE ANGELENOS. More Japanese Americans and immigrants lived in Los Angeles County than in any other part of the state or nation. They played an important role in L.A. produce markets in the 1920s.

FINDING NEW WAYS TO FLY. By the end of the 1920s, Los Angeles was a center of aviation innovation. Despite skeptics, Jack Northrop, left, founder of Northrop Aviation in 1929, championed the concept of a flying wing nearly fifty years before it was successfully adopted with the Stealth bomber.

Los Angeles with an unexpected identifier that became as well known as the Statue of Liberty and the Eiffel Tower.

Construction of an even more idiosyncratic Los Angeles landmark was begun in 1921. It would be the lifetime work of an Italian immigrant named Sabato "Simon" Rodia. As unconventional as L.A., Rodia's vision was unfinished when he died in 1965. The eccentrically assembled shards of pottery, tiles and found objects making up what would become known as Watts Towers could stand for culture in Los Angeles, adopting an ad hoc image that was very much its own.

In the 1920s, the movies were hardly considered cultured, but they continued to transform America and the world. In 1921, Hollywood released 854 motion pictures, an all-time record. If the movies weren't considered art, they were certainly a very big business. By the end of the decade, fifty-two Los Angeles movie studios were employing 15,000 people and paying $72.1 million in salaries and wages.

One of the era's most talented producers was Irving Thalberg. At twenty-one, Thalberg became the executive in charge of production at Universal Studios. In 1924, at age

WATTS TOWERS. Made from found materials, the largest tower is almost one hundred feet tall.

SIMON RODIA. L.A.'s openness allowed for new kinds of artistic expression. Beginning in the 1920s, Italian immigrant Sabato Rodia spent thirty years building the nine major structures known today as the Watts Towers.

twenty-five, he joined Louis B. Mayer at MGM. His tough management style and literary story sense influenced movies as diverse as the gritty World War I drama *The Big Parade,* the glossy *Grand Hotel* and wild Marx Brothers comedies, such as *A Night at the Opera.* Always burdened with poor health, Thalberg died in 1936 when he was only thirty-seven years old. Author F. Scott Fitzgerald, who spent time in Hollywood as a frustrated screenwriter, took the young mogul as the model for the hero of his unfinished final novel, *The Last Tycoon.*

MGM boasted a "galaxy" of stars, and movie celebrities were America's aristocracy.

Mary Pickford and Douglas Fairbanks reigned from Pickfair, their mansion in Beverly Hills. Charlie Chaplin was probably the most recognizable man in the world. When Rudolph Valentino died in 1926, at the age of thirty, he was mourned with more fervor than the unexpected death of United States President Warren G. Harding three years before.

While movie stars were royalty, audiences

LOUIS B. MAYER AND IRVING THALBERG. Louis B. Mayer, center, was one of the original Hollywood moguls. To Mayer's left, brilliant MGM studio chief Irving Thalberg. On Mayer's right, producer Maurice Rapf.

PICKFORD STUDIOS. The Pickford-Fairbanks Hollywood studios on Santa Monica Boulevard in 1926. The large set in the lower left is a remnant of the 1924 film *The Thief of Bagdad.*

were treated like an aristocracy of their own. The 1920s was the beginning of the great age of the movie palace. Grand and opulent, almost every large city in America had at least one. In downtown Los Angeles, the palaces that lined Broadway included the lavish 1927 Spanish-style United Artists Theater and the aptly named Million Dollar Theatre. The first in Hollywood was the Egyptian, looking like a survivor from the age of the pharaohs, and the most famous, Grauman's Chinese Theatre, an Oriental fantasy, was home to the grandest of Hollywood premieres.

The Chinese Theatre opened in 1927 with the premiere of Cecil B. DeMille's *The King of Kings*. The first movie stars to leave an impression in the theater's concrete forecourt were Mary Pickford and Douglas Fairbanks. More than 170 would follow. The first Academy Awards, in May 1929, was a modest affair,

THE OPENING OF SID GRAUMAN'S CHINESE THEATRE in 1927 featured Cecil B. DeMille's biblical epic *The King of Kings*.

BUSTER KEATON was Charlie Chaplin's mute rival. Here, he appears in the wildly inventive 1924 film *Sherlock, Jr.*

CHARLIE CHAPLIN was not only a master motion picture actor, he was one of the medium's greatest early directors.

WARNER BROTHERS STUDIOS in Hollywood in 1926. The two towers are transmitters for radio station KFWB, also owned by the film studio.

KNX RADIO STATION as it appeared in 1926. It began six years before when a former WWI wireless operator started broadcasting from his Hollywood home. KNX became an affiliate of the CBS network in 1936.

A RADIO ENTHUSIAST. If there was any doubt that radio was the latest and greatest in the 1920s, this exuberant publicity photograph says it all.

held across the street from the Chinese Theatre at the Hollywood Roosevelt Hotel.

In 1928, a technical revolution transformed Hollywood. The dream of sound movies can be traced to the earliest experiments of Thomas Edison in the 1890s. Hollywood made tests of its own throughout the '20s. The first widely distributed "talky" was *The Jazz Singer*, starring Al Jolson. When the black-faced vaudevillian loudly declared, "You ain't heard nothin' yet!" he was right.

Sound brought the careers of many silent movie stars to an end, but it increased the impact of movies on American and world culture. With its influences on everything from fashion to sex, Hollywood created a controversial picture of Los Angeles, and to the rest of the world a vivid image of a distinctly

American attitude — fast-talking and filled with high spirits, energy and optimism.

Picturing Los Angeles became nearly instantaneous with the first "wire photo," a process that used telephone lines to transmit scanned images. With wire photos and the movies, the Jazz Age was there for everyone to see. The monitors of American morality weren't pleased with the portrait.

Religious leaders in Los Angeles didn't hesitate to express their outrage — some more loudly than others. Radio amplified the voice of Robert "Fighting Bob" Shuler, a politically ambitious preacher who arrived in Los Angeles from Tennessee in 1920. Shuler didn't mince words. He hated corrupt politicians, Catholics, Jews, jazz, dancing, the movies and evolution. Forty-two thousand parishioners followed his every word. Historian Kevin Starr called him "a paranoid populist." In 1931, Fighting Bob's ranting finally cost him his broadcasting license, and most of his influence. The old preacher kept fulminating until

FATTY ARBUCKLE. A third jury finally declared popular comedian "Fatty" Arbuckle, center right, not guilty of the rape and death of an aspiring actress. But to moralistic Americans in the 1920s, he remained a symbol of sinful Hollywood.

the day he died thirty-four years later.

If Los Angeles was essentially a Midwestern American town writ large, ironically, an eager press pictured it as a twentieth-century Sodom. While Chicago and New York claimed the Roaring Twenties as their own, writer Carey McWilliams noted that "Los Angeles led the nation in the number of suicides, the number of embezzlements, the number of bank robberies, in the rate of narcotic addiction, and in the fancy character of its sensational murders."

Confirming McWilliams's claim wasn't difficult. In 1921, the country was shocked and horrified by the trial of one of Hollywood's most beloved comedians, Roscoe "Fatty"

BIBLICAL ORGIES showed moviegoers the wages of sin—and a lot more. The result was a motion picture code of censorship.

Arbuckle. Arbuckle, known for his bad-boy innocence on screen, was charged with the rape and murder of a little-known starlet named Virginia Rappe. News stories of the sensational trials that followed ended his career. Although he was eventually found innocent, and the final jury went so far as to offer an apology for his ordeal, it was too late. Long before, Arbuckle had been convicted in the press.

Besides, another scandalous Hollywood murder had already captured the headlines. On February 2, 1922, a dapper movie director, William Desmond Taylor, was found dead in his home. The investigation that followed turned up evidence of drug use and a revolving door of Hollywood beauties, including seventeen-year-old Mary Miles Minter and well-loved comedienne Mabel Normand, who, it turned out, was supporting a serious cocaine habit. In the media furor that followed, more than

HOLLYWOOD MYSTERY MAN. The actor turned director who called himself William Desmond Taylor had a past as mysterious as his death. His murder in February 1926 was a scandal that involved some of Hollywood's most famous stars.

300 people confessed to the crime. No one was convicted. More than forty years later, fellow director King Vidor offered evidence that Taylor actually preferred gay relationships, and he named Mary Miles Minter's mother as the killer. Despite this, in L.A. police files, the case remains unsolved.

One of the most gruesome crimes of the decade involved a young psychopath with movie-star good looks but no Hollywood connections. Nineteen-year-old Edward Hickman

EDWARD HICKMAN, found guilty of the December 1927 kidnapping, murder and mutilation of twelve-year-old Marian Parker, appears more concerned with the appearance of his hair than his scheduled execution. Hickman was probably responding to a photographer looking for an interesting picture.

claimed he needed $1,500 for his college tuition when he kidnapped twelve-year-old Marian Parker, the daughter of a Los Angeles banker. Calling himself "the Fox," he taunted police until Parker's parents agreed to pay a ransom.

On the night of December 18, 1927, Hickman showed up in a car, with his victim apparently sitting beside him. After taking the money, the Fox drove off, promising to release the girl down the road. Her father followed and found her— dead. Hickman had cut Marian Parker's body in half and placed her torso in the passenger seat. To make his victim look alive, he had powdered her face and used thread to sew her eyelids open.

On October 19, 1928, the Fox was hanged in San Quentin State Prison. He never made it to college.

In 1926, Los Angeles police faced another kidnapping. This time the victim was one of the most famous women in the city, Aimee Semple McPherson. In "Sister Aimee's" Angelus Temple, worship was theater. Dressed in diaphanous gowns and bathed in spotlights, she gave dramatic sermons and enacted struggles for the soul with winged angels and brass bands. Like her bigoted competitor, Fighting Bob Shuler, radio amplified Aimee's messages and multiplied her congregation.

On May 18, the lady evangelist disappeared from a beach between Santa Monica and

EVANGELICAL LOVERS. Aimee Semple McPherson and her radio engineer, broadcasting from the Angelus Temple station shortly before the two disappeared on a month-long romantic tryst.

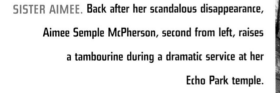

SISTER AIMEE. Back after her scandalous disappearance, Aimee Semple McPherson, second from left, raises a tambourine during a dramatic service at her Echo Park temple.

WITH PROHIBITION THE LAW in 1927, Sheriff Eugene Biscailuz, far left, helps pour 400 gallons of alcohol down the drain. A deputy since 1907, Biscailuz became head of the L.A. Sheriff's Department, the largest in the world, in 1932. He remained on the job for thirty-six years.

Venice. Believing that she'd drowned, mourning followers hired airplanes to drop flowers over the site. One devotee died while diving in the surf to search for her body. Five weeks later, the ever-theatrical Aimee made an unexpected re-appearance near the Mexican border. Her return to Los Angeles was like a second coming. She claimed to have been kidnapped. A police investigation raised doubts. In fact, clues strongly suggested that she'd spent her missing weeks trysting with her radio engineer. Sister Aimee's trial for misleading police made headlines until Asa Keyes, the politically sensitive Los Angeles district attorney, dropped all charges. Some

said he was bribed. As the Julian Pete trial later proved, it wasn't out of the question.

Contrary to what some evangelistic boosters might think, the explosive growth of Los Angeles was not an act of God. It was made possible by a man-made supply of water. Shortly after L.A.'s aqueduct was completed in 1913, feelings of anger and betrayal quieted in the Owens Valley. However, by the 1920s, each new year brought fresh evidence that their community was being drained dry, while the newly watered San Fernando Valley was booming.

On May 21, 1924, increasing tensions and a long and heated legal battle turned violent. Near the town of Independence, a dynamite blast blew a gaping hole in the aqueduct, interrupting the water supply to Los Angeles. City leaders were infuriated at what they considered an act of terrorism, but to many Owens Valley residents, it was an act of desperation against the overwhelming power of Los Angeles. In the weeks that followed, the damage was repaired but the fury and frustration remained. On November 16, armed men from the town of Bishop, in the heart of the valley, arrived in Model Ts and took possession of aqueduct gates in the nearby Alabama Hills. Women followed with food, and the insurrection became a triumphant picnic as sympathy for Owens Valley residents continued to grow. Adding to the festivities, Hollywood cowboy star Tom Mix, who was shooting a movie nearby, turned up with a mariachi band.

Los Angeles leadership was not amused. Order was restored and repairs made, but there were more dynamite attacks during the spring of 1927. The Water Bureau responded with more lawsuits and armed guards. At last, the situation cooled off when the two banker brothers who were leaders of the protest were arrested and charged with embezzlement. Well before then, Los Angeles had developed a strategy for preserving the safety of the city's water supply. Plans had been made to construct two new reservoirs closer to the city. They would be created by formidable concrete dams.

The first was in the hills above Hollywood. A reservoir there would bring water to the very edge of Los Angeles, and certainly enhance the attractions of a new real estate development adjacent to Hollywoodland. The second was forty-five miles to the north, in isolated San Francisquito Canyon. Construction of the Weid Canyon (later Mulholland) Dam in Hollywood began in 1923. Work on its northern sister, the St. Francis Dam, started in

DYNAMITED AQUEDUCT. Los Angeles investigators inspect damage to the Owens Valley Aqueduct in May 1927. It was the fourth of ten attacks by Owens Valley vigilantes during a decade of water wars.

April 1924. It was positioned between two hydroelectric power plants, which together supplied 90 percent of L.A.'s electricity.

The pressures of growth pressed on both dams. Mulholland declared that the St. Francis would hold a year's supply of water, and he worked quickly to complete it. It was still unfinished when unexpected population increases made the Chief's commitment impossible to honor. He responded by raising the height of the dam until it towered almost 200 feet above the canyon floor. The massive wall of concrete was finally completed in May 1926. During the next two years, the reservoir behind it was gradually filled until it held 12.5 billion gallons.

As water crept up the back of the St. Francis Dam, leaks appeared. Minor leaks in a new concrete dam weren't uncommon, and the cracks were repaired. On March 12, 1928, a possibly more serious leak was reported. The dam keeper at the site thought the water flow looked muddy, which could indicate the structure's foundation was failing. That morning, William Mulholland personally went to investigate. His assistant, Harvey Van Norman accompanied him. Mulholland and Van Norman saw no muddy flow and the Chief assumed the dam was safe. Despite this, less than twelve hours later, just before midnight, the St. Francis Dam shuddered, cracked and burst apart. The horrifying flood that followed,

MULHOLLAND DAM. In the distance, the dam, a V-shaped wall of concrete, holds back a reservoir only a short distance from the corner of Hollywood and Vine. After the collapse of its younger sister, the St. Francis Dam, the water level at Mulholland Dam was permanently lowered. The dam was reinforced with an earthen berm and shielded from sight by eucalyptus trees.

ST. FRANCIS DAM COLLAPSE. The morning after the 1928 midnight collapse of the St. Francis Dam, a devastated William Mulholland, left, and his assistant, Harvey Van Norman, view what remains. More than 400 people died in the tragedy.

with crests as high as 185 feet, surged fifty-four miles to the Pacific Ocean, overwhelming everything in its path. As many as 450 people lost their lives.

How could a dam apparently safe only twelve hours before fail so catastrophically? With Owens Valley dynamiters on trial, there were rumors of sabotage. But the underlying causes of the disaster needed no conspiracy— they were the result of human errors and misjudgments, exacerbated by the social and political pressures rushing Los Angeles into an uncertain future.

At age seventy-two, William Mulholland was a legendary figure — the man who played a major role in making modern Los Angeles possible when he oversaw completion of the Owens Valley Aqueduct. Yet, in the end, the

power of water that gave him his greatest fame brought him down. With unquestioned authority, confident that his years of experience were enough to face any challenge, the Chief had chosen to build the St. Francis Dam without consulting independent engineers, even as new technologies were transforming dam design. The ancient Greeks had a name for his overconfidence — *hubris*.

Mulholland could have made excuses, but true to his character he accepted full responsibility for the failure. Even so, he went to his grave in 1935 without accepting any of the explanations for what had caused the collapse, and remained silent about theories of his own.

Long after Mulholland's death, his first concrete dam, built in the Hollywood Hills, still

LOOKING NORTH ACROSS DOWNTOWN. By 1929, Los Angeles was already reaching out to the south and west.

In the distance the new City Hall towers over the cityscape.

stands. As for the St. Francis, investigations showed it was positioned on a site fraught with overlooked geological hazards.

Following Mulholland's lead, the City of Los Angeles accepted responsibility for the St. Francis Dam disaster. Repairs were made along the flood path, and restitution was paid to those who made claims for lost property and for the deaths of family members. The final cost was an estimated $12 to $15 million. The largest single claimant was the nearly bankrupt Newhall Land and Farming Company. A settlement of more than $700,000 saved the family-owned business, ironically allowing the enterprise to go on to become one of California's largest and most successful land developers, accommodating further growth and adding more demands on Southern California's water system.

By the end of the 1920s, contrary to popular perceptions, Los Angeles was far more than a superficial boomtown. The time had long passed when a man like William Mulholland could command knowledge of every pipe and valve in the city's water system. The Chief's self-taught skills and unstinting dedication had helped L.A. achieve unprecedented growth and success, but as both he and the city aged, change, like the floodwaters unleashed by the St. Francis collapse, was rushing ahead.

In 1928, from the isolated upper reaches of San Francisquito Canyon, far from the lights of Hollywood and the bustling traffic on Broadway or Wilshire Boulevard, Los Angeles received a tragic lesson in the consequences of misunderstood technology and uncontrolled growth.

Soon the United States would confront another kind of catastrophe—an economic and political failure that would set America on the edge of collapse. Again, a young Los Angeles would serve as a laboratory for change.

BROTHER, CAN YOU SPARE A DREAM?

"Many citizens in the city of Los Angeles find themselves in the embarrassing situation of being unemployed."

LOS ANGELES CITY COUNCIL MINUTES, *January 30, 1930*

For more than fifty years, local boosters claimed there was no better place in the world to live than Los Angeles. The 1930s challenged them to prove it. Even after the explosive changes of the 1920s, L.A. had the capacity to grow. In 1928, shortly after William Mulholland experienced his worst nightmare, one of his oldest dreams was realized with the creation of the Metropolitan Water District of Southern California (MWD), a regional association that brought more water through a new aqueduct from the Colorado River, and later transported electricity from Hoover Dam. MWD would allow other Southern California cities to continue to survive and grow, even as it slaked L.A.'s thirst for water and power. Yet, if positive change was possible, was it inevitable? An answer came a year later when the city — and the United States — faced the consequences of the stock market crash of 1929.

By 1932, 25 percent of Americans were out of work. In the past, the City of Angels had welcomed newcomers. As the impact of the Depression increased, formerly open arms were closed to immigrants from the dust-blown farms of Oklahoma and the Southwest. They came anyway.

GINGER ROGERS AND FRED ASTAIRE. Elegant and stylish, Rogers and Astaire swept movie audiences to a carefree world during the dark years of the 1930s.

In 1932, the Southern Pacific Railroad reported that it had evicted 80,000 "hobos" looking for a free ride to the Promised Land at the edge of the Pacific.

Crossing the Colorado River in the ramshackle cars made famous by John Steinbeck's 1939 novel *The Grapes of Wrath,* 600,000 "dust bowl refugees," as songwriter Woody Guthrie called them, made it to the Golden State. Most were heading for farm work in California's Central Valley, but Los Angeles wanted no part of them. In 1936, in an attempt to hold back the tide, Los Angeles Police Chief James "Two Gun" Davis sent more than 100 armed officers to set up a "bum blockade" at the California border. In one week, more than a thousand "undesirables" were denied entrance.

The *L.A. Times* cheered. The State Attorney General declared the action unconstitutional.

In the booming 1920s, America had actively recruited Mexican agricultural workers. When the Depression hit, the country began repatriating them. In Los Angeles, immigrant workers were rounded up and sent back over the border. A deal was made with the Southern Pacific to transport immigrants for

A SALES PITCH FOR WATER WAS A SALES PITCH FOR GROWTH. This bond measure allowed Los Angeles to purchase more water rights in the Owens Valley and Mono Basin.

DUST BOWL REFUGEES. Most headed north, hoping to find work in California's central valley. A "bum blockade," enforced by L.A. police, stopped many at the California border in an attempt to keep them away from the city.

THE HOMELESS WARE FAMILY tries to make the best of a bad situation on Terminal Island in Los Angeles harbor. A simple Christmas tree suggests the Wares would have a meager holiday season.

JAMES E. "TWO GUN" DAVIS took a tough approach to law enforcement, but the mayor's office and the police department were rife with corruption.

DECEMBER IN LOS ANGELES. Despite Depression-era realities, the Los Angeles Chamber of Commerce never tired of reminding snowbound Easterners that Christmas in L.A. could be bathing suit weather.

OLVERA STREET AFTER. Remade into an idealized Mexican market when opened in 1930, Olvera Street attracted tourists and Angelenos alike to colorful shops and restaurants. In time, the tourist site developed historical traditions of its own.

OLVERA STREET BEFORE. With City Hall in the background, Olvera Street was an unpaved slum when Christine Sterling decided it should be saved for future generations.

CHRISTINE STERLING proved a powerful persuader when she set out to save the 1818 Avila Adobe and other historic buildings along Olvera Street.

$14.70 a head. In 1932 alone, more than 11,000 were moved out.

On Easter Sunday, April 19, 1930, while thousands of Mexican workers were soon to be taken away by the trainload, Los Angeles proudly announced the opening of Olvera Street, a tourist and craft district celebrating the city's Hispanic heritage. Four years before, Olvera Street was a muddy alley lined with collapsing buildings. Named in 1877 for Agustín Olvera, L.A. County's first judge, the narrow thoroughfare extended north from the Old Plaza, a short distance from where the city was founded in 1781. Nearby were some of the oldest structures in Los Angeles, including the most venerable, the crumbling 1818 Casa Avila.

In March 1926, Casa Avila had been tagged for demolition when Christine Sterling, a local socialite, passed by. Appalled, Mrs. Sterling determined to lead an effort to reimagine and rebuild Olvera Street. It took four years of persistent pressure before she engaged the support of city officials and business leaders. With laborers conscripted from a local jail, armed with shovels and pickaxes, work began on November 7, 1929. Even the stock market crash eight days earlier didn't dampen Mrs. Sterling's enthusiasm. The result was an idealized Mexican marketplace where mostly Anglo tourists and English-speaking Angelenos experienced L.A.'s romanticized past — peaceful missions, festive ranchos, bright-eyed senoritas and noble Spanish dons.

The commercialized charm of Olvera Street couldn't obscure the historic realities and multicultural contradictions of L.A.'s true history. One of the street's most popular Mexican restaurants occupied the Pelanconi House, the city's first brick building, built in 1855 by an immigrant from Italy. Across the plaza was another brick structure, the Garnier Building. Named for a Frenchman, it had been home to Chinese apartments and businesses since its completion in 1890. And it wasn't long before Mexican American merchants created their own Olvera Street traditions. With time, Christine Sterling's romanticized tourist site was added to the reality of L.A.'s multicultured past.

Two years after it opened, uncomfortable ideas attempted to intrude on Olvera Street. Mexican muralist David Alfaro Siqueiros was commissioned to paint a large fresco on a blank wall above the colorful shops and restaurants. Working with a close group of assistants, the radical artist finished his work at night. He called it *La América Tropical*. A protest against imperialism, the mural featured an Indian peasant crucified on a cross, capped with an American eagle. Mrs. Sterling and the Los Angeles business community were not

MILDRED "BABE" DIDRIKSON. During the 1932 Olympics, eighteen-year-old Didrikson, second from right, sets a new world record as she wins a gold medal in the eighty-meter hurdles.

OLYMPICS GREETINGS. What better way to welcome the world to L.A.'s first Olympic Games than with a bevy of bathing beauties?

CLOSING CEREMONIES. The 1932 Olympiad comes to an end.

pleased with what they saw, and the offending imagery was quickly covered with whitewash. It had no place in L.A.'s official portrait.

If "Okies," Mexicans and radical artists were not welcome in 1930s Los Angeles, during the summer of 1932, the city opened its arms wide for the tenth modern Olympic Games. L.A. had been preparing for the event since the early 1920s. Now, with American and international communities sliding deeper into an economic depression, Angelenos wondered if anyone would show up. They did. When the games opened on July 30, all 105,000 seats in the Memorial Coliseum were filled. Thirty-seven nations and 1,408 athletes competed. Prohibition dampened some European spirits, and some Japanese visitors were angry at being snubbed at local restaurants, but with Hollywood nearby, movie stars and cameras were everywhere.

Adding to the excitement, for the first time photography was used to decide close races. During the competition all but three previous Olympic records were broken. United States athletes earned forty-one gold medals. On her own, American track star Mildred "Babe" Didrikson won two gold medals and one silver. She had qualified to compete in five events, but women competitors were limited to three. After sixteen days, the games came to an end, and a jubilant

HORSEMAN CHARLES HOWARD with the legendary California mare Seabiscuit, right, before a 1939 race at Santa Anita Park. After a long ban on pari-mutuel betting, the track opened for the first time in 1934.

Los Angeles proudly pictured itself as an international capital.

Before the Olympics, sports in Los Angeles had been mainly a local affair. The city had boxing matches, as well as football, baseball and even a hockey team. Horse racing was a favorite of the movie crowd. The track at Santa Anita, on Lucky Baldwin's old turf, opened on Christmas Day, 1934. Movie producer Jack L. Warner, and a partnership of stars, established Hollywood Park four years later.

One of the most popular Los Angeles sports and entertainment centers in the 1930s and '40s was built on an oil field. At the turn of the century, dairy farmer A.F. Gilmore was drilling a well for water when he hit something else—oil. In 1934, partly to advertise the Gilmore Oil Company's filling stations and

GILMORE FIELD. The diamond wasn't fancy, or especially big, but during the 1930s it was enough to keep Angeleno fans cheering for their home team.

GILMORE STADIUM. The Bulldogs take on the Stars.

MOTORCYCLE DAREDEVIL. Anything went at Gilmore Stadium, including this motorcycle daredevil.

NIGHT BASEBALL AT WRIGLEY FIELD. More than 17,000 fans filled L.A.'s Wrigley Field for the first local nighttime baseball game. The Angels beat the Sacramento Solons 5–4 in the eleventh inning.

petroleum products, the family built Gilmore Stadium on their property southwest of Hollywood. The stadium held 15,000 seats for fans of auto races, boxing and wrestling matches, football games and rodeos.

A few months after the opening of Gilmore Stadium, the outdoor Farmers Market was set up nearby. It was soon popular with Angelenos as well as tourists who enjoyed strolling past outdoor stalls featuring the produce of still-semirural Los Angeles. In 1938, the Gilmore sports and entertainment complex became home to the Hollywood Stars, a minor league baseball team owned by Brown

FARMERS MARKET. During the Depression, many tourists and Angelenos headed to Third and Fairfax for affordable fresh produce and ten-cent "supermalts."

Derby restaurateur Robert Cobb (originator of the Cobb Salad) and a partnership of movie people, among them Bing Crosby and Gary Cooper.

During the '30s, an athletic landmark of another sort was established on a wooden platform south of the Santa Monica Pier. It was Muscle Beach. Frolics on L.A. beaches had long been a favorite of newspaper editors looking to picture life in Los Angeles as essentially silliness in a bathing suit. Muscle Beach was more than that. Over time, it provided a staging ground for healthy-living pioneers such as Jack La Lanne, Vic Tanney and Joe Gold. Each would eventually turn their biceps into successful businesses, and inspire an era emphasizing health and fitness. Later generations of all-American he-men, and women, would follow, including a future action movie star and California governor, Arnold Schwarzenegger.

Since the 1920s, maintaining the picture of a healthy and robust Los Angeles had not always been easy. Keeping the city looking clean and appealing, in contrast to images

THE PACIFIC COAST HIGHWAY curves along the shore north of Santa Monica. A lighthouse served as a lifeguard station.

County Supervisor Frank L. Shaw. In return for their support, business organizations such as the semisecret Better American Federation made it known that they wanted their man, James Edgar Davis, as chief of police. The 1936 "bum blockade" was Davis's kind of policing. He also supported the activities of a special intelligence unit called the Red Squad. These were cops dedicated to strikebreaking and beating up and arresting social agitators and other "troublemakers." One newspaper quoted the chief as believing that life in Los Angeles would be a lot better if "the whole

of crowded New York or corrupt Chicago, involved a covert collaboration between L.A.'s business interests and the Los Angeles Police Department. As long as the police kept organized crime and social unrest under control, or out of sight, civic leaders allowed them a relatively free hand. It was a delicate and unhealthy balance that resulted in an unsavory record of injustice and police brutality. At the time, writer and social critic Louis Adamic observed: "Few persons in Los Angeles know about these things. The press of course is mum on the subject; for the tourists must not get the idea that there is anything wrong with Los Angeles."

In 1933, L.A. elected a new mayor, former

CAPTAIN WILLIAM "RED" HYNES at the wheel of an LAPD squad car. He and his men, known as the Red Squad, were given a free hand to crack down on protestors, Communists, trouble-makers and other L.A. "undesirables."

question of constitutional rights was forgotten and left to the discretion of the police."

When they weren't harassing "trouble-makers," L.A. police had old-fashioned crimes to solve. One that remains a mystery had the Hollywood connection that newspaper editors and readers loved. Sexy actress Thelma Todd was part owner of a beachside nightclub and restaurant called Thelma Todd's Sidewalk Café. High above her club she kept an apartment and garage for her cars, including a Lincoln Phaeton convertible. Todd's partner was Roland West, a second-tier movie director rumored to be in love with her. But Thelma wasn't one for monogamy. Flirtatious, she had a weakness for stiff drinks and was always ready for a good time. During her years in Hollywood, she earned her nickname: "Hot Toddy."

On Sunday, December 15, 1935, after leaving a party at the Trocadero, one of Hollywood's most popular nightclubs, Todd appeared anxious. Her chauffeur later reported that she seemed to be in an unusual hurry to get home. The next morning her body was found in her garage, slumped in the front seat of her Lincoln. The official cause of death was carbon monoxide poisoning. Her face was bloody and there were signs of bruising. Was it really an accident or suicide? The theory was that she had forgotten her keys and, locked out, climbed 270 steps up a steep stairway to the garage. There, looking for warmth, she turned on the car's engine and heater, fell asleep and hit her face against the steering wheel when she became asphyxiated by toxic exhaust.

There were plenty of other possibilities. Todd had argued publicly with Roland West, and was reportedly seen in Hollywood with a mysterious man *after* her chauffeur said he'd driven her home. Even more mysterious was a letter she'd written to family members in Massachusetts, saying "I've fallen in with a tough bunch of characters . . . I'm really frightened for the first time in my life." New York mobster "Lucky" Luciano was looking for business in Los Angeles, and there was talk that the mob was pressuring Todd to let them set up a gambling operation at the Sidewalk Café. No pushover, it was said that the actress told him to forget it. Had an angry Luciano sent a hit man? Whatever the real cause of Thelma Todd's death, the Hollywood establishment didn't want another 1920s-style scandal, and police seemed willing to let the suicide or accident explanations put an end to further speculation. Still, to this day, doubts remain.

In 1931, there seemed little doubt about the guilt of twenty-six-year-old Winnie Ruth Judd, the young wife of a Santa Monica physician, even though her big, innocent-looking

NOIR L.A. It could be a scene from a movie, but it's a news photo of a real Westwood murder scene. An LAPD detective had been shot to death in the office of the Village Theater.

THELMA "HOT TODDY" TODD was a sexy and talented Hollywood comedienne. When she turned up dead on December 15, 1935, police called it suicide, but rumors of murder refused to die.

ACCIDENT OR MURDER? A homicide captain checks the position of actress Thelma Todd's body where it was found, in her car parked in the garage above her beachside restaurant and club.

JUDD ON TRIAL. **On the first day of her trial, "trunk murderess" Winnie Ruth Judd, right at the table, seems to be the picture of innocence. Could she have been?**

eyes and gentle smile would never mark her as a multiple murderer. And yet, on October 16, 1931, during a stay in Phoenix, Arizona, it was alleged that she shot and killed her two best girlfriends, Hedvig "Sammy" Samuelson and Agnes Anne LeRoi. But what to do about the bodies? The case against her said that Winnie jammed them into her steamer trunk, cutting up Samuelson's corpse to make more room, and then calmly boarded a train to Los Angeles. When she reached her destination, a porter noticed a foul smell and spotted seepage that looked like blood. When he asked what was inside, Judd hurried away. After the abandoned luggage was opened and the bodies unpacked, newspapers across the country

couldn't make headlines big enough. William Randolph Hearst's Los Angeles *Examiner* led the way.

After Judd was apprehended, ironically near a funeral parlor, Hearst paid for her defense, and kept the money flowing for exclusive interviews with witnesses and participants in the case. The crime was a tabloid dream and another lurid addition to L.A.'s image, even if the murders took place in Phoenix. Headlines said Judd had killed in a fever of jealousy. The victims were rumored to be lesbians who cavorted with married men, one of whom was Winnie's lover. Judd's response that she had acted in self-defense after her two friends attacked her, and that the bodies had been cut up by someone else, was ignored. A serious bullet wound in her left hand was caused, she said, when one of the friends fired a gun at her. Again, no one took that into account.

"The Tiger Lady," as the press called her, was eventually declared insane and spared the death penalty. Instead, she was sent to an Arizona mental hospital for the rest of her life. But that wasn't the last headline for Winnie Ruth Judd. She managed to escape an incredible seven times. In 1962, using an alias, she finally found a secure hiding place as a caregiver and companion to a wealthy California woman who promised her lifetime support. Six years later she was caught again, complaining that she had been unjustly punished.

So, was Winnie Ruth Judd a deranged killer? In 1990, Jana Bommersbach, an Arizona investigative reporter, uncovered troubling evidence that Judd's self-defense alibi just might be true. Weighing only 103

pounds, and handicapped by her wounded hand, it seemed impossible that Judd could have moved the bodies, let alone cut up a corpse. At the minimum, Bommersbach concluded, the Tiger Lady had help.

The end of the story is almost as astonishing as the beginning. In 1971, Judd was finally declared sane and paroled. She went to live with Ethel and John Blemmer, the daughter and son-in-law of the woman who had taken her in 1962. They, too, had vowed to support Winnie for life. When Ethel died, however, John

HARRY CHANDLER AND WILLIAM RANDOLPH HEARST.
A meeting of the titans. Chandler, left, publisher of the *Times,* and Hearst, publisher of the rival *Examiner,* shake hands in a show of collegiality during a 1930 gathering. In fact, they were usually bitter rivals.

reneged, and Judd went back to court, this time as a plaintiff. She might not have received justice in 1931, but in 1983 she won her case and received a settlement of $50,000, plus $1,250 a month for the rest of her life.

That kind of money would have been a fortune to the millions who couldn't find work in the 1930s. The Depression didn't hit Los Angeles as hard as most American cities, but by January 1931, one out of every five workers was unemployed. Later that year, voters passed a $5 million bond that gave temporary work to some 18,000 men—10 to 15 percent of the city's unemployed—who planted trees and created bridle trails, a fern dell and bird sanctuary in Griffith Park, as well swimming pools, baseball diamonds and other recreational facilities.

L.A. also benefited when President Franklin Roosevelt attacked joblessness with a phalanx of federal programs. Residents and newcomers who joined the Works Progress Administration (WPA) created projects that left lasting contributions to an art deco–influenced picture of Los Angeles. WPA workers built roads and bridges, artists painted murals and carved sculptures, actors presented plays and other entertainments, and writers researched and wrote a history and guide to the city.

One of L.A.'s most visible art deco landmarks debuted on May 14, 1935. The Griffith Observatory was Griffith J. Griffith's great dream, but he didn't live to see it come true. In 1912, sixteen years after he donated the land that would become Griffith Park, Griffith added a Christmas gift of $100,000 for an observatory. Cynics said he was trying to buy his way back into the city's good graces after the 1903 attempt on his wife's life. As a result, his gift was accepted only after he died. Located on a vantage point high above the city, the observatory was visible for miles. The $655,000 monument to science and astronomy featured a planetarium, capped by a brilliant copper dome, and a twelve-inch refracting telescope inside. The lights of the

THE GRIFFITH PARK OBSERVATORY shortly after it opened in 1935.

FLOODING—AGAIN. Still without adequate flood control, Los Angeles was hit by major floods in the late 1930s. Here, a bridge in North Hollywood was washed away.

city were already competing with starry nights, but the observatory's scientific displays and planetarium shows provided information and awe to generations of visiting children and their families.

The Griffith Observatory wasn't a federal project, but WPA artists contributed a towering monument that stands on the structure's front lawn, honoring history's great astronomers. Not far away, other WPA and California Conservation Corps workers were involved in one of the city's greatest tragedies.

On October 3, 1933, more than 3,700 government laborers were clearing brush in Griffith Park when a fire broke out. As the smoke and flames spread, the men were ordered to "smack it down" with their shovels. With no fire-fighting experience, and little training or organization, the workers were quickly overwhelmed. When some marched into a steep canyon, the flames rushed after them. It was a death trap. "You could follow the course of the fire by the screams," one survivor said. Three hours later, after the flames were finally extinguished, at least twenty-nine men were reported dead, although

the actual number may have been higher. Measured in loss of life, it was the worst fire disaster in Los Angeles history.

As always, after fires came the rain. And with the rain came flooding. The deadliest and one of the most damaging Los Angeles floods took place in 1938. In a five-day period beginning February 27, the city was inundated with thirty-one inches of rain — more than twice the annual average. More than 100 people lost their lives, and damage was reported at $35 million. The floodwaters subsided, but the disaster marked the beginning of a major change to the picture of Los Angeles.

The city's meandering, sometimes elusive river was an attraction to Spanish settlers in 1781. What they didn't know was that the innocent-looking stream could turn deadly. In roughly fifty miles, from its source in the western San Fernando Valley until it empties in the Pacific near Long Beach, the watershed of the Los Angeles River drops more than 7,000 feet—far more than the Mississippi during its entire length. Runoff from the steep mountain slopes north of the city can inundate the Los Angeles basin in a matter of

THE 1933 LONG BEACH EARTHQUAKE convinced Southern California that old construction codes needed to be upgraded.

hours. A Los Angeles County Flood Control District had been formed after another great flood in 1914. But hampered by indecision, politics and scandal, the agency's efforts were mostly ineffective. In the 1930s, the U.S. Army Corps of Engineers took on the challenge, determined to tame the Los Angeles River. During the next three decades, the result was an extensive flood-control system that created temporary reservoirs and confined once-shallow tree-lined streams into concrete channels designed to send runoff to the sea as quickly as possible.

Earthquakes were less common than fires and floods, but far more frightening. At 5:54 p.m. on March 10, 1933, comedian W. C. Fields was working on a new movie when the chandelier above his head began to swing. It was no joke. A 6.3 temblor, centered three and a half miles off the coast of Newport Beach, shook the earth for ten to fifteen long seconds. When it was over, sections of Long Beach were in ruins, more than 2,000 homes were destroyed or damaged, and 120 people were dead or dying. Fortunately, damage in L.A.'s more densely populated downtown was light.

Even without an earthquake to shake things up, 1930s America was on unsteady ground. And, like the turmoil of the first decade of the twentieth century, Los Angeles was a social and political war zone, as well as a laboratory for new solutions. Muckraking novelist Upton Sinclair was an enthusiastic Southern California transplant. His 1906 novel, *The Jungle,* had exposed the horrors of the Chicago meatpacking industry and led to the passage of the Pure Food and Drug Act.

In 1915, Sinclair moved to Pasadena, where he continued writing, enjoyed tennis, and embraced such "harebrained" schemes as vegetarian diets and full rights for women. In 1934, Sinclair, an avowed Socialist who had previously lost campaigns for congress and the senate, decided to switch to the Democratic Party and run for governor of California. He summed up his program in a booklet titled *End Poverty in California,* or EPIC.

UPTON SINCLAIR. Novelist, activist and socialist Upton Sinclair ran for governor of California in 1934 on a platform to end poverty in the state. He faced a powerful big business backlash.

Supported by a large middle-class grassroots effort, EPIC proposed a redistribution of wealth that threatened California's powerful business interests. "This is not politics," said Harry Chandler, "it's war." Hollywood moguls agreed. The studios paid for a series of phony "newsreels" to undermine public enthusiasm for EPIC and influence the election. "Nothing is unfair in politics," declared MGM production chief Irving Thalberg. The counterattack of media and money worked. Sinclair's opponents spent an estimated $10 million to defeat him, yet he still attracted a solid 39 percent of the vote in a three-candidate contest.

Los Angeles had long been fertile ground for utopian visions. Dr. Francis Townsend, a retired physician, had been bankrupted by the Depression when he came up with the idea of a government-sponsored pension supported by a sales tax. Again, there was a large and

sympathetic audience in the Los Angeles area, especially in middle-class and Midwest-dominated Long Beach. The Townsend Plan seemed simple. Every citizen over sixty would receive $200 a month. They were required to spend the stipend in thirty days, returning the money to the economy. Townsend raised almost $1 million on behalf of his proposal. "The Good Doctor," as both supporters and critics called him, was eager to discuss his idea with Franklin Roosevelt. The President put him off, but FDR couldn't ignore the new ideas emerging from Los Angeles and California.

In 1935, he finally responded with one of his own—Social Security.

Los Angeles was a laboratory of ideas, both outlandish and imaginative. The city's most evident contribution to America during the Depression came from the creativity of the movies. The glossy films of MGM provided glamour. The lavish musicals of Busby Berkeley offered entertainment and escape. Ever-optimistic Shirley Temple kept hopes high and Frank Capra's populist comedy-dramas were a source of inspiration. The gangster movies of Jimmy Cagney and Edward

SHIRLEY TEMPLE was the darling of the Depression years. Her cheerful optimism and energy lifted spirits in America and around the world.

FANTASIES ON FILM. Lavish production numbers like this one in *Gold Diggers of 1935*, choreographed and directed by Busby Berkeley, entertained Depression audiences with specta-cles that were unique to motion pictures.

G. Robinson vented frustration and anger while Fred Astaire and Ginger Rogers seemed to dance away their troubles.

The single-best year in Hollywood history is generally considered to be 1939. While the big Oscar winner was *Gone with the Wind,* the competition included *The Wizard of Oz, Wuthering Heights, Mr. Smith Goes to Washington, Ninotchka* and *Stagecoach.* In contrast to all the great Hollywood movies and stars of the era, it was a cartoon character, Mickey Mouse, who always gave audiences a chance to laugh.

Mickey's creator, Walt Disney, was born in Chicago in 1901. Disney began his cartooning career in Kansas City. Like hundreds of thousands of other Midwesterners, he headed for Los Angeles. With his brother Roy, he set up a studio in a garage where they created the first Mickey Mouse cartoon, *Plane Crazy,* capitalizing on public enthusiasm for Charles Lindbergh and aviation. In 1933, from new facilities in Edendale, northwest of down-town L.A., Disney Studios created *The Three Little Pigs,* whose theme song, "Who's Afraid of the Big Bad Wolf?" inspired playful optimism in

MICKEY AND WALT. More than fifty years after they became partners, Walt Disney and Mickey Mouse were still world famous.

GEORGE BURNS AND GRACIE ALLEN, seen here broadcasting from Hollywood's CBS studios, began in vaudeville and became one of America's most popular radio teams during the 1930s.

CBS. The West Coast studios of CBS and KNX radio in 1939.

the early days of the Depression. In 1937, Disney stretched his ambitions to a full-length feature, *Snow White and the Seven Dwarfs.* Until he did, most critics considered animated cartoons as no more than amusements for children. In fact, Walt Disney was creating an art form that was archetypically Angeleno — untraditional, deeply populist and enthusiastically entrepreneurial. This is to say, it was essentially American.

While the humor and glamour of the movies provided refuge from the Depression, it was radio that brought the entertainment home. The first radio experimenters in Los Angeles were tinkering with shortwave and crystal sets as early 1901. Commercial broadcasting began in 1922 with KFI, a station started by entrepreneurial car dealer Earle

C. Anthony. Anthony also commissioned America's first neon sign.

Before cross-country hookups, the West Coast had its own networks. At first Hollywood tried to ignore radio, but national broadcasters CBS, NBC, then ABC (an offshoot of NBC) soon built studios at or near the corner of Sunset and Vine in Hollywood. By 1935, with the active participation of the film industry, Los Angeles was the home of radio drama. Programs included *Lux Radio Theater* as well as comedy and variety shows hosted by Jack Benny and Bob Hope. Listeners could also tune into the folksy adventures of Lum 'n' Abner and enjoy exchanges between ventriloquist Edgar Bergen and his smart aleck wooden sidekick, Charlie McCarthy.

In the 1930s, while radio was in its prime,

there were already hints of a new empire in the making. The word *television* first appeared in print in 1900, and experiments with transmitting pictures were underway by the 1920s. A widely publicized TV demonstration was part of the 1939 New York World's Fair. However, "Out West" Los Angeles was already picturing itself on the airwaves. Visionary entrepreneur Don Lee owned a West Coast radio network when he moved to Los Angeles in 1931. There he continued a successful Cadillac dealership he'd begun in San Francisco, and turned his attention to TV. With a brilliant twenty-four-year-old electrical engineer, Harry Lubcke, Lee began work on an experimental station, W6XAO, which was soon on the air for one hour every day except

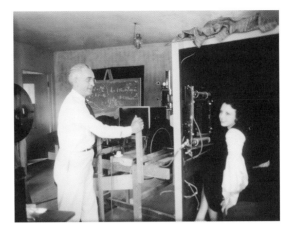

EARLY TV. In 1930, a model poses for an experimental television camera.

PAN-PACIFIC AUDITORIUM. A beautiful example of Streamline Moderne architecture, the Pan-Pacific Auditorium opened in 1935. It burned down in 1989 and was replaced ten years later with a tasteful contemporary re-creation.

Sunday. To increase the audience, Lubcke prepared plans for $200 kits that allowed viewers to build their own TV, complete with a fourteen-inch screen.

Like Don Lee, Harry Lubcke is an often-overlooked TV pioneer. Another of his contributions to television history occurred in 1949. As president of the new Academy of Television Arts & Sciences, founded in Hollywood the year before, Lubcke is credited with christening the Academy's annual award. The name Emmy was suggested by an engineering nickname for TV's image orthicon tube ("immy").

In the '30s, Lee erected transmitters on the hill above the Hollywoodland sign, with 360-degree access to the Los Angeles area. All that was missing were more viewers. After Don Lee died in 1934, his son Thomas continued his father's pioneering efforts, but progress was interrupted by World War II.

In 1932, Lee and Lubcke's television equipment was sent high over Los Angeles to receive the TV images broadcast to an airplane. It was a historic first, and as it was most days, the weather was ideal for flying. If the development of television would eventually be forced to take a temporary pause, aviation in Southern California continued to soar. Already a billion-dollar industry, airplanes were transforming the image of Los Angeles.

In 1932, Donald Douglas and his Santa

A DOUGLAS DC-3, designed by Donald Douglas, founder of Douglas Aircraft in 1925, comes in for a landing at Lockheed Air Terminal in Burbank. Nearby Lockheed Aircraft was another manufacturer that made the Los Angeles area an international aviation center.

MINES FIELD, later Los Angeles International Airport, was dedicated in 1930.

Monica–based Douglas Aircraft Company won a TWA contract that resulted in the twin-engine, all-metal DC-1. An improved DC-2 followed two years later, and the passenger-friendly DC-3 debuted in 1935. By the end of the decade, 90 percent of the world's commercial air traffic was flying Douglas DC-3s.

Another energetic and innovative entre-preneur drawn to Los Angeles was Howard Hughes. When Hughes arrived in 1925, he was a tall, handsome nineteen-year-old son of a millionaire Texas wildcat oilman and inventor. There was no better place than Los Angeles for him to indulge his three great passions: movies, aviation and making money.

In the late '20s, Hughes combined all three with an air war epic called *Hells Angels*. Premiered at Grauman's Chinese Theatre in 1930, it was the world's first multimillion-dollar movie. While keeping one hand on his movie interests, Hughes used the other to build and fly innovative airplanes. When either hand was free, he was regularly photographed with an arm around one of the many Hollywood beauties he escorted about town, including Jean Harlow, Bette Davis and Katherine Hepburn.

In 1937, Hughes broke the transcontinental aviation speed record, flying from Los Angeles to New Jersey in just under seven and a half hours. In 1938, he set another

UNION STATION. **By the summer of 1938, the new depot, designed to bring all Los Angeles passenger railway operations under one roof, was well underway. America's last great railroad station opened the following year.**

record, a flight around the world in ninety-one hours and seventeen minutes. By 1939, Howard Hughes was richer than ever and a major stockholder in TWA, poised to cash in on the emerging commercial airline market.

In the 1930s, although aeronautical technology was improving fast, trains remained the primary mode of transcontinental travel. Most large American cities had a grand rail station to impress those arriving, departing or passing through. In 1939, a proud Los Angeles unveiled a new terminal of its own — Union Station. With a Spanish-style clock tower, tile

CHINA CITY. When Chinese Americans were forced to move to make way for Union Station, Christine Sterling decided they needed a Chinese equivalent of Olvera Street. Called China City, it opened in June 1937.

roof, and painted interior wood beams and ceilings, Union Station acknowledged the city's Hispanic past. At the same time, it was dedicated "to the spirit of private enterprise and the continuing growth of Southern California." The inaugural party was L.A.'s biggest celebration since the Olympics. A great pageant entitled "Romance of the Rails" was performed in a temporary 6,000-seat amphitheater. It featured Mexican dancers and musicians, a parade of old trains and a reenactment of the driving of the Golden Spike that linked East and West in 1869. Mostly missing was acknowledgement of the thousands of Chinese laborers who did much

NEW CHINATOWN. Chinese-owned and operated New Chinatown opened in the same month as China City. New Chinatown still stands, while China City was damaged twice by fires and finally abandoned.

of the work that made Western railroads possible. To add irony to the oversight, the new station stood on ground that only shortly before had been the city's Chinatown.

In 1936, as the dimly lit apartments and dilapidated shops and restaurants of "old" Chinatown were shoved aside by bulldozers, indefatigable Christine Sterling, the "mother of Olvera Street," was appalled and inspired again. Her latest vision was a brand-new "China City"— an Asian equivalent to the tourist success of Olvera Street. After token consultation with Chinese community leaders, Mrs. Sterling declared, "The Chinese need a Chinatown." With the support of Harry Chandler and local business leaders, she set out to give them one. It would be two blocks from the Plaza, convenient to the new train station. Looking to enhance the Los Angeles tourist experience, movie set designers provided appropriate "Oriental atmosphere," complete

with rickshaws, available for twenty-five cents a ride. When it was finished, the few Angelenos who were displeased were members of the city's Chinese community who had been allowed little say and less benefit from Mrs. Sterling's new creation.

In 1939, the night sky of downtown Los Angeles glowed with light from a fire. Whether it was due to accident or arson, China City was in flames and everything, including rickshaws, was seriously damaged. The tourist site would be rebuilt only to burn down again ten years later. Before then, in terms that Los Angeles understood, there was already a different kind of "take two." On June 25, 1938, New Chinatown had opened a short distance away. Developed by the Chinese community itself, led by businessman Peter Soo Hoo, L.A.'s New Chinatown was the first Chinese enclave in the United States owned by Chinese Americans.

Although the Asian communities of Los Angeles were relatively small in the 1930s, they were already making their mark. Cinematographer James Wong Howe contributed his imagery to Hollywood's picture of America and the world, and actress Anna May Wong was "the mystery of the Orient" personified. On August 12, 1934, Japanese Angelenos held the first Nisei Week to celebrate and share their heritage with the rest of the city. In 1937,

the American headquarters of the Korean community moved from San Francisco to Los Angeles.

Even with incidents like the China City fire, Los Angeles continued to emphasize a peaceful and positive picture of itself. However, during the 1930s, East Coast cynicism and condescension continued, and the less savory side of the city was getting harder to ignore. In 1938, polemical newspaper columnist Westbrook Pegler wrote: "It is hereby earnestly

ANNA MAY WONG. Los Angeles—born Wong, the first Chinese American movie star, poses in her New York Broadway role in the play *On the Spot*. In 1932, she costarred with Marlene Dietrich in the film *Shanghai Express*.

KOREAN ANGELENOS. By 1937, many California Koreans had moved to Los Angeles. Here, a trio of young women enjoy a day at Venice. At the time, nonwhites were often segregated to separate areas of the beach.

JOHN FANTE, shown in a 1937 snapshot, was a novelist who lived in Los Angeles and loved the city, even with its shortcomings.

RALPH BUNCHE. Graduate of L.A. public schools and UCLA, Ralph Bunche and his family pose for a 1938 snapshot. Bunche would become a professor, diplomat and winner of the 1950 Nobel Peace Prize.

proposed that the USA would be better off if that big, sprawling, incoherent, shapeless, slobbering civic idiot in the family of American communities, the City of Los Angeles, could be declared incompetent and placed in charge of a guardian like any individual mental defective."

Novelist John Fante couldn't care less what Westbrook Pegler thought. He reveled in the underbelly of Los Angeles and embraced his adopted hometown—sunshine, eccentricities, sinister secrets and all. In his 1939

novel, *Ask the Dust,* Fante's ebullient alter ego, Arturo Bandini, couldn't help but burst forth: "Los Angeles, give me some of you! Los Angeles come to me the way I came to you, my feet over your streets, you pretty town. I loved you so much, you sad flower in the sand, you pretty town."

Nathaniel West also was intrigued by Los Angeles. His 1939 satirical novel, *The Day of the Locust,* portrayed a city filled with citizens who were deeply disappointed and living empty lives. West pictured L.A. as a jumbled movie back lot — a "dream dump." Both Fante's dark-tinged romanticism and West's bitter exaggerations reflect glimpses of reality in 1930s Los Angeles.

Profiting from rootless and restless Angelenos, and others just out for a good time, was the business of former bootlegger Tony Cornero. In 1930, Cornero celebrated his release from prison on Prohibition violations by launching a fleet of gambling ships. The most famous was the *Rex.* Operating literally just beyond the reach of the law, in international waters off the shore of Santa Monica, the *Rex* was only a water taxi away for thrill-seeking Angelenos. During peak hours, two to three thousand "squirrels," as Cornero called his patrons, kept the bingo parlors, roulette wheels and dice tables busy. It took a reformed city government and a 1938 court order to put an end to the fun. Ironically, during World War II, the *Rex* was drafted for more patriotic purposes. It was sunk by a Nazi submarine, proving that the house doesn't always win.

One year before the *Rex* was seized, time ran out for Los Angeles Mayor Frank L. Shaw. His administration was riddled with corruption. Shaw's brother Joe had turned City Hall into a cash-and-carry operation. Municipal jobs and promotions were up for sale, and police abuses were more blatant than ever. An outraged group of reformers led by crusading County

TONY CORNERO. Owner of the gambling ship *Rex,* Cornero, left, consults with an unknown man, perhaps a curious law enforcement officer.

OUT OF LUCK. In 1938, California Attorney General Earl Warren had the offshore gambling ship *Rex* raided and its slot machines dumped into Santa Monica Bay.

CLIFFORD CLINTON. Reformer Clifford Clinton, owner of Clifton's cafeterias, examines the dynamited car of investigator Harry Raymond. Raymond's attempted assassination led to the recall of Mayor Frank Shaw.

CLIFTON'S CAFETERIA. Beginning in 1931, this and six other cafeterias established by Clifford Clinton followed the owner's "pay what you can" policy during the Depression. The South Pacific façade was added in 1939.

EARL KYNETTE. Looking inappropriately smug, the L.A. police officer was found guilty of planting the bomb that exploded in investigator Harry Raymond's car.

FRANK SHAW AND FLETCHER BOWRON. Shaw, left, recalled as L.A.'s mayor after years of corruption, puts on a game face as he shakes hands with his reform-minded successor.

1930S DOWNTOWN MODEL. Los Angeles is often considered an unplanned city, but in fact there have been many attempts to understand and organize L.A.'s unprecedented growth. During the 1930s, WPA artists created this scale model to help visualize downtown.

Supervisor John Anson Ford and Clifford Clinton, owner of Clifton's, a popular chain of cafeterias, demanded change. To help build their case, the reformers hired hard-nosed private detective Harry Raymond. Raymond was uncovering a lot when, on the morning of January 14, 1938, he tried to start his car. It exploded. Someone had tried to kill him with a bomb. Raymond was seriously injured, and he knew who had tried to do him in. It was Earl Kynette, a Los Angeles police lieutenant who'd been secretly keeping track of the reformers' investigator for months.

The attempted assassination of Harry Raymond blew the lid off the administration of Frank Shaw. Angry Angelenos invoked the legislative legacy of the Progressive era and voted to recall the mayor, a first in American politics. He was replaced by an upstanding and conservative former superior court judge, Fletcher Bowron. Police Chief James "Two Gun" Davis got a first-hand taste of the public's constitutional rights in action. He was fired.

By the end of the 1930s, Los Angeles was still facing the challenges of the Depression, but getting its house in order. And, as the next decade would prove, it was just in time.

FROM BATTLEFIELDS
TO BARBECUES

"After four frantic years of war and four wild years of peacetime boom, it is plain that Los Angeles will never be like anything on earth."

Time *magazine, July 4, 1949*

On December 7, 1941, it was late morning when the news from Pearl Harbor arrived in Los Angeles. The United States had been attacked by the Empire of Japan. After more than two years of conflict in Europe, and strong feelings of isolationism in America, there was no longer a choice. The country was at war, and the Depression was soon a thing of the past.

Along with families of the casualties in Hawaii, among the first Angelenos to feel the impact were Japanese Americans. Many community leaders in Little Tokyo quickly affirmed their loyalty to the United States. In fact, half were native-born American citizens. Despite this, the FBI and other government agencies decided all were enemy aliens. Within hours, roundups began. The Santa Anita racetrack became a temporary assembly area until barracks were built in isolated sites in California and other Western states.

On March 21, 1942, the first trainloads left Los Angeles for Manzanar, 220 miles north in the Owens Valley, on land purchased by the city during the water wars of the 1920s. Families were

L.A.'S ARSENAL FOR DEMOCRACY. This composite image links Los Angeles–based World War II defense workers with the patriots of 1776. The city was a major source of support for America's war effort.

forced to sell or leave behind houses, farms, businesses and much of what they owned. While a few homes and possessions were protected by friendly neighbors, opportunists bought or appropriated much of what had to be left behind. In a matter of weeks, 35,000 Japanese Americans in Los Angeles County were gone.

Ironically, the war would give members of L.A.'s Chinese community their first opportunity to fully participate in American life. With the United States government eager to maintain good relations with China, an ally in the Pacific Theater, young Chinese Americans were welcomed into the armed services and defense industry. Nearly 13,500 would serve in uniform.

Mexican farm laborers were invited by the U.S. government to replace Japanese agricultural workers. "Okies" and other immigrants from the South and Southwest were also welcome now. They found work in the city's burgeoning defense plants, along with a new influx of African Americans. As the war continued, many new workers were women, filling in for brothers and husbands serving in the military. In Los Angeles, "Rosie the Riveters" were an early indication that old-fashioned views of women were changing, at least for the duration of the war.

IN 1942, A JAPANESE AMERICAN CHILD, surrounded by her family's belongings, waits for a train that will take her to an internment camp.

CHINESE AMERICAN ANGELENOS proudly joined the war effort. Here, a local color guard stands at attention on April 12, 1942.

AFRICAN AMERICAN DEFENSE WORKER. A popular 1940s song, "Rosie the Riveter," gave female defense workers a lasting nickname. The all-out war effort in Los Angeles also gave new opportunities to minorities, including African Americans.

A FAREWELL TO REMEMBER. On his way to war, Private Joe Sunseri grabs a last-minute kiss from his girl, Alma Teresi.

MEXICAN AMERICAN SERVICEMEN participated with honor in World War II, a proud response to prewar discrimination.

ON GUARD. The dynamiters of the Owens Valley "water wars" of the 1920s were no longer a threat to L.A.'s aqueduct lifeline. Now, these World War II soldiers guard against foreign saboteurs.

The major battlefields were thousands of miles away, but only sixteen days after Pearl Harbor, a roving Japanese submarine cruised off the Oregon Coast, and even succeeded in sinking an oil tanker. On February 23, 1942, a Japanese sub surfaced near Santa Barbara and fired thirteen rounds into an oil installation north of the city. Three days later, an anxious Los Angeles fought a skirmish that couldn't have been more appropriate for the world capital of make believe. In the middle of the night, anti-aircraft barrages suddenly lit up the sky. More than 1,400 rounds ripped into the darkness. Many Angelenos were convinced "the Japs" were coming. They weren't. There was plenty of excitement, but nothing to shoot at. What became known as "The Battle of Los Angeles" was an embarrassing false alarm. The next day, sheepish citizens returned to more real and important contributions to the national defense.

In 1939, there were 13,000 workers in local aircraft factories. Two years later, responding to President Roosevelt's call for 50,000 warplanes a year, there were 113,000. At plants such as Douglas, Lockheed, Northrop and North American, shifts were around the clock.

ANGELENO DEFENSE WORKERS ready fighter planes for America's world-war arsenal.

Douglas was supplying the DC-3 and B-17 bomber. Lockheed had the P-38 fighter. During the war, Hughes Aircraft grew from four employees to 80,000. By 1945, Southern California aviation contracts topped $7 billion. Only five years before, agriculture had been the largest segment of the Los Angeles County economy. That was changing fast. The City of Los Angeles was soon flush with $10 billion in defense contracts. At full capacity, L.A.'s aviation plants were producing a new warplane every seven minutes.

With shifts working twenty-four hours, seven days a week, the streets of Los Angeles were filled at all hours with military personnel, bleary-eyed defense workers and other men and women infused with the exuberance

SOLDIERS DISCOVER L.A. Riding in one of the city's famous Red Cars, these GIs seem happy to be in Los Angeles. Who knows, they may meet a movie star?

DOING THEIR PART TO WIN THE WAR, kids from Bunker Hill work on a Victory Garden as part of a project sponsored by the city's Recreation Department.

A FRONT-PAGE DISPLAY. Too young to fight, twelve-year-old Burton Weinstein follows America's efforts to fight back after Pearl Harbor. His collection of newspaper headlines won a prize in 1942.

WIDE-EYED SOLDIERS AT THE HOLLYWOOD CANTEEN IN 1944 line up for signed photos from pinup favorites. From left: actresses Jane Russell, Toni Seven, and Martha Tilton, a singer with Benny Goodman's band.

HOLLYWOOD CANTEEN. Servicemen could send this postcard picture back home to prove that they were mingling with movie stars.

STARLET GREETINGS. Even if it was staged for the camera, what GI wouldn't want to be met in Los Angeles with a handshake, a hug or even a smooch from a beautiful Hollywood starlet?

and fatalism of war, all out for a good time. No American city had a larger concentration of soldiers, sailors, marines and airmen. Most only knew Los Angeles from the movies. Now they experienced the city firsthand. The Hollywood Canteen, started in 1942 by stars Bette Davis and John Garfield, was a short distance from Hollywood and Vine. A former barn, the Canteen was a well-publicized place where a waiter or dishwasher might be a visiting movie star, and there were plenty of starlets to give a GI a smile, or even a hug on the dance floor.

There were even livelier hot spots in the clubs and bars downtown and on Central Avenue, the heart of L.A.'s African American community. Places like Club Alabam were bursting with the music of Duke Ellington, Count Basie, Louis Armstrong and other jazz greats. Recently evacuated Japanese neighborhoods were now called Bronzeville, as Japanese-owned stores and restaurants

THE PALLADIUM BALLROOM on Sunset Boulevard in Hollywood opened on September 23, 1940, with Tommy Dorsey and his orchestra.

CLUB ALABAM was a favorite nightspot on Central Avenue in the heart of L.A.'s African American community.

JITTER-BUGGERS "cut a rug" during a war-time dance contest.

became temporary homes to black nightclubs and cafés.

On the streets of Los Angeles, all kinds of Americans were meeting each other for the first time. In the beginning, war-time jobs were limited to whites, and efforts to enlist African Americans and Mexicans were slow to come. At the same time, Mexican American teenagers, caught between two cultures, and not fully at home in either, were asserting themselves. Inspired by black hipsters, they wore outfits called zoot suits, with long jackets, pegged pants and broad-brimmed hats.

Many newly arrived servicemen had never seen a Mexican. Cooped up in barracks and filled with pent-up anxiety and energy, they angrily watched zoot-suiters, convinced that

MOTORMANETTES. Women were not only recruited for jobs in defense plants. These patriotic Angelenas are filling in at the city's war-time transit system.

ZOOT-SUITERS. For many young Mexican Americans who went out on the town in zoot suits, they were simply "stylin'." To anxious Anglo soldiers, every zoot-suiter was either a gangster, trouble-maker or draft-dodger.

GUILTY AS CHARGED? On August 10, 1942, twenty-three youths were indicted by a county grand jury for the death of José Diaz, twenty-two, at "Sleepy Lagoon," an abandoned gravel pit near Slauson and Atlantic boulevards.

they were gang members or at least arrogantly dodging the war effort. Tensions exploded on a hot June 3, 1943. Sailors swept through predominately Mexican neighborhoods, beating up anyone whose looks they didn't like. For the next three days servicemen and zoot-suiters traded attacks while the Los Angeles Police Department mostly stood on the sidelines. Local newspapers reported the clashes like one-sided war news. One article read: "Two hundred Navy men sailed up the Los Angeles River early today, and in a task force of taxicabs launched a reprisal attack on 'zoot suit' gangsters...." In the end, more than one hundred Mexicans were arrested. As for the servicemen, they were told to save their fighting for overseas.

The LAPD and the local judicial system were rarely known to have an even hand with blacks or Mexican Americans. A year earlier, in August 1942, twenty-three members of a local gang were arrested for a murder that

took place near an abandoned quarry known as "Sleepy Lagoon." There was little evidence to support the charges, yet nine young men were convicted of murder and eight were found guilty of lesser crimes. Los Angeles activists, led by lawyer and writer Carey McWilliams and members of the Hollywood film community, including Orson Welles and Anthony Quinn, protested. It took two years before the verdicts were overturned.

It was clear that, in the midst of a worldwide fight for freedom and democracy, there was unfinished business at home. What was happening on the streets of Los Angeles offered proof of that. However, Hollywood had the power to smooth things over. Movies played a major role in inspiring, educating and encouraging Americans to work together and keep up the fight. In 1942, *Mrs. Miniver* pictured an English family under assault by the Nazi blitz. The message was clear: the English were like us, and contrary to the vestiges

of an American isolationist movement, the popular film effectively argued that Britain and the war in Europe deserved our support.

Offering their services to the home front, Hollywood designers created inventive camouflage for defense plants, transforming factory roofs and parking lots into illusory farm fields, complete with counterfeit cows. Hollywood also went to the front lines in person. Comedian Bob Hope traveled thousands of miles with a troop of entertainers, getting the biggest response when pinups like Betty Grable or Veronica Lake appeared. It was the beginning of a tradition that lasted most of Hope's long career.

Hollywood was both transforming and transformed by World War II. During the next

four years, as the war spread and the death toll mounted, the documentary series *Why We Fight,* directed by Frank Capra — famous for populist entertainments like *It Happened One Night* and *Mr. Deeds Goes to Washington* — argued the case for final victory. John Ford, known best for his westerns, faced real shootouts with heavy weapons while serving in the navy. Director George Stevens, once a cameraman for comedians Laurel and Hardy, documented the realities of war in Europe and the horrors of the Holocaust. John Huston,

THE WAR IN EUROPE, 1945. Far away in Germany, an Angeleno GI points the way home.

FRANK SINATRA, in a sweater and white shirt, greets returning members of the Japanese American 442nd Regimental Combat Team, the most decorated U.S. military unit of World War II.

master of hard-boiled detective films like *The Maltese Falcon,* got himself in trouble with army brass when he showed actual American casualties in his documentary *The Battle of San Pietro.*

A future generation of motion picture talent learned their craft working in Culver City at sound stages owned by comedy producer Hal Roach. Nicknamed "Fort Roach," the studio produced hours of training films and newsreels, starring unknowns and more famous former civilians, such as Ronald Reagan.

When World War II ended in 1945, Americans took a deep breath. The 1946 film *The Best Years of Our Lives* captured the relief and

CELEBRATING VICTORY in World War II.

WARY JAPANESE AMERICANS at Union Station returning to Los Angeles from internment camps.

uncertainty of a country suddenly at peace. It didn't take much insight to notice that Los Angeles and the United States had changed. Women had tasted independence and the pride and responsibility of earning a living outside the home. In a segregated military, African Americans had graduated from laboring jobs to combat, and even army air force duty. Mexican young men denied the draft-dodger stereotypes of the zoot-suit riots by fighting and dying in numbers beyond their percentage in the population. Even more telling, Japanese veterans of the 442nd "Go For Broke" Regimental Combat Team came home with more than 18,000 individual medals, the most decorated military unit in American history. This while their parents and friends were imprisoned in internment camps.

The war changed Los Angeles in other ways. The conflict in Europe brought a remarkable gathering of scientists, artists, writers and musicians to Los Angeles. In 1941, Albert Einstein arrived to teach at Caltech in Pasadena. That same year Nobel Prize–winning novelist Thomas Mann moved to Santa Monica. He joined a community of fellow German refugees that included playwright Bertolt Brecht and theater director Max Rheinhart.

Igor Stravinsky, considered the greatest composer of the twentieth century, became an Angeleno in 1940, and a U.S. citizen five years later. In Los Angeles, he participated in performances of new music in a series called "Concerts on the Roof." The composer of the revolutionary ballet *Le Sacre du Printemps* collaborated with poet W. H. Auden, and enjoyed outdoor lunches at the Farmers Market with Auden's partner and mystical poet, Christopher Isherwood. Stravinsky's rival, Arnold Schoenberg, escaped Nazi Germany in 1933 and lived in Brentwood for the rest of his life. Other master musicians, such as pianist Artur Rubenstein and violinist Jascha Heifetz, also made L.A. their home.

During the '30s and '40s, British author Aldous Huxley hung out with a wonderfully L.A. crowd that included Stravinsky, Isherwood, Harpo Marx, Greta Garbo and astronomer Edwin Hubble. While he made extra money writing screenplays, Huxley explored mysticism and mind-altering drugs. Later, in his book-filled home beneath the Hollywood sign, he looked down at Los Angeles with a sardonic eye. His 1939 novel, *After Many a Summer Dies the Swan,* written shortly after his arrival in L.A, was a futurist story about the search for human immortality — an ideal subject for a city infatuated with the new and regularly reinventing itself.

Even with misgivings about their adopted city, L.A.'s European émigrés enriched what most American intellectuals considered a

EINSTEIN ON THE BEACH. During a 1930s stay at Caltech, Albert Einstein enjoyed meeting movie stars and riding a bicycle, as well as lecturing at the prestigious Pasadena campus. With him are his wife and an unidentified man.

ALDOUS HUXLEY, below, author of *Brave New World*, complained about L.A.'s lack of traditional culture, but thrived in the city's unconventional environment.

NOBEL PRIZE—WINNER THOMAS MANN, a refugee from Nazi Germany, settled in Santa Monica where other émigrés had established a vital community of intellectual exiles.

IGOR STRAVINSKY came to Los Angeles in the early 1940s for his health. Here, he would write some of his most important neo-classical pieces, such as the 1945 "Symphony in Three Movements," as well as allowing *Le Sacre du Printemps* to be included in Walt Disney's *Fantasia*.

STOKOWSKI AND DISNEY. Symphony conductor Leopold Stokowski, left, and Mr. and Mrs. Walt Disney at the 1941 premiere of *Fantasia,* Disney's ambitious crossbreeding of classical music and animation.

cultural wasteland, or at least a place without culture as they defined it. What was especially underappreciated, even in Los Angeles, were the highly skilled artists who worked in the film industry, including composers such as Max Steiner, Miklós Rózsa, Erich Korngold and Bernard Herrmann, as well as other musicians, dancers and painters. Outside the studios they added to the city's artistic and cultural environment. In the 1940s, the movies were becoming more than light entertainment. In 1941, twenty-six-year-old Orson Welles stunned old-fashioned Hollywood with *Citizen Kane,* an innovative and thinly disguised biography of one of America's most powerful men, William Randolph Hearst.

Hearst newspapers had the power to make or break reputations. In Los Angeles, the evening *Herald-Express* and the morning *Examiner* claimed the city's largest circulation. Their headlines had prematurely sealed the fate of Fatty Arbuckle in the 1920s. Welles and his studio, RKO, refused to yield to demands to sell or destroy all prints of *Citizen Kane.* Even though early distribution was limited, the film went on to be considered one of the greatest achievements in the history of the movies, a

ORSON WELLES. Twenty-six-year-old Welles orates as Charles Foster Kane in his landmark film *Citizen Kane,* inspired by the life of newspaper magnate William Randolph Hearst.

THE FILM *D.O.A.* (Dead on Arrival) is a film noir classic of the 1940s. This climactic shooting was filmed in the Bradbury Building on Broadway, an 1893 L.A. architectural landmark.

RAYMOND CHANDLER. A master of the hard-boiled detective fiction of the 1930s and '40s, Chandler confessed to being "the most fanatical cat lover in the business." He had more mixed feelings about Los Angeles.

source of entertainment that would soon be acknowledged as the art form of the twentieth century, with Los Angeles as its capital.

The death and devastation of the war years left filmmakers and their audiences with a darker, more sobering view of life. *Citizen Kane* was just one example of a new style of American movie that emerged in the '40s. Pictured with dark shadows and rain-slicked streets, they were infused with anxiety, cynicism and betrayal. French intellectuals called them *film noir.*

Rooted in the hard-boiled fiction of writers such as Chicago-born and British-educated Raymond Chandler, film noir was at home in Los Angeles. The idea that life in sunny L.A. was darker than it seemed wasn't new. The city government and police scandals of the 1930s showed that. Chandler relished the contrasts of life in Los Angeles, and at the same time regretted the changes that were transforming America and the city he'd known since 1912. "Hollywood is wonderful," he wrote. "Anyone who doesn't like it is either crazy or sober."

In 1932, when a drinking habit cost him an executive job with an oil company, Chandler decided to devote himself to a longtime ambition and become a writer. Starting with cheap magazines known as pulps, where he was paid by the word, his taut style and hard-boiled similes complemented the grim environment

EDWARD ROYBAL. Born in Albuquerque, New Mexico, Roybal moved to Los Angeles with his family in 1922. His successful 1945 campaign for city council was a political breakthrough for Mexican Americans.

of the Depression and the war-time uncertainties of the years that followed. After *The Big Sleep* became a best-seller in 1939, Chandler's novels were regularly snapped up by Hollywood. By then, they pictured a noir Los Angeles that was impossible to ignore.

Whether the city was being boosted or blasted, L.A. was more than even the most indelible imagery. Postwar Americans may have been repelled by the shadowy city portrayed in Raymond Chandler's fiction. But when they imagined a new life, many pictured themselves in sunny Los Angeles. In 1940, L.A. was America's fifth-largest metropolis, with a population of 1.5 million. By 1947, 10,000 newcomers were arriving every month. Significantly, these new Angelenos were far more diverse than the Midwestern immigrants of the past.

During the war years more than 100,000 African Americans traveled to Los Angeles. Many decided to stay. Mexicans came too, settling close by the concrete walls of the Los Angeles River in barrios with incongruous nicknames like Alpine Flats, Happy Valley and

Dogtown (because it was near a city animal shelter). The Eastside community of Boyle Heights had been predominantly Jewish in the 1920s. During the 1940s, as Jews moved to the Fairfax district west of downtown, East L.A. became the center of the city's Mexican American community. In 1949, with a broad grassroots effort and help from liberal Jewish support, Edward Roybal became the first Mexican American elected to the Los Angeles City Council since the nineteenth century. It was the beginning of modern Latino politics in Los Angeles, and California. Roybal later served for thirty years in the U.S. Congress as a staunch advocate of civil rights and the elderly.

Postwar Los Angeles was bursting. Housing was in short supply, schools crowded and public services virtually overwhelmed. In 1947, Los Angeles Congresswoman Helen Gahagan Douglas described a city where "more families are homeless . . . than after the San Francisco Earthquake . . ." In fact, 162,000 families, including 50,000 veterans, were living in tents and temporary shelters, such as the Quonset huts of Rodger Young Village, named for a war hero, on the edge of Griffith Park. And the people kept coming.

The war had put a damper on American sports, but in 1946, Los Angeles celebrated the arrival of the defending National Football League Champions. The former Cleveland Rams now belonged to Los Angeles. The Rams got off to a fresh and fast start by drafting UCLA stars Kenny Washington and Woody Strode, breaking a twelve-year NFL ban on African American players.

The postwar years were both hopeful and haunted by a renewal of old anxieties.

During the war, the Soviet Union had been an invaluable ally. Victory resurrected fears that Communists were dedicated to triumphing over American capitalism, and worse, undermining our country from within. There were especially strong suspicions that "Reds" had infiltrated the very heart of Hollywood, where they supposedly had been poisoning the minds of moviegoers for years.

As a result of these fears, the U.S. House Un-American Activities Committee (HUAC) began a series of hearings with the aim, in part, to probe the loyalty of Hollywood's creative community. Well-known stars, including Humphrey Bogart, Frank Sinatra, Henry Fonda, Burt Lancaster and Gregory Peck, responded with an organization called Hollywood Strikes Back. They charged that HUAC was an attack on the First Amendment guarantee of freedom of speech. The anti-Communist furor was so overwhelming that most of the original protestors soon backed down, some insisting on their hatred of Communism and love for America. Others, fearful for their careers,

THE 1940 UCLA BACKFIELD, from left: Jackie Robinson, Ned Mathews, Bill Overlin and Kenny Washington. In 1946, Washington and UCLA teammate Woody Strode were signed by the Los Angeles Rams. The next year, Robinson made his break-through appearance with the Brooklyn Dodgers.

A DEMONSTRATION IN SUPPORT OF THE HOLLYWOOD TEN, writers convicted of contempt of congress for refusing to answer questions by the House Committee on Un-American Activities.

"named names" of friends and acquaintances with leftist leanings.

Some of those who refused to cooperate, mostly screenwriters, were labeled "The Hollywood Ten." In 1950, members of The Ten began serving prison terms of six months to a year for contempt of congress. Other Hollywood professionals, implicated by evidence, rumors or frightened friends, were added to an industry-wide blacklist that denied them jobs. A few were Communists, or sympathizers, which was not uncommon in the activist 1930s. Many, however, simply shared an idealistic passion for issues such as racial equality and trade unionism. Neither enthusiasm was popular in the powerful Los Angeles business community, which preferred de facto segregation and factories without unions. To survive, some on the blacklist left for Europe, or wrote using pseudonyms, or hired "fronts"

to conceal their identity. Although the list ended in the 1960s, many never again worked in Hollywood.

While the postwar era brought Los Angeles increased importance, American political and economic power remained in New York and Washington, D.C. Since 1898, when Los Angeles convinced congress to help fund a man-made harbor in San Pedro, national political representation was vital for L.A.'s growth and development. In 1946, local business interests found their man for the postwar era—Richard Milhous Nixon. Like Bostonian and fellow political novice John F. Kennedy, the ambitious young navy veteran and Whittier lawyer represented a new generation of leadership and, beyond that, early indications of the growing significance of California and Los Angeles in national politics.

With the support of conservative Southern Californians, and the influential endorsement of the *Los Angeles Times,* Nixon proved to be an effective campaigner. Insinuating that his opponents were "soft" on Communism, he was elected to the U.S. House of Representatives in 1946. As a congressman, Nixon played an active role on the House Un-American Activities Committee. He also made national headlines in 1948, when he accused former State Department official Alger Hiss of being a Communist spy. In 1950, Hiss, a well-connected graduate of Harvard Law School, was sent to jail for perjury. That same year, Nixon challenged incumbent senator Helen Gahagan Douglas. Calling his opponent "The Pink Lady," for her liberal politics, he won.

Fears of Communism weren't the only threat to the good life in Los Angeles. The boom of the war years attracted fortune seekers of all kinds, including a local brand of organized crime. Benjamin "Bugsy" Siegel had Hollywood good looks and a movie star's sense of fashion. Underneath he was a contract killer who'd been born in the poverty-stricken streets of Brooklyn. He hated his nickname, but it stuck.

CONGRESSMAN RICHARD NIXON on November 8, 1950, declaring victory after a controversial senate race against Democratic contender Helen Gahagan Douglas.

BUGSY SIEGEL AND JERRY GEISLER. In 1942, Siegel celebrates with his lawyer after being acquitted of any involvement in the murder of fellow mobster Harry "Big Greeny" Schachter.

In 1937, Bugsy headed west to Los Angeles.

His mission was to cultivate new opportunities on turf loosely controlled by local mobster Jack Dragna. An accommodating Dragna didn't object. Siegel set up gambling rackets and made himself at home in the highest circles of Hollywood, hosting lavish parties with his adoring millionaire girlfriend, Countess Dorothy Dendrice Taylor DiFrasso. Dragna was a hood with a small-town vision. Siegel thought big. During World War II, he was even eager to arrange mob-style hits on top Nazi leaders, including the Führer himself. The Allied armies won the war without his assistance.

In 1945, Siegel had the even crazier idea of turning isolated, windblown Las Vegas, Nevada, into a gambling mecca. To make it happen, he borrowed heavily from New York syndicate chief Charles "Lucky" Luciano. When Siegel's Flamingo hotel operation showed promise, Luciano demanded a return on his investment. Bugsy refused. It was not a wise response. On June 20, 1947, the dapper mobster was relaxing in the Beverly Hills living room of a girlfriend, Virginia Hill, when representatives from New York paid a visit — with a shotgun. Bugsy had been a well-known figure in Hollywood society, with many important friends. The only people who showed up at his funeral were five Siegel family members.

In the 1940s, Meyer Harris Cohen, better known as Mickey, claimed to be nothing more than a nightclub owner and the proprietor of a Sunset Boulevard men's clothing store. He was somewhat more. A veteran of Al Capone's Chicago, Mickey Cohen was Bugsy Siegel's "shadow." He had his hand in an extensive network of rackets in Los Angeles, including gambling and loan sharking. Lacking Siegel's smooth veneer, Cohen muscled his way around town and wasn't shy about appearing in the press.

After Siegel's execution, Cohen found himself under attack by Jack Dragna. Starting in 1949, he miraculously escaped repeated assassination attempts. He was ambushed as he was

"BUGSY" SIEGEL hobnobbed with Hollywood stars and envisioned modern Las Vegas. But when he crossed East Coast mob bosses, he paid the price.

GANGSTER MICKEY COHEN, second from left, joins a roundup of fellow mobsters in 1948.

COHEN IN HANDCUFFS, accompanied by a U.S. marshal. After dodging the law and assassination attempts, the L.A. gangster was sent to jail for tax evasion in 1952.

driving home, his house was bombed and he was wounded in a barrage of gunfire outside a fancy restaurant. Newspapers called the repeated attacks "The Battle of Sunset Strip."

If bullets couldn't bring him down, the law finally caught up with Mickey Cohen in 1952. He was sent to jail for tax evasion. Upon his release three years later, Cohen returned to open a seemingly innocent ice cream parlor near his home in upscale Brentwood. Behind the containers of chocolate and vanilla was a bookie joint, but it was another conviction for tax invasion in 1961 that sent him to Alcatraz. There, always the tough guy, the feisty gangster got into a fight with another inmate. The encounter left Cohen crippled for life. Finally,

he was out again in 1972, officially retired. Still good for a provocative quote for reporters, he declared: "There's no politics in Southern California you can deal with. It's anarchy."

Los Angeles's most infamous unsolved murder happened in 1947, and it wasn't a mob hit. On January 17, the naked body of an aspiring young actress named Elizabeth Ann Short was found in an empty lot. With surgical precision, she'd been cut in half and disemboweled. When reporters found a picture of her dressed in black and learned of her love for dahlias, she became "The Black Dahlia." It was the perfect crime for noir L.A. Over the years, there have been many theories to explain her death, none of them conclusive.

ELIZABETH SHORT, better known as "The Black Dahlia," came to Los Angeles to become an actress and ended up a victim in one of L.A.'s most famous noir mysteries.

THE BLACK DAHLIA MURDER filled the front pages of L.A. newspapers for months.

One recent solution came from a retired L.A. policeman who claimed his sadistic doctor father was the killer. Although he provided provocative new evidence, doubts remain.

In the late 1940s, even if Los Angeles had its share of gruesome murders, there also was a sense of new life in the air. After four years of rationing, Americans were eager to celebrate with a buying spree. Postwar Southern California became America's second-largest clothing producer, specializing, not surprisingly, in swimsuits and casual wear. Cole of California had made parachutes during the war. Now, along with Catalina, Rose Marie

Reid and others, Los Angeles companies dressed former Rosie the Riveters and their daughters, while Hollywood designers such as Edith Head set trends on the movie screen.

Government-backed loans allowed veterans of World War II to get a college education and buy a house. The Los Angeles real estate market was hot again. Lots that went for $850 before the war were selling for $5,000 and more. While urban planners shook their heads at sprawling fields strewn with new homes, L.A. newcomers refused to return to crowded

CARS AND MOVING VANS line up at a 1940s suburban tract development.

L.A. AUTO ASSEMBLY PLANT. During the war, auto production was redirected to jeeps and tanks. Afterwards, assembly plants in Los Angeles joined those in Detroit to fulfill pent-up demands for new cars.

BOB'S BIG BOY. Uniformed carhops line up outside the popular Bob's Big Boy Glendale drive-in.

city apartments. They wanted a place of their own, and a lawn, even if it was a small one. It was the American Dream, and as before, Los Angeles promised to deliver.

Along with a suburban home, an automobile — preferably a convertible — filled out the picture. In 1948, Los Angeles auto plants were turning out 650,000 new cars a year. The postwar years marked the beginning of a new kind of American mobility and lifestyle, one that even changed what and where we eat.

In 1948, the McDonald brothers started selling fast and cheap food to walk-up customers in San Bernardino. That same year, a husband-and-wife team inaugurated drive-through service at the first In-N-Out Burger in Baldwin

DON LEE TV SHOW. The total budget for this experimental drama was $200.

BOB HOPE. In a 1947 Paramount newsreel, the famous comedian reenacts the inaugural broadcast of L.A.'s first commercial television station, KTLA.

TV TO GO. Experimental Paramount Studios television station W6XYZ was already moving TV broadcasts away from studios during the 1940s.

Park, east of downtown L.A. Also during the '40s, Bob Wian of Glendale made his two-patty "Big Boy" a model for future hamburgers like the Big Mac.

As the housing market began to boom, factories that had made bombsights and radar systems retooled for kitchen appliances and television sets. Los Angeles picked up where TV pioneer Don Lee had left off in the 1930s. After five years of experimentation, on January 22, 1947, KTLA became the first commercially licensed Los Angeles television station with an inaugural broadcast hosted by Bob Hope. The station was owned by Paramount Pictures, which, like most movie studios, was unsure how to deal with the small-screen medium.

With transcontinental broadcasting still in the future, local stations were left to innovate on their own. KTLA's general manager, Klaus Landsberg, a veteran of early television experiments in Germany, including a broadcast of the Berlin Olympics of 1936, was allowed to try anything — and he did. Landsberg took cameras out of the studio to pioneer live, on-site entertainment and news.

In 1949, the station broadcast continuously for twenty-seven and a half hours during the attempted rescue of three-year-old Kathy Fiscus, who was trapped in an abandoned San Marino well. One of the reporters on the scene was Stan Chambers, a fixture of local

A KTLA TELEVISION CREW records desperate attempts to save the life of three-year-old Kathy Fiscus, trapped in a well in San Marino. The real-life drama was a landmark in early television news.

WITH A "RADIO-FLASH-CAR" equipped with two-way radios, reporters and photographers for the Los Angeles *Herald-Express* try to keep up with rapidly changing Los Angeles in 1949.

OVERLOOKING THE FARMERS MARKET, as well as Gilmore Stadium, upper left, and Gilmore Field, right, home of the Hollywood Stars baseball team.

THE CARTHAY CIRCLE THEATER wasn't in the heart of Hollywood, but it provided a dramatic location for major premieres—this one for *The Heiress* in October 1949.

broadcast journalism for more than fifty years.

Although it ended tragically, the Fiscus telecast was the first indication of the power of live TV news. During the '50s, KTLA also was the first to televise an atomic bomb test as it happened. In 1958, the station bought the world's first "Telecopter," to quickly reach and report news in a city so spread out that it could take hours to drive across town. Klaus Landsberg died of cancer in 1956, at age forty. By then L.A.'s innovative role in the history of early television was well underway.

The big news on October 14, 1947, was a breakthrough in aviation. Taking off from Edwards Air Force Base north of L.A., test pilot Chuck Yeager flew his Bell X-1 rocket plane faster than the speed of sound. A renewed commercial airline industry, and experimentation with faster planes, promised to bring Los Angeles closer to the rest of America. However, postwar aviation wasn't without lingering controversies.

In 1946, aviator/movie producer Howard Hughes nearly died in the Beverly Hills crash of his latest experimental aircraft, and his most ambitious project, the H-4 Hercules, an enormous and expensive air transport built in part with wood, remained unfinished. Dubbed the "Spruce Goose," it led critics to call Hughes a war-time profiteer, and the H-4 a boondoggle.

HOWARD HUGHES IN THE SPRUCE GOOSE. As confident as ever, Hughes prepares to pilot his giant wooden aircraft, known as the "Spruce Goose." The controversial plane barely made it airborne and never flew again.

The lanky former Texan angrily vowed to prove that his giant was airworthy. On November 2, 1947, he did—barely. The huge, eight-engine, 300,000-pound flying boat lifted seventy feet off the surface of Long Beach Harbor and touched down a minute and a mile later. Although the Spruce Goose would never fly again, to himself at least, Hughes was vindicated. After a while, the government was willing to forgive and forget. Investigators backed off, and Hughes Aircraft grew into one of Southern California's largest aviation and high-technology companies.

Innovative, potentially powerful and definitely big, by the end of the 1940s, L.A. was taking off toward a new decade. How far and how high the city would rise, remained, it could be said, very much in the air.

SURFING. After the war, it was time to return to the surf. This longboard looks like it could be as lethal as a torpedo.

SNOW? Quick, hide this photo! Belying L.A.'s ever-sunny image, a rare snowstorm hits unprepared Angelenos on January 11, 1949. These frustrated drivers are trying to make it up aptly named Coldwater Canyon Drive.

SPRAWLING TOWARD TOMORROW

"If you lived here, you'd be home."

REAL ESTATE BILLBOARD

In the early 1950s, "The City as New as Tomorrow" was born. Fourteen miles south of Los Angeles, Lakewood was the largest planned community in the United States, twice the size of New York's widely publicized Levittown. Where once there was a small village, 17,000 homes seemed to appear overnight. In three years, Lakewood grew from a population of 15,000 to more than 70,000. When it opened in 1952, the Lakewood Shopping Center, a model for future suburban malls, had 12,000 parking spaces.

Lakewood wasn't alone. Between 1940 and 1960, nearly nine million people moved to California — the largest migration in American history. In 1943, Bing Crosby sang about making "the San Fernando Valley my home." The Valley, just north of the Los Angeles basin, had boomed in the 1920s and '40s, but nothing compared to what happened in the 1950s. Young families followed Bing's advice, replanting sandy agricultural land with fresh crops of tract homes. And not all new arrivals to Los Angeles were from the United States.

The end of the Korean conflict in 1953 brought Korean war brides and other Asians looking for a better life. By 1961, children from Asia, especially Korea, represented 59 percent of America's

BACKYARD BARBECUE. An image of the good life in suburban L.A.—a backyard barbecue with burgers on the grill, even in the depths of December.

CANOGA PARK. During the housing rush of the 1950s, a former ranch in the western San Fernando Valley was subdivided into side-by-side homesites.

OBLIVION. One of the last of the old Los Angeles streetcars leaves the Hill Street subway tunnel on its way into history.

DISCARDED RED CARS. With the age of the freeway underway, some trolleys were destined for the scrap heap. Others were saved and sold to cities in Latin America.

"immigrant orphans." On November 11, 1954, 1,600 Issei, first-generation Japanese Americans, were proudly sworn in as citizens in Los Angeles. Only ten years before, they had been held in internment camps.

As L.A. expanded in all directions, the city needed a transportation system to hold it together. The Red Car transit trains had done the job since the turn of the century, but their days were numbered. The idea of a freeway system for Los Angeles had been proposed as early as 1930 by a team of consultants that included Frederick Olmstead Jr., son of the designer of New York's Central Park. Their plan expressed a regional vision, separating modes of transportation with parkland and landscaped high-speed roadways. It looked great on paper, but many real estate—driven city

CONSTRUCTION OF THE HOLLYWOOD FREEWAY through Cahuenga Pass, connecting the Los Angeles basin with the San Fernando Valley.

CELEBRATING SPEED. Motorcycle police escort VIPs on opening day of the yet-to-be-completed Hollywood Freeway in December 1950.

leaders considered government management and planning as interference with free enterprise and public parks as unprofitable use of valuable land. As a result, the plan was ignored. The freeway idea, however, stuck.

Inaugurated in 1939, the first Los Angeles freeway was the Arroyo Seco Parkway connecting downtown with Pasadena. Commonly known today as the Pasadena Freeway, it was inspired by East Coast and international models. In New York, uninterrupted parkways had been built in the 1930s. Chicago opened Lakeshore Drive in 1933. The first "cloverleaf" interchange was constructed in New Jersey. In Germany, there were the high-speed stretches of the autobahn. But dense New York and Chicago worked best with mass transit, and the autobahn was designed for interurban rather than intra-urban travel. Open, dispersed Los Angeles offered perfect terrain for a high-speed automobile-driven transportation system.

World War II had interrupted highway construction. But by the 1950s, new freeways were threading through the city like an urban circulatory system. During the decade, more than 160 miles were added. As freeways established arterial pathways throughout Los Angeles, they promised unprecedented new mobility. They also devoured land at the rate of forty acres per mile, replacing open space with concrete. For better and worse, it wasn't long before it was difficult to frame a picture of L.A. without a freeway.

In 1953, Los Angeles acquired one of its most recognizable downtown features, an interwoven interchange nicknamed "the stack," or "mixmaster." From there, drivers

A NEW INTERCHANGE for the Golden State Freeway promises more urban mobility as it swallows land by the acre.

IN 1956, THE HARBOR FREEWAY links some neighborhoods and divides others.

THE "STACK," OR "MIXMASTER," as it appeared in 1954, shuffled downtown freeway traffic, part of a high-speed transportation network that was defining the look and structure of Los Angeles.

CHOKING, STINGING SMOG made many a 1950s day miserable in Los Angeles. The result of a natural inversion layer and man-made pollution, L.A.'s toxic air spurred an environmental movement that spread across America.

could easily turn northwest toward Hollywood, southwest toward San Pedro, northeast toward Pasadena, or southeast toward Orange County and San Diego.

Los Angeles had been the automobile capital of the world since the 1920s. By the '50s, Angelenos were more than voracious consumers of automobiles, and the city was second to Detroit, Michigan, as an auto-manufacturing center, and second to Akron, Ohio, as a producer of tires. Along with hundreds of thousands of new residents, by the end of the 1950s, Los Angeles County was populated with 3 million cars. Much of urban America, still dependent on crowded trains, subways and buses, viewed auto-driven L.A. as an anomaly. In time they would insist on wheels and freeways of their own.

Although drive-in movies didn't originate in Southern California, year-round good weather allowed them to flourish. Beginning

in the '20s, there were drive-through markets, fast-food restaurants, pharmacies and drycleaners — even drive-in churches. However, prayers couldn't prevent cars from producing unwanted consequences.

In 1943, a headline in war-wary Los Angeles declared a mysterious "gas attack." It wasn't Japanese saboteurs, it was "smog," an amalgam of the words *smoke* and *fog*. In fact, smog had been part of the Los Angeles environment for centuries. In 1542, Spanish explorer Juan Rodríguez Cabrillo, sailing into San Pedro Bay, noticed that smoke from Native American campfires flattened above the basin that would be called Los Angeles. His crew named the place Baya de los Fumos (Bay of Smoke). The flattening was caused by colder upper atmosphere pressing down on warmer air trapped below. Later, scientists defined it as an inversion layer.

Long associated with London, by the 1950s, smog was a major health problem in Los Angeles. Industry was initially considered the primary cause, but the city's beloved automobiles were major culprits. California and

THE DISAPPEARING RIVER. In 1959, what was once a wandering, sometimes dangerous stream called Rio de Porciúncula gets a concrete straitjacket.

Los Angeles would eventually lead the nation in environmental advocacy and air-pollution controls, but improving air quality often seemed an endless race against the consequences of unprecedented growth.

Along with a thick brown haze of smog, images of mushroom clouds haunted 1950s Los Angeles, and the rest of the United States. In response to fears of a nuclear attack, school kids were taught to "duck and cover" under their desks. Downtown buildings, and even the Eastland Shopping Center in the booming community of West Covina, had spaces designated for use as bomb shelters.

A different kind of threat appeared in the sky over Los Angeles on October 4, 1957. The Soviet Union had launched Sputnik, the first man-made satellite. Sputnik was a major blow to America's sense of technological supremacy. But the result was a boom for Southern California's defense and aerospace industries. In 1958, Pasadena's Jet Propulsion Laboratory launched America's first successful satellite, Explorer I, and it wasn't long before Hughes Electronics, part of Howard Hughes's aviation

KTLA TELEVISES A-BOMB. In a major television landmark on April 22, 1952, KTLA cameras broadcast the first nationwide live images of an atomic blast from the Nevada test site.

ATOMIC SUNRISE. On March 7, 1955, the Los Angeles skyline gets a man-made dawn when an atomic bomb is tested in Nevada— more than 300 miles away.

CIVIL DEFENSE DRILL. During the 1950s and early '60s, school children were taught to "duck and cover" in case of a nuclear attack. Here, fifth and sixth graders at Elysian Heights Elementary School practice survival techniques.

empire, became the single-largest supplier of weapon systems for the U.S. Air Force and Navy.

The "arms race" was already underway when a "space race" began. Soon, even L.A. architecture took on a space-age look. There were restaurants with starbursts and rocket-shaped signs, and new buildings, like the Los Angeles Sports Arena, with a shape that suggested a flying saucer. One of the most visible space age–influenced structures was the new Theme Building at the Los Angeles International Airport. Supported by thin curved legs, it looked like one of the alien spacecraft so familiar to fans of 1950s Hollywood science fiction films. In his 1950 book, *The Martian Chronicles,* Los Angeles author Ray Bradbury anticipated a sense of time warp that characterized 1950s L.A., as the last vestiges of a Midwestern sensibility were being translated and transformed by a futuristic landscape.

As an indication of L.A.'s uncertain sense of community, public architecture had usually been overshadowed by the creativity invested in individual homes. For example, Frank Lloyd Wright had done some of his most interesting work in Southern California, including the 1924 Ennis House and the 1921 Hollyhock House.

A movement to define a new architecture for postwar America was the goal of a series of Case Study houses built between 1945 and 1966, inspired by Los Angeles magazine editor John Entenza. Designed by local architects such as Richard Neutra, an Austrian-born immigrant who came to Los Angeles in the 1920s, these simple and economical residences blurred the distinction between inside and out. With walls of glass, flat roofs and exposed beam ceilings, mid-century Case Study homes inspired and epitomized the dream of openness and freedom that was a picture of life at home in Los Angeles. The dream came inside with furniture created by artists such as Charles and Ray Eames, the

SPORTS ARENA. Like a recently landed flying saucer, the Los Angeles Sports Arena arrived in 1959, in time for the Democratic Party National Convention the following year.

ARCHITECT PAUL WILLIAMS, known for his homes for wealthy Angelenos, was part of the team that designed the new Theme Building for the Los Angeles International Airport.

THE 1928 LOVELL "HEALTH" HOUSE, one of the great works of architect Richard Neutra, expressed an elegant simplicity and openness that was an architectural representation of L.A.'s cultural and environmental openness.

RICHARD NEUTRA, an immigrant from Austria, embraced life in Southern California, creating clean-lined and open designs that set a standard for mid-century American architecture.

husband-and-wife team who designed innovative pieces that could be mass-produced, using curved plywood, plastic and tubular steel.

Although it was rarely revealed in news and publicity photos, Los Angeles attracted more than movie stars and middle-class white suburbanites. Many prominent figures in 1950s America came from L.A.'s growing minority communities. Mexican Americans could point with pride to boxer Art Aragon and tennis champion Ricardo "Pancho" Gonzalez, who against all odds rose to the top of an elite and virtually all-white sport. L.A.'s African American community produced U.S. diplomat Ralph Bunche, a 1927 UCLA graduate; baseball star Jackie Robinson, another UCLA alumnus; and pioneering black architect Paul R. Williams, the designer of homes for some of the city's wealthiest and broad-minded clients. By 1950, 218,000 black Americans called Los Angeles County home.

Despite this, in housing and job opportunities, Los Angeles had a long tradition of segregation and discrimination. Home sales and occupancy contracts contained "restrictive

PANCHO GONZALEZ. In this 1949 photo, L.A. native Ricardo "Pancho" Gonzales shows the fierce and determined style that took him to the heights of international tennis, a sport formerly reserved for the wealthy and white.

BOXER ART ARAGON never won a major title, but he was "The Golden Boy" to L.A.'s Latino community during the late 1940s and '50s.

RACISM IN PARADISE. In the 1950s, when black fireman Bailey Rogers bought a house in an all-white Los Angeles neighborhood, angry local residents set fire to his new home in an effort to make him leave. He didn't.

covenants," limiting some neighborhoods to white-only buyers and renters. Even city employers such as the fire and police departments had hiring and assignment restrictions. The 1954 *Brown v. Board of Education* Supreme Court decision initiated a wave of change across racially segregated America—south and north.

In 1892, when Sam Haskins, a former Virginia slave, became the city's first black fireman, he was integrated into the Los Angeles Fire Department. A short time later, he died in the line of duty, one of many firefighters who served the city well since the first volunteer organization. By 1902, new black firefighters, like George Bright, the second to join the department, were assigned, along with Mexican Americans, to segregated fire stations in minority neighborhoods. One of the most prominent was Central Avenue Station House 30, established as an all-black company in 1924. Even with additional black station houses, top leadership remained white. Twenty-nine years later, in 1953, that policy was challenged by the National Association for the Advancement of Colored People.

MULTICULTURAL L.A. Eleven-year-old Edward Gomez lines up a shot in a news photo presenting an uncommon positive image of L.A.'s growing African American, Asian and Mexican populations.

Los Angeles fireman and attorney Arnett Hartsfield was a leader in the fight that followed.

In 1954, although the city fire chief, John Alderson, initially resisted, steps began to integrate the LAFD. During the early years of the process, African American firefighters were ostracized and harassed by their white colleagues. To Hartsfield, "integration was isolation." As a result of his activism, he was never promoted, leaving him with a lifelong nickname: "The Rookie." Finally, in September 1956, after a long and bitter struggle, integration of the department was declared complete. Even so, like much of the rest of America, there remained a long way to go. Nearly twenty years later, it took a federal consent degree to improve the number of black Los Angeles city firemen from forty-five in 1974 to nearly 400 in 2005, including, most notably, fifty-six captains and thirteen chiefs.

Progress came more quickly to the L.A. economy. Just as World War II enriched Los Angeles, the Korean War and the space race continued the upward trend. Between 1950 and 1957, Los Angeles County accounted for one-sixth of all manufacturing jobs in the United States. Yet, even with the speed and convenience of new cross-country air travel, L.A. was considered on the distant edge of America. Products were sold with "Prices slightly higher west of the Rockies."

With an almost-colonial relationship with East Coast institutions and influences, Angelenos continued to support and entertain themselves. During the 1950s, the Los Angeles Rams football team drew fans, if not championships. Quarterback Norm Van Brocklin and receivers Tom Fears and Elroy "Crazy Legs" Hirsch led the offense.

Until the late 1950s, the nearest major league baseball team to Los Angeles was in St. Louis. The western states made up for this with the Pacific Coast League, founded in

ARNETT HARTSFIELD, fireman and civil rights activist, celebrates his graduation from law school in 1956.

1903. Fifty years later, the big leagues considered Pacific Coast teams "minor," yet many of the game's biggest stars had been nurtured there, including Joe DiMaggio, Ted Williams and even future New York Yankee manager Casey Stengel.

Since the 1930s, Angelenos enjoyed cheering for the Angels and their arch rivals, the Hollywood Stars. The Angels were the Pacific Coast League powerhouse. In the 1930s alone, they won more than 1,000 games. In 1921, Chicago chewing gum magnate William Wrigley Jr. bought the team and built a West Coast Wrigley Field. Ten years later he installed lights for night games, decades before they illuminated the diamond in major-league Chicago.

Gilmore Field, north of the Farmers Market, had been home to the Hollywood Stars since 1938. The Stars, fondly called the "Twinks," took on the Angels in a rivalry as heated as the Yankee-Dodger matchup three thousand miles away. One of the most famous Twinks was outfielder Frankie Kelleher, who hit forty homers in 1950. His speedy teammate Carlos Bernier chalked up a career total of 594

ELROY "CRAZY LEGS" HIRSCH, left, and Tom Fears put on their game faces for the Los Angeles Rams in this 1952 photo. Both were NFL Hall of Famers. Fears was the first Latino to be so honored and the first to coach in the NFL.

THE 1952 HOLLYWOOD STARS outside their Gilmore Field home near the Farmers Market. Anticipating the arrival of the Dodgers, the Stars moved to Salt Lake City in 1957. Their intimate stadium was razed the following year.

STEVE BILKO, left, home run king of the Los Angeles Angels, has a smile for Dick Stuart, first baseman for the minor league Angels' cross-town rivals, the Hollywood Stars.

MARILYN MONROE'S glamorous life, which included a brief marriage to baseball's Joe DiMaggio in 1954, was troubled. Mystery still surrounds her untimely death in 1962 at age thirty-six.

stolen bases. For the Angels, there was 1956 Triple Crown–winner Steve Bilko. Bilko's fifty-five home runs that year came close to Babe Ruth's big league record, and even the "Bambino" once declared that Pacific Coast play was just as good as the majors. Major league teams practiced in L.A.'s spring-time weather, and occasionally played exhibition games. But for the rest of America, the Pacific Coast remained too distant to make direct comparisons.

The impact of that distance began to fade on September 4, 1951, when President Harry Truman delivered a speech to the United Nations. He'd spoken to the U.N. before, but this speech marked a first. With a new AT&T transcontinental connection, Truman was heard and seen simultaneously in New York and Los Angeles. On New Year's Day three years later, winter-bound Americans enviously watched what life was like in sunny Southern California when the Pasadena Rose Parade was featured on the first coast-to-coast television broadcast. Even as communications technology connected Los Angeles to the rest of the nation, the picture of Southern California remained both exotic and alluring. Despite this, when many Americans peered at images of L.A. on television, like it or not, they were tuning into their future.

In 1950, only 9 percent of American

TIME FOR BEANY. Warner Brothers' cartoon factory alumnus Bob Clampett created the popular 1950s *Time for Beany* puppet TV series. Among the show's loyal fans was visiting Caltech professor Albert Einstein.

THE MILLIONTH TV. In July 1951, Mayor Fletcher Bowron, right, celebrates a landmark in L.A.'s television history.

households owned a television, but 16 percent of Angelenos were able to watch seven local stations, the most of any city in America. By 1954, the national TV audience was up to twenty-nine million, nearly half the population.

With declining ticket sales, the movies struck back with expansive gestures that tiny home screens couldn't match, including Cinerama, Cinemascope and Vista Vision. There were also Technicolor spectaculars, 3-D and special-effects-filled science fiction adventures. In the '50s, Hollywood also churned out action-packed westerns and lavish musicals while continuing a postwar tone with tougher, darker, black-and-white films with brooding stars, such as Marlon Brando in

A Streetcar Named Desire, The Wild One and *On the Waterfront.* In contrast to this dose of reality, if Americans embraced Marilyn Monroe in neighborhood movie theaters, they weren't ready to welcome her into their living rooms on television. As the decade crossed over into the '60s, hints of change were evident in the popularity of slightly naughty Doris Day and Rock Hudson comedies. Much of this was a result of Los Angeles–based image-making.

During the '50s, old movies filled empty airtime on TV while New Yorkers Milton Berle and Sid Caesar were reborn from the vestiges of vaudeville, and second-string Hollywood players like Lucille Ball became small–screen superstars. Genial actor Ronald Reagan kept

LUCILLE BALL. In a 1958 episode of *The Lucy-Desi Comedy Hour*, the gang is on a hunt for uranium. Television made Ball one of America's most popular and best-loved comediennes.

GORGEOUS GEORGE. During the 1950s, flamboyant wrestler George Wagner, better known as "Gorgeous George," was a top draw at L.A.'s Olympic Auditorium and an early gender-bending TV star.

his place in the public eye as host of *General Electric Theater*. Walt Disney was one of the most successful manipulators of the new medium with his *Davy Crocket* and *Mickey Mouse Club* series.

Disney's use of television was especially shrewd. In 1954, while realizing his most ambitious dream, a $17 million amusement

WALT DISNEY was well aware of the power of television. By 1954, he was one of the first to capitalize on it.

WALTER KNOTT, patriarch of what would become Knott's Berry Farm restaurant and amusement park.

park, he convinced the ABC network to buy a weekly series called *Disneyland.* It was a virtual infomercial for the amazements that were under construction on a 160-acre former citrus grove in Anaheim, twenty-five miles south of Los Angeles. After less than a year, Disneyland was only partially finished when it officially opened to an invitation-only list of guests on a sweltering July 17, 1955. The event was celebrated with a ninety-minute television special. Disney, and cohosts Art Linkletter and Ronald Reagan, welcomed the world, and introduced a compelling new reason for tourists to come to Los Angeles. Despite the doubters — and there were more than a few — it wasn't long before "The Magic Kingdom" was drawing a minimum of 87,000 visitors a day.

A short distance from Disneyland was another popular Southern California tourist destination, Knott's Berry Farm. In 1920, enterprising and entrepreneurial Walter Knott bought twenty acres in the agricultural community of Buena Park. Improving on earlier experiments by an Anaheim neighbor, Rudolf Boysen, Knott perfected the boysenberry. To help the family survive the Depression in the 1930s, Knott's wife, Cordelia, began selling jams, jellies and chicken dinners to passing travelers. With the coming of the postwar boom of the 1940s, tourism returned and the

Knott family's expanded restaurant was selling as many as four thousand dinners on a typical weekend. To amuse customers while they were waiting, the family constructed an idealized "Old West" town. By the 1960s, Knott's Berry Farm was a full-fledged theme park, featuring roller coaster rides and a patriotic re-creation of Philadelphia's Independence Hall.

Disneyland, with its many "lands" representing past, present, future and fantasy, all made possible through corporate sponsorship, pictured an increasingly commercialized United States. At the same time, Knott's Berry Farm shared its neighbor's idealized image of America.

IN 1958, A JAPANESE FAMILY ENJOYS DISNEYLAND, already one of the world's most visited tourist attractions.

KNOTT'S BERRY FARM DINING ROOM. With the war over, tourism returned to Southern California. By the 1950s, Cordelia Knott's restaurant featured home-style fried chicken dinners and boysenberry pie.

HISTORY AS AMUSEMENT. Following a distinctive Southern California path, Knott's Berry Farm began as an agricultural enterprise, added a restaurant in 1934, and then a Ghost Town in the 1940s—the modest beginnings of a major American theme park.

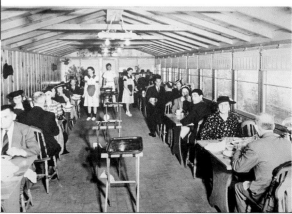

JAMES DEAN AND NATALIE WOOD in the 1955 film *Rebel Without a Cause*. Dean's emotionally raw acting style expressed tensions beneath the surface of 1950s life. After only three movies, he died in a car crash at age twenty-four.

Teenagers had been around long before the swing era enthusiasm of Mickey Rooney and Judy Garland, but young people found an aggressive new musical voice in '50s rock 'n' roll. The urban juvenile delinquents in the 1955 movie *Blackboard Jungle* terrified parents and enthralled their kids. In *Rebel Without a Cause,* released the same year, James Dean was filled with small-town angst, roaming tree-lined neighborhoods, drag racing and facing death in a knife fight in the parking lot of the Griffith Park Observatory. It was a darker picture of America, projected on a suburban landscape that reflected Los Angeles.

During the 1950s, teenagers were emerging as a major consumer market, and

DRAG RACING IN BURBANK. In 1954, members of the Prowlers car club engage in a popular but illegal L.A. sport.

BOB'S BIG BOY IN TOLUCA LAKE was a favorite drive-in restaurant for San Fernando Valley teenagers during the 1950s and '60s.

HULA HOOP. Free-spirited, entrepreneurial L.A. was the perfect place to create and nurture this 1950s fad.

Los Angeles became the home of research and development for the latest in popular culture. One of the most memorable merchandising success stories of the 1950s came from a little L.A. company, Wham-O. In 1957, inspired in part by public fascination with flying saucers, Wham-O introduced the Pluto Platter, which became better known as the Frisbee. The plastic flying disk was a multimillion-dollar success. One year later, the company adapted a bamboo exercise device

Australians were using in school gym classes, and transformed it into the hula hoop. It was a phenomenon that was certainly not considered equal to the latest serious novel or thoughtful Broadway play. Most dismissed it as only another silly Los Angeles–based fad. But the success of the hula hoop was a creative and indelible expression of the playful side of Americans in the 1950s. In four short months, twenty-five million were sold.

Hollywood was still the motion picture capital of the world, but the music business remained in New York. In 1955, that began to change when British-owned EMI bought L.A.-based Capitol Records, and a year later built a new recording studio and offices near the corner of Hollywood and Vine. A modern cousin to the eccentric Los Angeles architecture of the 1920s, the Capitol Records Building was a thirteen-story cylindrical structure that looked like a stack of 45-rpm records. At its top, a needle-shaped spire featured a beacon that flashed "Hollywood" in Morse code.

The first recording company in Los Angeles was created in 1921 by Andrae Nordskog, a Norwegian immigrant from Story City, Iowa. That year, Nordskog, who was also a persistent critic of the Owens Valley Aqueduct, released the first jazz record featuring black musicians. The band was led by New Orleans trombonist Kid Ory. Twenty-one years later, Capitol

Records was founded by a partnership including songwriter Johnny Mercer, movie producer Buddy DeSylva, and Glenn Wallichs, owner of L.A.'s largest music store, Music City, two blocks south on the corner of Sunset and Vine. Capitol was the largest West Coast record label. EMI made it international. In the 1950s, the company's Hollywood sound studios produced some of the greatest recordings by Frank Sinatra, Nat "King" Cole, bandleader Stan Kenton, Bobby Darin, parodist Stan Freberg, and the Kingston Trio, leaders of the decade's folk music resurgence. During the '60s, EMI was the label of the Beatles, and Capitol would become a major recording studio for everything from pop to classical music.

What was most underappreciated and misunderstood about the art and music that emerged from Los Angeles was its broad-based appeal. After a career as the leader of modestly successful dance bands in the Midwest, Lawrence Welk, an accordion-playing North Dakotan, arrived in Southern California in 1951 for a six-week booking. It turned into a lifetime. As a reminder that Los Angeles still had a strong streak of Middle America, Welk regularly drew crowds who enjoyed his old-fashioned polkas and sweet style of swing. In 1952, he began broadcasting a weekly dance show on L.A.'s pioneering television station KTLA.

THE CAPITOL RECORDS TOWER lit up for Christmas. A short distance north of Hollywood and Vine, the cylindrical building has been a unique L.A. landmark since 1955.

KLAUS LANDSBERG AND LAWRENCE WELK. Klaus Landsberg, left, a television innovator at L.A.'s first commercial TV station, KTLA, eyes bandleader Lawrence Welk, one of the station's early stars.

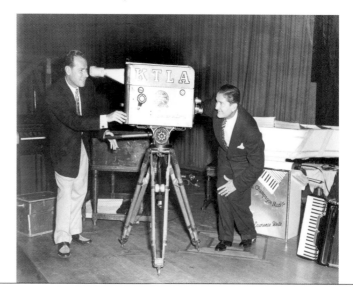

LIGHTHOUSE JAZZ CLUB. Along with venues like the Haig, the Lighthouse in Hermosa Beach, shown here in 1959, was a center for the cool sound of West Coast jazz.

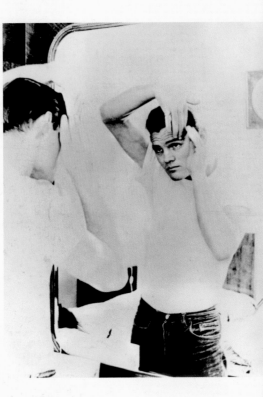

WEST COAST TRUMPETER CHET BAKER was the epitome of 1950s L.A. cool.

SHELLY'S MANNE-HOLE. By the 1970s, Shelly's jazz club may have looked a little ragged, but it was still attracting top performers such as pianist Bill Evans and singer Abbey Lincoln.

Three years later, with little change in a simple format, *The Lawrence Welk Show* moved to the ABC network and became one of America's most popular and long-lasting programs. Critics made fun of his German-accented introductions and called his arrangements corny; however, like much of 1950s Los Angeles, Welk's music represented the still-influential tastes of a prewar America, and a refuge between a comforting past and an uncertain, onrushing future.

Another underappreciated aspect of 1950s music in Los Angeles was certainly more hip. It was West Coast jazz, a softer, sophisticated style that grew out of the bebop of the 1940s. Gerry Mulligan, Chet Baker, Buddy Collette, Chico Hamilton and Shelly Manne were among the front men for the sound. At the same time, rhythm and blues and doo-wop, primarily African American precursors of rock 'n' roll, not usually associated with Los Angeles, were being nurtured in L.A. by musicians who would go on to be some of the more popular artists of the '50s and '60s, including the Platters ("The Great Pretender"), The Coasters ("Searchin'") and The Penguins ("Earth Angel"). Ironically, many of the greatest early rock and doo-wop classics were written by two L.A. white guys who moved to New York—Jerry Leiber and Mike Stoller.

Just as indicative of unexpected new directions in American popular music was the tragically short career of San Fernando Valley–born Richard Valenzuela, better known as Ritchie Valens. Killed in a 1959 plane crash shortly after the release of his major hit "La Bamba," Valens offered early evidence of a nascent Mexican American cultural and political movement that would gain strength in the 1960s and '70s.

In fact, in contrast to what would become "Happy Days" nostalgia on TV, the 1950s were far from uncomplicated or even innocent. Again, Los Angeles provided proof.

The politics of the '50s continued the anti-Communist furor that began the decade before. Wisconsin senator Joseph McCarthy

RITCHIE VALENS. San Fernando Valley–born Richard Valenzuela, renamed Ritchie Valens for more Anglo appeal, was America's first Chicano rock star. He died in a plane crash in 1959. He was only eighteen.

VICE PRESIDENT RICHARD NIXON, his wife, Pat, and daughters, Tricia and Julie, enjoy a day at the beach. Their dog, Checkers, is a reminder of a scandal that the politician survived with a famous 1952 speech televised from the El Capitan Theatre in Hollywood.

claimed there were Communists in all corners of American life. In 1951, the Hollywood Blacklist was reinvigorated with a new round of House Un-American Activities Committee hearings. Los Angeles teachers were required to sign loyalty oaths or be fired. The *Los Angeles Times* advised readers what to do if they ran into an agitator: "Don't punch him in the nose. Reds are used to that. Get his name and address and phone the FBI."

In 1952, even Hollywood legend Charlie Chaplin was pressured to leave the country, as much for his politics as for his infatuation with younger women and persistent income tax problems. That same year, Republican presidential candidate Dwight Eisenhower reluctantly accepted Richard Nixon as his running mate. Like Los Angeles, Nixon's rise to prominence was meteoric, but he soon faced a crisis that threatened to return him to his Whittier hometown.

Accused of benefiting from an illegal "slush fund" of political gifts, the California senator went to the NBC studios at the El Capitan Theatre on Hollywood Boulevard to defend himself on TV. Nixon's success that night showed the power of television that would eventually transform American politics. His refusal to return one gift, a puppy, touched some viewers and appalled others, but the speech saved his political life and made Checkers, the Nixon family dog, world famous.

DAWSON'S BOOK SHOP. L.A. is America's biggest book market. Dawson's dates to 1905. Originally located downtown on Grand Avenue, the store later moved to Larchmont Village, south of Hollywood.

After decades of scandal and corruption, the Los Angeles Police Department also faced challenges to its reputation. Tough, dedicated, professional and hard-drinking William H. Parker was promoted to chief in 1950. Like Nixon, Parker appreciated the power of television. With clipped, Raymond Chandler—inspired dialogue, the TV series *Dragnet,* produced with Parker's cooperation, pictured the LAPD as dedicated to firm but fair law and order. The chief believed in "proactive policing." L.A. cops regularly handcuffed first and asked questions later. In 1956, when the crime rate was low, records show that the LAPD made 220,000 arrests, a number close to 10 percent of the population of Los Angeles.

Dragnet and the popular 1950s television series *The Adventures of Ozzie and Harriet* offered Americans a picture of Los Angeles that reflected law and order and family togetherness. This image did not match the photographs and stories on the front pages of *Confidential Magazine.* Claiming ten million readers, *Confidential* printed lurid accounts of the real and suspected sins of high-profile personalities. Accusations of interracial sex and homosexuality, as well as hypocrisies and assorted "unnatural acts," were favorite headlines.

Confidential Magazine had few scruples, but it was a tradition for L.A. cops to cooperate with Hollywood studios to keep movie star

L.A. SHERIFF EUGENE W. BISCAILUZ, left, Police Chief William H. Parker, center, and District Attorney William E. Simpson, right, discuss law and order in 1950s Los Angeles.

OZZIE AND HARRIET. On their popular 1950s television series, Ozzie and Harriet Nelson and their sons Ricky, left, and David represented an ideal American family enjoying an L.A.–inspired suburban life.

indiscretions quiet. If you were an African American, Mexican or homosexual, treatment was less discrete. The LAPD regularly raided "queer" hangouts. Partly in response to this, in 1950, Los Angeles activist Harry Hay founded the Mattachine Society, the first organization in an American gay pride movement that would develop international prominence thirty years later.

On the night of the Academy Awards, April 6, 1958, the cops couldn't keep quiet about what they found at 750 Bedford Drive in Beverly Hills. The body of Johnny Stompanato, an ex-marine and former Mickey Cohen body-guard, lay in a pool of blood in the bedroom of movie star Lana Turner. Turner's fourteen-year-old daughter Cheryl had shoved a knife into Stompanato's stomach and killed him. Even before police arrived, legendary Holly-wood defense lawyer Jerry Geisler was on the case. With Cheryl and her mother as the only eyewitnesses, a coroner's jury was told how an abusive Stompanato had repeatedly hit his Hollywood star girlfriend after she returned from the Academy Awards. He was angry

because she refused to invite him. The verdict was justifiable homicide.

The death of Johnny Stompanato was a big story in 1958, but it was nothing compared to another event that year — one that marked a major transition in Los Angeles history and changed forever the way the city was pictured. On April 18, the Dodgers played their first home game in Los Angeles. No longer "Da Bums" of Brooklyn, they would become "Dodger Blue."

When owner Walter O'Malley first flew over the city in a helicopter, scouting sites for a new stadium, he picked the crest of a small canyon north of downtown. At the time, Chavez Ravine was a semirural community of mostly poor Mexican Americans. Only a few years before O'Malley's decision, plans had been drawn to replace the Ravine's dilapidated homes with new government-sponsored housing, designed by modern architect Richard Neutra.

With the promise of new apartments, many families agreed to move. However, to conser-vative real estate and political interests, public housing smelled of socialism. Even Rodger Young Village near Griffith Park, originally built

LANA TURNER, the "sweater girl" of 1940s movies and Oscar nominee for her 1950 role in *Peyton Place,* had many suitors and husbands. Shortly after this photo was taken, Johnny Stompanato, a rejected but persistent lover, center, would be stabbed to death by Turner's daughter, Cheryl Crane, right.

for World War II vets, was under attack. In 1953, critics called the residents freeloaders and noted the mixing of whites and blacks. The fight that followed cost longtime Los Angeles Mayor Fletcher Bowron his job.

With the support of the *Los Angeles Times,* former Congressman Norris Poulson successfully campaigned on his opposition to government-sponsored housing. The result left Chavez Ravine residents without their promised new homes, and their old community available for other plans — such as a new baseball stadium.

The few families that remained fought eviction, but in the end, Walter O'Malley and the city fathers of Los Angeles got what they wanted, and the Dodgers soon had a new home overlooking downtown. L.A.'s first World Series victory came in 1959, and Latinos became some of the team's most ardent fans, but the power struggle over Chavez Ravine foreshadowed greater conflicts in the decades to come.

CHAVEZ RAVINE. To make way for Dodger Stadium, on May 8, 1959, Los Angeles county sheriff deputies forcibly remove one of the last residents in the Mexican American community in Chavez Ravine.

HOMESTEADING ON THE NEW FRONTIER

"And she'll have fun, fun, fun 'til her daddy takes the T-bird away."

BRIAN WILSON AND MIKE LOVE, THE BEACH BOYS, "Fun, Fun, Fun," 1964

In the summer of 1960, Los Angeles hosted the Democratic National Convention — a first in the city's history. It was an acknowledgement of a transcontinental power shift that had been moving west since the end of World War II. In 1964, California surpassed New York as America's most populous state. Los Angeles was edging up on Chicago, the country's second-largest city, and the population of L.A. County was larger than that of forty-four American states.

Democrats convened at the newly completed Sports Arena. The nominee was John F. Kennedy. In his acceptance speech, the future president recalled the importance of the West in American history, then declared: "We stand today on the edge of a New Frontier—the frontier of the 1960s—a frontier of unknown opportunities and perils . . ." Kennedy was speaking about the United States and the world, but in the decade to come, his words would have special significance for Los Angeles.

In 1961, when President Kennedy dedicated America to the goal of sending a man to the moon and back, it galvanized the nation and empowered the Southern California economy with

NATIONAL GUARD TROOPS PATROL CENTRAL AVENUE. After six days of violence in August 1965, the Watts neighborhood was in ruins and Los Angeles in a state of shock.

technology and employment from a new aerospace industry. Later in the decade, the war in Vietnam would begin to devastate a small Asian country and tear America apart, but increased defense spending meant even more money for the L.A. economy.

For the City of Angels, the 1960s were boom times again. It was a decade when the leadership of Los Angeles determined to show the world that their hometown was truly America's "city of the future." It also was a time when L.A.'s sunny suburban image was hit hard by urban realities that had been too long ignored.

As the decade began, the business-dominated oligarchy that had run Los Angeles for decades had big plans. The old Bunker Hill district, home to the city's elite before the turn of the century, was now filled with neglected Victorian mansions, more recently used as apartments and flophouses. Like an embarrassing ancestor, old Bunker Hill would be

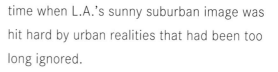

KHRUSHCHEV IN HOLLYWOOD. During a landmark 1960 visit to the United States, the Russian premier got a glimpse of Shirley MacLaine's gams on the set of the movie *Can-Can.* Khrushchev had wanted to see Disneyland, but despite his protests, the Magic Kingdom remained "top secret."

JOHN F. KENNEDY at the Los Angeles Sports Arena before his 1960 nomination as the Democratic candidate for president. The convention was the first by either party held in Los Angeles. The Democrats returned in 2000.

cropped from L.A.'s new image, razed and leveled to make way for an ambitious business and cultural complex.

Angels Flight, the little funicular known as "the shortest railway in the world" since it opened in 1901, was literally left alone in space, then dismantled and packed away. It would unexpectedly be resuscitated in 1996, only to close again after an accident five years later. While San Francisco was nurturing and preserving its Victorian past, Los Angeles was determined to picture itself in a futuristic frame.

Art and culture in L.A. had long been the source of derision and one-liners. During the 1960s, the laughter began to fade, if ever so slightly. Beginning in 1963, artist David Hockney, a transplant from Britain, reveled in the bright and sensual Southern California light. Well before that, in 1957, California artist Ed Kienholz and curator Walter Hopps opened the Ferus Gallery behind an antiques store on La Cienega Boulevard. Featuring the work of Angeleno artists such as Billy Al Bengston, Robert Irwin, Ed Moses and Ed Ruscha, Ferus ("uncivilized" in Latin) was also home to New York avant-gardists Roy Lichtenstein, Jasper Johns, Frank Stella, Andy Warhol and others. Although the gallery closed in 1967, almost forty years later one curator summed up its importance: "Ferus

OPENING NIGHT OF THE DOROTHY CHANDLER PAVILION at the new Los Angeles Music Center. From left, L.A. Philharmonic conductor Zubin Mehta, philanthropist Dorothy Buffum Chandler and architect Welton Beckett.

MUSIC CENTER. An aerial view of the new complex along with the headquarters of the Los Angeles Ahmanson Theatre and the circular Mark Taper Forum.

stands as a symbol of the transition of Los Angeles from provincial center to what it is today — an internationally recognized center for the arts."

In the early 1960s, while New York was building Lincoln Center, the City of Angels was planning a major cultural complex of its own. In an unprecedented effort led by Dorothy Buffum Chandler, wife of former *Los Angeles Times* publisher Norman Chandler, two great power centers came together. The Eastside communities of Hancock Park, Pasadena and San Marino were "old money" L.A.— mostly conservative and Protestant. On the west— from Hollywood and Beverly Hills to the Pacific—there was newer wealth, much of it from the entertainment business. Here, power was more liberal and notably Jewish. Private donors from both sides, who usually eyed each other with suspicion, joined to contribute $20 million toward the new complex. The county provided the land and $14 million more.

On December 6, 1964, the Music Center, as the new complex was called, inaugurated the Dorothy Chandler Pavilion. Opening night was highlighted with a concert by the Los

Angeles Philharmonic featuring virtuoso violinist and Santa Monica resident Jascha Heifitz and twenty-eight-year-old Indian-born conductor Zubin Mehta. Three years later, the addition of the Ahmanson Theatre and the Mark Taper Forum gave Los Angeles major venues for new plays and traveling shows. Producer/Director Gordon Davidson would serve as artistic director of the Taper and Ahmanson from 1967 to 2005.

L.A. was creating a new look, but with an attitude more appropriate for a provincial small town than for America's third-largest metropolis, city leaders preferred local, well-connected architects for big projects like the Music Center. The complex was designed by Welton Beckett & Associates, a firm responsible for much of the large-scale architecture of mid-century Los Angeles.

A 1933 transplant from Seattle, Beckett made powerful friends among L.A.'s business and Hollywood elite. Unlike self-absorbed architects, such as Frank Lloyd Wright, Beckett's style was modern but flexible, and he was happy to be responsive to his clients' tastes and budgets. These qualities, and his design and organizational skills, made the firm of Welton Beckett & Associates one of the world's largest. In addition to the Music Center, the company was responsible, alone and with others, for the 1930s streamline Pan-Pacific

LAX, 1962. **The airport began commercial service in 1946 and welcomed the first jets in 1959. By the twenty-first century, the city's airport was the fifth busiest in the world, and still growing.**

Auditorium, the 1940s Pasadena Bullocks Wilshire department store, the iconic Capitol Records building, the geodesic Cinerama Dome, and the spidery Theme Building at the Los Angeles International Airport.

Beckett was not alone in his influence on the image of mid-century institutional Los Angeles. In 1965, the firm of A.C. Martin, one of those responsible for the 1928 City Hall, designed the glass-faced headquarters of the Los Angeles Department of Water and Power across the street from the Music Center. Surrounded by reflecting pools and fountains, lights in the building were often left on at night, a glowing symbol of civic pride and power.

DODGER STADIUM. **In early 1962, the Dodgers' new home nears completion in Chavez Ravine.**

Also in 1965, William Pereira, an architect and city planner who started as a movie production designer and special effects supervisor in the 1940s, added the Los Angeles County Museum of Art to the growing list of 1960s Los Angeles landmarks. "Tinseltown" was getting the kind of culture that the rest of the world recognized. Even so, as always, tourists still came for the sun, the beach and a chance to glimpse a movie star, or in 1966, animal celebrities at a new Los Angeles Zoo in Griffith Park.

In sports as well as tourism, Los Angeles was no longer minor league. In April 1962, after four seasons in the Coliseum, where they set two new national attendance records, the Los Angeles Dodgers finally played their first game in L.A.'s new stadium in Chavez Ravine. Fans quickly noticed a lack of drinking fountains. Not surprisingly, concession stands were easy to find. The team went on to win two World Series titles during the decade behind the pitching of L.A. local boy Don Drysdale and left-hander Sandy Koufax.

OPENING THE DOOR TO L.A. **On April 9, 1962, Dodger owner Walter O'Malley, center, receives a symbolic key to the team's new stadium from Baseball Commissioner Ford Frick and National League president Warren Giles.**

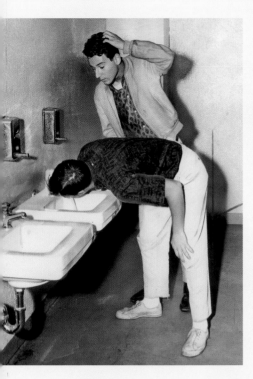

VIN SCULLEY AND JERRY DOGGETT.
Radio broadcaster Scully, left, joined the Dodgers in 1950 and moved to Los Angeles, where he continued captivating fans with his eloquent play-by-play. With Scully in this 1960 photo is "color man," Jerry Doggett.

WATER, WATER? Fans needed a little ingenuity to get a free drink when Dodger Stadium opened. There were no water fountains, but plenty of concession stands.

DON DRYSDALE. Born in Van Nuys, the right-hand pitcher joined the Brooklyn Dodgers in 1956 and came West with the team in '58. "Big D" and teammate Sandy Koufax dominated the National League for nine seasons.

SANDY KOUFAX. In 1963, the Dodger left-hander poses for posterity. Koufax led the team to a World Series win that year and was later named Player of the Decade.

In 1961, singer and former western movie star Gene Autry bought California's first American League franchise. Taking the name of L.A.'s venerable Angels, "the Halos" began playing in the old Wrigley Field, then in Dodger Stadium, before moving in 1966 to Anaheim as the California Angels. Autry's wealth and achievements were a Los Angeles success story. With little formal education, he certainly didn't fit the mold of an East Coast entrepreneur with a Harvard MBA. Known in the movies as "America's Favorite Singing Cowboy," in the '30s, '40s and '50s his records were widely popular, most notably "Rudolph the Red-Nosed Reindeer," which sold more than twenty-five million copies.

GENE AUTRY AND BABE HERMAN. In 1938, the cowboy star, left, exchanged uniforms with baseball player Babe Herman. Autry's business skills and love for baseball would lead to ownership of the Los Angeles Angels nearly thirty years later.

Autry shrewdly maintained the rights to his movies, and made a fortune when early television was desperate to fill airtime. He invested in a string of hotels and set up his own studio, Flying A Productions, and went on to acquire radio and television stations under the banner of Golden West Broadcasting. As an example of his business acumen, in 1964, he bought pioneering L.A. television station KTLA for $12 million and sold it twenty years later for $245 million. By the '60s, Autry was one of the city's richest men. With stadiums thirty-one miles apart, his Angels and Walter O'Malley's Dodgers were the L.A. equivalent of a cross-town rivalry.

In 1961, Los Angeles got its first NBA basketball team — from, of all places, Minnesota. Despite Silver Lake and Echo Lake, Los Angeles isn't known for small bodies of water. But the Lakers kept their name and thrived. Jack Kent Cooke acquired the team for $5 million in 1965, and added Wilt Chamberlain to the roster three years later.

The 1960s witnessed the birth of another basketball dynasty. The UCLA Bruins and coach John Wooden began the most impressive record in college basketball history, winning an unmatched ten national championships — five in the '60s, and five more in the decade that followed. Three-time All-American, 7'2" Lew Alcindor, who changed his name to Kareem

JACK KENT COOKE, left, sports entrepreneur, confers with L.A. architect Charles Luckman, who designed the Forum for L.A.'s new hockey franchise, the Kings. Completed in 1967, the arena was home to the L.A. Lakers as well.

USC COACH JOHN MCKAY, surrounded by members of his undefeated Trojans, considered one of the greatest teams in college football history.

JOHN WOODEN. On the sideline with his trademark rolled-up program, "The Wizard of Westwood" led UCLA to ten NCAA basketball titles.

Abdul-Jabbar in 1971, stood out in a series of teams that featured speed and precision.

Across town, always-competitive USC won two 1960s national football championships under Coach John McKay, going 10-1 in 1962 and 11-0 in the 1967 season. In 1961, the team introduced a new mascot, Traveler, a horse. A Trojan warrior was in the saddle.

The decade also produced two USC Heisman Trophy winners, Mike Garrett and O. J. Simpson, who would make bigger headlines thirty years later.

In 1967, a sport arrived that might seem out of place in balmy Los Angeles. Canadian entrepreneur Jack Kent Cooke, already owner of the Lakers, added a new National Hockey League expansion team to his sports portfolio. After playing their first two months on "borrowed ice," the Los Angeles Kings moved to The Fabulous Forum, a new $16 million stadium built by Cooke in Inglewood.

IN 1964, J. C. AGAJANIAN, right, counsels Parnelli Jones, at the wheel. A San Pedro High School dropout, Jones drove jalopies on the dirt track of Gardena Stadium before graduating to the winner's circle of the Indianapolis 500 and the NASCAR circuit.

Perhaps a more fitting sport for car-filled 1960s Los Angeles was auto racing. Promoter J. C. Agajanian, son of an Armenian immigrant who parlayed earnings as a dishwasher at the Hotel Alexandria in downtown L.A. into profitable hog farm and garbage businesses, joined with driver Rufus Parnell "Parnelli" Jones, a San Pedro High School dropout, to dominate the competition, from midgets and stock cars to the Indianapolis 500.

Not many considered surfing a true sport, even so, along with freeways and Hollywood, it came to symbolize the L.A. lifestyle.

FRANKIE AND ANNETTE. In *Bikini Beach,* Annette Funicello and Frankie Avalon—behind the moustache, glasses and Beatles wig—perform in one of a series of movies that spread the enthusiasm for surfing into realms far from coastal breakers.

Angelenos had been riding the waves since George Freeth demonstrated the ancient Polynesian tradition at Venice Beach in 1907. In the 1920s, with the help of newspaper photography, Hawaiian Olympic swimmer Duke Kahanamoku became a more celebrated surfing pioneer.

The sport continued to grow in popularity in the 1920s, '30s and '40s. The 1959 movie *Gidget,* written by a recent émigré from Czechoslovakia, and the '60s string of beach-blanket frolics with Frankie Avalon and former Mouseketeer Annette Funicello, had land-locked kids across the country dreaming about "hanging ten." The popular 1966 documentary *The Endless Summer* exported the Southern California surfer lifestyle as

an international, laid-back search for the perfect wave.

In 1961, when three brothers, Brian, Carl and Dennis Wilson, their cousin, Mike Love, and friend Al Jardine formed a rock 'n' roll band in the suburb of Hawthorne, a uniquely Southern California sound emerged. The Beach Boys' clean-cut good looks contrasted with the sexuality of Elvis and the racially shadowed appeal of black stars like Chuck Berry and Little Richard. "Fun, Fun, Fun," "Little Deuce Coupe" and "California Girls" blended close harmonies with echoes of Chuck Berry to picture a carefree life, selling L.A. as

effectively as the boosters of the 1880s and 1920s. In the '60s, the Beach Boys were an inspiration to the Beatles, and an American answer to the music of the British Invasion. However, just as none of the Beach Boys was an avid surfer, the realities of the city they sang about were far more than fun, fun, fun.

The music of the other great L.A. band of the '60s, The Doors with Jim Morrison, reflected a darker city. The band was named after a mescaline-inspired memoir, *The Doors of Perception,* by fellow Angeleno Aldous Huxley. Jim Morrison, the son of a navy rear admiral, had the good looks of a Southern California

THE BEATLES arrive in Los Angeles for a sold-out August 23, 1964, concert at the Hollywood Bowl. Cannibal and the Headhunters, a local band from L.A.'s Chicano Eastside, opened for the British superstars.

THE BEACH BOYS, formed in 1961 in Hawthorne, made their Hollywood Bowl debut in July 1965, headlining a "teenage program" that included the Righteous Brothers, Sam the Sham, Sonny and Cher and many others.

THE DOORS. Formed in Los Angeles in 1965, the band lit fires in the rock world before Jim Morrison flamed out in Paris in 1971. Shown here clockwise from top, Robbie Krieger, Jim Morrison, John Densmore and Ray Manzarek.

surfer. However, his perfect wave was a monster in himself. Burned out by drugs and alcohol, he died in Paris in 1971 at the age of twenty-seven. A mixture of innocence and excess, some saw his short life as a metaphor for a city that sometimes seemed eager to push boundaries, often without looking ahead.

Self-styled bum, alcoholic, poet and novelist Charles Bukowski was an L.A. author the Chamber of Commerce was unlikely to tout. Inspired by poetical realist John Fante, Bukowski was a product of the Beat Generation of the 1950s. He worked for the U.S. Post Office before turning to writing in the 1960s as a way to survive, personally and financially. Like Fante and Raymond Chandler, the Los Angeles he wrote about—back streets, bars and flophouses—was missing from tourist brochures, yet his words brought a brooding reality to the picture of a city he knew and loved. "You live in a town all your life," he told an interviewer, "and you get to know every street corner. You've got the layout of the whole land. You have a picture of

DRIVE-IN CHURCH. In 1965, a parking lot provided a sunny sanctuary for the North Hollywood Emmanuel Lutheran congregation.

where you are. . . . I can't see any other place than L.A."

In seemingly boundless Los Angeles, nature always sets limits. Hot, strong Santa Ana winds are annual Southern California events. On the night of November 5, 1961, the winds were brisk and the mountain brush dry. It was fire season. Around 8 o'clock the next morning, the hills seemed to burst into flames. Starting on the San Fernando Valley side of the Santa Monica Mountains, the fire pushed south across Mulholland Drive and down into the wealthy communities of Bel-Air and Brentwood, fueled by luxury homes and tinder-dry wood-shake roofs.

Shortly after noon, another fire broke out in Topanga Canyon, driven west by fifty-mile-per-hour winds. For two days, clouds of smoke billowed into the sky as 2,500 fire-fighters cut breaks through the brush and airplanes dropped thirty-five million gallons of water—up to 50,000 gallons per minute—on the flames. At last, on November 8, the most destructive fire in Los Angeles history was declared under control. Nearly 16,000 acres of valuable watershed had been burned, and more than 480 homes lost. Amazingly, no one died. The total loss was set at $24 million.

With a size and economic base able to absorb disasters that would devastate smaller

BEL-AIR FIRE. Observers can only watch helplessly as sections of a high-priced neighborhood burns to the ground.

FIRE! It's too late to heed this sign, as the November 1961 Bel-Air fire, declared the city's worst, races through the Santa Monica Mountains.

cities, and a history of boom and bust, Los Angeles continued to rebuild and redefine itself. In April 1960, the *Los Angeles Times* announced a new publisher, not surprisingly, his name was Chandler, a familial connection that represented a tradition of entrepreneurial enthusiasm and staunch anti-union conservatism. But Otis Chandler, son of Norman and Dorothy, was determined to take the *Times* far from its narrow-minded and provincial past.

Fond of motorcycles, fast cars and surfing, Otis was not just another Chandler. A series of articles critical of the extreme-right-wing John Birch Society shocked and alienated many Chandler family members and other L.A. conservatives, and showed that this young member of the dynasty was his own man. If Los Angeles was going to be a world-class city, it needed a world-class newspaper, and Otis Chandler was determined to provide one.

While the publisher of the *Times* was transforming the paper, Los Angeles was sprouting skyscrapers, continuing to push beyond the original height limit set in 1906. In the capital of Southern California earthquake country, engineers assured developers that modern steel-frame construction allowed the city a fledgling skyline. The first new L.A. skyscraper climbed to thirty-two stories. Designed by William Periera in 1965, it was named the Transamerica Tower. In time, there would be more than one high-rise cluster, poking up like tufts of prairie grass on the gently rolling contours of Los Angeles, extending to Warner Center, on the farwestern reaches of the San Fernando Valley.

On April 8, 1961, Los Angeles waved good-bye to the last of the venerable Red Cars, now considered relics as irrelevant as the Victorian mansions of Bunker Hill. Despite persistent conspiracy theories involving General Motors and the Firestone Tire Company, Angelenos didn't need to be tricked into driving their cars. It was love at first sight. And Los Angeles wasn't the only American

THIRTY-TWO-YEAR-OLD OTIS CHANDLER, right, accepts the reins of the *Los Angeles Times* from his father, Norman, on April 12, 1960. Before long, the younger Chandler will take the conservative paper in dramatically new editorial directions.

city abandoning noisy, under-funded and poorly maintained inner-city trolleys. Only hilly San Francisco kept their cable cars, mostly as a tourist attraction.

In 1970, more than 200 miles of new freeways were completed or under construction. They had already begun to give Los Angeles an automobile-driven arterial system and, at their best, they provided a sense of speed and personal freedom that intimidated visitors and exhilarated Angelenos. But L.A. was in a race against itself. Each new freeway seemed to arrive just in time to overflow its capacity.

Just as the tragedy of the St. Francis Dam had shown in 1928, the growth of Los Angeles during the 1960s strained and threatened the city's infrastructure. On December 14, 1963, the strain turned disastrous again. That morning a worker walking along a dam in Baldwin Hills, eight miles southwest of downtown Los Angeles, heard a gurgling sound. It was coming from a crack in the massive

embankment that held back nearly 300 million gallons of water. Constructed by the Los Angeles Department of Water and Power in 1951, the Baldwin Hills Dam was considered safe enough for homes to remain in the canyon below. Fortunately, unlike the St. Francis failure, signs of seepage led to immediate calls for evacuation.

Television station KTLA's Telecopter earned its price tag when aerial cameraman Lou Wolf focused on the widening crack, then unexpectedly captured one of the most dramatic moments in early television news. As Wolf and millions of others watched, the dam embankment gave way, releasing a fifty-foot wall of water, roaring north through streets and populated neighborhoods. Fire department helicopters were soon swarming overhead, plucking survivors from crumbling buildings, rooftops and trees. Thanks to the evacuation warning and heroic rescue efforts, only five lives were lost. The cause of the collapse was found to be a legacy of the city's past. The foundations of the Baldwin Hills Dam had been weakened by decades of subterranean oil drilling, dating back as early as

SINGER AND PIANIST NAT "KING" COLE was the first African American to host his own network television program in 1956. But national audiences weren't ready. The show went off the air a year later. Cole's version of the song "Route 66" chronicled the travels of many Americans heading west to Los Angeles. He died in 1965, as a new civil rights movement was growing.

the nineteenth century and the exploits of Lucky Baldwin, the neighborhood's irrepressible namesake.

Los Angeles survived disasters such as the Bel-Air fire and the Baldwin Hills Dam failure, yet even with new cultural landmarks and championship sports teams, not everyone was satisfied with the social and political changes that were transforming the city.

With Los Angeles's great size and a predominately booster press, "out of sight, out of mind" had been a common approach to social problems. The modern struggle for equal justice had been intensifying since the late 1950s. The signing of a new Civil Rights Act in 1964 was a major victory, but tensions remained. In 1965, in "fun-in-the-sun" Los Angeles, America would be confronted with

one of the most destructive urban uprisings of the twentieth century.

It began on August 11. The temperature was in the mid-'90s in the predominately African American south L.A. neighborhood of Watts. Two white California Highway Patrol officers stopped a suspected drunk driver. The young man and his stepbrother, a passenger in the car, resisted arrest. A short time later their mother, a nearby resident, arrived and angrily protested. A crowd gathered. As the bystanders became increasingly hostile, the highway patrolmen hastily handcuffed the young men and arrested their mother. Surrounded, the officers shoved their prisoners into their squad car and quickly drove off. LAPD backup arrived but the crowd refused to disperse. The confrontation intensified, and an empty squad car was set on fire. Suddenly Watts seemed to explode. Shops and stores were set ablaze, especially white-owned businesses. Looting and vandalism spread even faster than the fires. For two days the outburst raged virtually unchecked.

Ill-prepared national guard troops were ordered into the streets. Some community members cowered in their homes, others fought back as law-enforcement officers and armed guardsmen responded with an arsenal of clubs, tear gas and guns. Finally, after six terrible days, it was over. Thirty-four people had been killed by gunfire, all but one shot by police. More than 1,000 were wounded and nearly 4,000 arrested. Six thousand buildings were damaged or destroyed. The loss was set at $40 million. The smoldering streets of Watts looked like the aftermath in a war zone.

The uprising stunned most Angelenos, but it was an advance warning for the rest of America. Similar violence would break out in Detroit, Michigan, and Newark, New Jersey.

L.A. Police Chief William H. Parker initially blamed the hot weather. However, exhaustive official reports condemned the looting and vandalism. They emphasized long-seething hostilities between police and the black community, poverty, unemployment and a failing education system. Whatever the causes, for the City of Los Angeles "out of sight, out of mind" was no longer an acceptable public policy.

Three years earlier, Angelenos had elected a law-and-order mayor, Sam Yorty. Once a New Deal liberal, Yorty was already moving to

A NATIONAL GUARD SOLDIER stands patrol in Watts.

WATTS. Whether it was a riot or a rebellion, the 1965 outbreak of violence in the African American community of Watts exposed anger and injustice long ignored in Los Angeles—and America.

the right in response to pressures from more conservative suburban — and mostly white — voters. Watts was an unexpected shock for Los Angeles, and the city's leaders remained uncertain what to do. California Governor Edmund G. "Pat" Brown appointed a commission to investigate the deep-rooted causes. A new county hospital named after Dr. Martin Luther King Jr. was built and other changes were recommended, but solutions were slow to come, and some never implemented.

In 1966, four years after L.A. area native Richard Nixon lost an election for governor of California, angrily promising the press that they wouldn't have him to "kick around any-

GOVERNOR RONALD REAGAN. During a period of student protests, in 1968, Reagan faces the press after a contentious meeting with the University of California Regents at UCLA.

more," Californians got a most-unexpected new leader. He was Ronald Reagan, the charming television host, former star of Hollywood B-movies and the emerging front man for a growing conservative movement rising from Southern California and the Southwest that would transform American politics.

In the early '60s, the liberal legacy of President Franklin Roosevelt appeared secure. A few years later, the political winds in California, as they had many times before, indicated a shift. The evidence across the country was in the ballot box. It was hastened with bullets — first with the assassination of President John Kennedy, then the killings of Malcolm X and Dr. Martin Luther King Jr. In 1968, when President Lyndon Johnson decided not to run again because of the growing unpopularity of the Vietnam War, Robert Kennedy stepped forward, offering new hope for a shaken Democratic Party.

In June, Kennedy was in Los Angeles where, eight years earlier, his brother had called for a New Frontier. It was after midnight, June 6, when the New York senator celebrated his victory in the California primary and thanked his supporters at the Ambassador Hotel. As Kennedy and his entourage left, they passed through a hotel kitchen. Palestinian-born Sirhan Sirhan was waiting with a .22-caliber pistol. There was no way to

stop him and he pulled the trigger. After more than twenty-four hours in the emergency room, Kennedy was declared dead from a single gunshot wound to the head. In future history books, the picture of Los Angeles would be forever linked with that of Dallas and the assassination of Senator Kennedy's brother John.

In the midst of the upheavals of the 1960s, the press discovered a counterculture and called them "hippies." The L.A. community of Venice — a bohemian enclave for decades — shared in the spread of "flower power" and "tune-in, turn-off, drop-out" drugs. Meanwhile, students at UCLA joined in the Free Speech Movement that had spread south from Berkeley, and anti–Vietnam War sentiment continued to grow.

In the late 1960s, a new generation of Hollywood filmmakers was opening eyes. In 1969, Peter Fonda, son of Hollywood stalwart Henry Fonda, produced *Easy Rider* with actor-writer Dennis Hopper. With an anti-establishment attitude, this motorcycle road movie didn't match the box office of *The Sound of Music,* also released that year, but *Easy Rider* offered an independent vision that

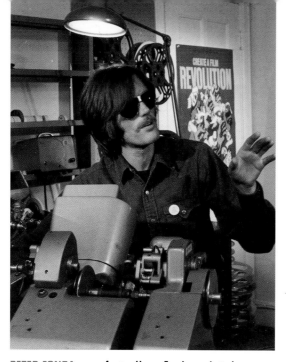

PETER FONDA, son of actor Henry Fonda, projected a new view of Hollywood with the film *Easy Rider*.

A 1962 MEETING OF MOVIE MOGULS—PAST AND FUTURE. Samuel Goldwyn, left, gives a first-place writing award to a young Francis Ford Coppola.

would increasingly influence movies in the decades to come.

The days of the old studios were fading. In 1958, executives at 20th Century Fox decided to sell their enormous back lot for a commercial real estate venture called Century City. Construction began in 1961. The land, once a ranch owned by silent film star Tom Mix, was soon producing an alternative Los Angeles skyline, halfway between the old downtown and the ocean.

To those who welcomed the energy and change of the 1960s, Los Angeles was showing the way to a freer, more tolerant America. To others, the decade was infuriating and frightening. The use of drugs seemed to be everywhere, from the hip clubs of the Sunset Strip to schoolyards and suburban homes. To anxious Americans, their worst fears seemed confirmed one night in the summer of 1969.

On Saturday, August 9, twenty-six-year-old actress Sharon Tate, the pregnant wife of film director Roman Polanski, was socializing with friends in their secluded Benedict Canyon home. After midnight, neighbors thought they heard gunshots and a woman screaming. It wasn't until the next morning that a maid discovered the gruesome truth. Tate and four friends were found dead, slashed and drenched in blood. The next night, a non-celebrity couple, Leno and

CENTURY CITY. By 1963, the new office, entertainment and housing complex was emerging from land that was once the back lot of the 20th Century Fox film studios.

Rosemary La Bianca, apparently chosen at random, were savagely stabbed in their upscale Los Feliz neighborhood home. The words "Death to Pigs," written in blood, were scrawled on a wall, and in the kitchen the misspelled phrase "Healter Skelter," a reference to a Beatles song, was smeared across the refrigerator door.

After two months of confused investigation and rampant rumors, Los Angeles detectives were drawn to an isolated ranch once used for western movies. The eventual arrest of Charles Manson, and the demented "family members" who committed the murders on his behalf, resulted in America's

CHARLES MANSON. Under arrest, Manson parades for cameras with a swastika on his forehead. A self-proclaimed messiah and rock star wannabe, he masterminded the brutal Tate–La Bianca murders.

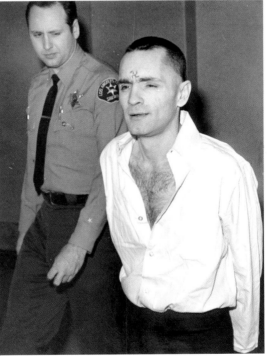

MEMBERS OF THE MANSON "FAMILY" gather in a cave near their commune on a former movie ranch in the hills west of the San Fernando Valley. In 1975, Lynette "Squeaky" Fromme, third from left, would attempt to shoot U.S. President Gerald Ford.

longest trial to date, and certainly one of the most disturbing.

The Manson murders threatened to end the 1960s with a nightmare. But the final years of the decade also brought one of the greatest technological triumphs in human history. On July 20, 1969, Neil Armstrong was the first man to walk on the surface of the moon. Edwin "Buzz" Aldrin followed a short time later. It was an unforgettable event for America and the world, and an especially proud moment for high-tech Southern California. Many of the ideas and much of the engineering that lifted the Apollo spacecraft into space, and allowed the fragile landing module to settle in the lunar dust, came from the innovation and ingenuity of Angelenos.

During the 1960s, ten Mariner spacecraft, designed and built by Pasadena's Jet Propulsion Laboratory and launched aboard Atlas rockets built by Southern California aerospace companies, returned amazing information and images from the planets Mars, Venus and Jupiter, before sailing beyond the solar system and into deep space.

Founded 188 years earlier, when space travel was hardly a dream, Los Angeles in

1969 remained in many ways immature and awkward, and Watts showed that there was injustice and anguish in what was touted as a suburban paradise. Now L.A. was about to confront a new decade. It would begin as a continuation of the 1960s, then challenge and transform the city in ways that neither boosters nor critics ever imagined.

EDWIN "BUZZ" ALDRIN in a photo taken by Neil Armstrong, the first man on the moon, thanks in part to Angeleno expertise.

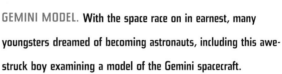

GEMINI MODEL. With the space race on in earnest, many youngsters dreamed of becoming astronauts, including this awe-struck boy examining a model of the Gemini spacecraft.

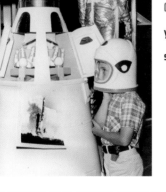

JAMES MONROE HIGH SCHOOL CHEERLEADERS in a classic picture from the mostly white suburban San Fernando Valley of the early 1960s. In the decades that followed, Valley demographics changed radically. By 2006, the Monroe student body had grown to nearly 5,000, 80 percent of whom were Latino.

WHOSE FUTURE IS IT?

"Welcome to the Hotel California..."

THE EAGLES, 1976

Since the 1880s, the Mexican heritage of Los Angeles had been evident in streets signs, tourist brochures and plates of tacos, enchiladas and refried beans, but Mexican Americans themselves were mostly relegated to the background. The zoot-suiters of the 1940s suggested that a bolder, more outspoken generation was emerging, yet it wasn't until the 1960s and '70s that the "sleeping giant" of California's Mexican American community began to stir.

In East L.A., new immigrants and the sons and daughters of the zoot-suiters were not fully accepted in either Mexico or America. In the 1970s, they continued a search for an identity of their own. Latino teenagers found it in rock 'n' roll, creating a local blend of rhythm and blues and Motown known as the Eastside Sound. One band, Cannibal & the Headhunters, had a hit, "Land of a Thousand Dances," that was big enough to attract the attention of the Beatles. In 1964, Frankie Garcia ("Cannibal") and his band — kids from East L.A. housing projects — toured briefly with the British superstars, and the group was an opening act at a sold-out Beatles concert at the Hollywood Bowl. During the '70s, other local musicians reclaimed the short-lived legacy of Ritchie Valens and achieved limited national success, including El Chicano, Tierra and most of all, Los Lobos. All played and sang with a new sense of independence and pride. Music from East L.A. offered early indications that American culture was beginning to change.

At the same time, talented young muralists picked up where controversial Mexican artist David Alfaro Siqueiros left off in 1934. One of the most remarkable projects was *The Great Wall*

BRIDE AND GROOM, a mural created by artist Kent Twitchell, covers the exterior of the Monarch Clothing Building in downtown Los Angeles. The groom was painted in 1973, the bride appeared three years later. During the 1970s, the image and the reality of an increasing Latino presence was rising over L.A.

CANNIBAL AND THE HEADHUNTERS. From left, Frankie "Cannibal" Garcia, band member Bobby "Rabbit" Jaramillo and disk jockey Casey Kasem. From right, Richard "Scar" Lopez and Joe Jaramillo.

THE GREAT WALL OF LOS ANGELES. Begun in 1974, the mural near the corner of Burbank and Coldwater Canyon boulevards is one of the most impressive works in the world's largest collection of urban murals.

of Los Angeles, created by more than 400 students, scholars and local muralists on the concrete side of a San Fernando Valley flood-control channel. Painted under the supervision of artist Judith Baca, the mural depicts the history of the city from prehistoric times to the 1960s. A half-mile long, the first phase of *The Great Wall* took ten years to complete, although, like the story it portrays, it remains a work in progress. Other paintings, many of them on buildings in L.A.'s Eastside, have become part of the largest collection of urban murals in the world.

A new generation was celebrating *La Raza* — the people. They proudly called themselves "Chicanos," a term once considered derogatory. In 1978, activist-writer Luis Valdez premiered a new play, *Zoot Suit,* starring a young Edward James Olmos. With music by veteran Angeleno singer-songwriter Lalo Guerrero, *Zoot Suit* made it clear that L.A.'s Mexican heritage was more than what was portrayed in *Ramona,* the nineteenth-century romantic novel and annual Southern California pageant.

During the 1960s, Dr. Martin Luther King

UNITED FARM WORKERS UNION LEADER CESAR CHAVEZ, second from the left, leads picketers at a local Safeway market to protest the chain's purchase of non-union-produced lettuce.

THE CHICANO MORATORIUM. Whittier Boulevard in East Los Angeles is filled with Chicano activists, and others, protesting the Vietnam War. The march began peacefully, but ended with violence when police moved in.

Jr. was an inspiration not only for African Americans but for Chicanos as well. Cesar Chavez, a quietly charismatic union leader, working with activist Dolores Huerta, began to organize long-exploited Mexican American farm workers. Other Chicanos were also active. In 1968, 10,000 students from East L.A., the San Gabriel Valley and downtown Los Angeles high schools walked out to protest poor classroom conditions and to demand courses in Mexican American history and culture. In the early 1970s, the Vietnam War was dividing the country, and antiwar protests were increasing. Activists in the Chicano community were concerned and angry that a disproportionate number of Mexican Americans were being sent to fight and die.

On August 29, 1970, the Chicano Moratorium, an antiwar march held in East Los Angeles, brought 20,000 protestors in what was then the largest Mexican American political demonstration in American history. As participants moved peaceably west on Whittier Boulevard, county sheriffs and Los Angeles city police prepared for trouble.

When the march ended in a local park, officers surrounded the protestors and demanded that they disperse. When they failed to comply, police moved in with clubs and tear gas. The result was an outbreak of violence that briefly recalled the horrors of Watts five years before. Three people died, including Ruben Salazar, a respected *Los Angeles Times* columnist and news director of Spanish-language television station KMEX. Salazar was killed when a deputy sheriff fired a tear gas canister into a neighborhood café.

At 6:01 a.m. on February 9, 1971, a different kind of violence shook the City of Los Angeles. A 6.7 earthquake shifted a ten-mile-long stretch under the northern San Fernando Valley. Beginning with a sharp jolt, it was the strongest earthquake to date within the city limits. As buildings and freeways shuddered, buckled or collapsed, sixty-five

THE TRANSITION FROM THE ANTELOPE VALLEY FREEWAY to the I-5 lies in ruins after the 1971 Sylmar earthquake. Fortunately, the temblor took place at 6 a.m. when traffic was relatively light.

OLIVE VIEW HOSPITAL IN SYLMAR was in no shape to receive emergency patients after the 1971 quake. Three died here. Forty-seven others at a Veteran's Administration facility in San Fernando also lost their lives.

people lost their lives — fifty of them in two hospitals in northeast Valley communities. Damage was estimated at more than $500 million. When an earthen dam threatened to give way, 80,000 residents were ordered to evacuate. New downtown skyscrapers swayed, but survived their first major earthquake test. On Olvera Street, however, damage to the 1818 Avila adobe required retrofitting and restoration.

In 1973, the political leadership of Los Angeles experienced another kind of shake-up. Former police lieutenant and city councilman Tom Bradley challenged the incumbent mayor, Sam Yorty, for a second time. In dispersed Los Angeles, local politics were rarely as intense as in cities such as San Francisco, New York or Chicago. What brought special attention to this election was the fact that Bradley was African American. Yorty had won the first campaign by picturing his opponent as a dangerous left-wing radical. This time he warned voters that police would hesitate to support a black mayor, opening the city to even more crime and violence. Yorty's second-round scare tactics didn't work. A dignified and quietly effective coalition builder, Bradley attracted south Los Angeles African Americans, and white, mostly Westside liberals, to become the city's first African American mayor. He would lead L.A. for the next twenty years.

MAYORAL DEBATE. **In a landmark election, Mayor Sam Yorty, left, debates second-time challenger Tom Bradley, standing.**

NEW MAYOR TOM BRADLEY. **In 1973, Bradley, L.A.'s first African American mayor, prepares to take office.**

Bradley's life was filled with examples of the barriers and the opportunities of mid-century African Americans. The grandson of a slave and the son of Texas sharecroppers, the future mayor picked cotton as a boy. In 1924, his family, which included three brothers and a sister, moved to Los Angeles. Bradley's ability as an athlete resulted in scholarships, and academic accomplishments prepared him to meet the educational challenges of UCLA. After graduation, he joined the Los Angeles Police Department, and later studied at night for a law degree. In 1963, he entered politics and was elected the first African American city councilman in Los Angeles history.

As a young man, Bradley was refused service in restaurants and denied admittance to Los Angeles hotels, even though he was a police officer, but he always kept his emotions under close control. This measured personality served him well as mayor. He worked effectively with business leaders and was devoted to the physical and economic growth of the city. The mayor's special passion was mass transit, but a different transportation issue was a major source of controversy during the 1970s.

African Americans and Chicanos were not the only ones in Los Angeles protesting for change. White suburban activists had issues of their own. One of the hottest was government-mandated school busing to achieve equal education through racial integration. Court orders required parents in predominately white and black schools to bus their kids to each other's neighborhoods. White parents, especially in the San Fernando Valley, resisted. One Encino activist-housewife, Bobbi Fiedler, formed an organization called Bustop, which attracted

ANTI-BUSING PROTESTS in Los Angeles spread during the late 1970s. In San Pedro, about 150 local residents, including this nine-year-old student, marched against the controversial school desegregation plan.

THE BONAVENTURE HOTEL. Downtown L.A. gets a new landmark in 1976. Featuring four thirty-five-story mirrored glass cylinders with exterior elevators, it replaced the Biltmore as the city's largest hotel.

THE TWIN ARCO TOWERS rise on Flower between Fifth and Sixth. Atlantic Richfield (ARCO) was an active corporate community member.

OCCIDENTAL TOWER. L.A.'s new skyline brought new challenges, including a November 1976 nighttime fire on the twentieth floor of the Occidental Tower. More than 300 firefighters responded. It took ninety minutes to douse the flames.

HOWARD JARVIS threatens to take a cleaver to the state budget. The spirit of Jarvis's Proposition 13, which slashed California property taxes, spread across the United States.

30,000 members in a matter of months. Bustop's appeal was so effective that Fiedler won an upset election for president of the Los Angeles School Board, and was later elected to the United States House of Representatives. In 1979, Californians voted to end mandatory busing and the system was dismantled within a few years. However, white Angelenos, again mostly in the San Fernando Valley, had more demands.

Howard Jarvis was a successful businessman and outspoken conservative Republican.

When he retired in 1962, he decided to devote his life to tax reform. In the always-active real estate market of Los Angeles, Jarvis's supporters wanted property taxes rolled back and capital gains on home sales repealed. Joining with fellow conservative activist Paul Gann, Jarvis brought the issue to a statewide referendum. In June 1978, their plan, Proposition 13, was approved by a resounding 65 percent to 35 percent of the voters. Virtually overnight, local property tax revenues to the State of California were cut in half, by $6.1 billion a year. And it didn't stop there. Proposition 13 inspired similar tax revolts across the United States. Again, Californians and Angelenos were picturing — for better or worse — America's future. The results would be felt for decades to come. While the tax burden was lightened for individual homeowners, large real estate interests got even bigger breaks. In the end, since property taxes were a primary source for education and public services, many county and local governments were left struggling to balance their budgets.

The 1970s were shifting and uncertain times. Soaring gas prices hit "auto-mated" L.A. especially hard. To many, the upper-middle-class angst of writer Joan Didion expressed a sense that Los Angeles, and America, had entered an anxious new era. To some of Didion's readers, L.A.'s annual season of hot Santa Ana winds suggested more than the weather: "There is something uneasy in the Los Angeles air this afternoon, some unnatural stillness, some tension," she wrote. "For a few days now we will see smoke back in the canyons, and hear sirens in the night."

Beyond this ominous foreboding, the 1970s produced a decade of unexpected creativity in Hollywood. A new generation of filmmakers, many graduates of film schools that began to flourish in the '60s, arrived on

SOARING GAS PRICES. **More than most Americans, car-dependent Angelenos were hard-hit by the Middle East oil embargo of 1973 and 1974. Prices attained a then-astronomical fifty-five cents a gallon.**

TRAFFIC CONGESTION. **Despite higher gas prices, traffic congestion continued to grow during the decade of the '70s. Freeways and surface streets often slowed to a standstill.**

movie sets with innovative ideas that gave old forms new style and excitement. In 1972, thirty-three-year-old Francis Ford Coppola directed *The Godfather,* returning to the kind of gangster movie that thrilled and shocked audiences in the 1930s. With visual flair and the operatic sweep of a violent family saga, *The Godfather* introduced a larger-than-life Marlon Brando to a new generation of movie-goers. In 1974, with Coppola directing again, *The Godfather Part II* set an Academy Award standard as the first sequel to join a predecessor as an Oscar winner.

Another 1974 classic was *Chinatown.* Writer Robert Towne, a native of San Pedro, gave the Owens Valley water wars, one of the great sagas of L.A. history, a freely fictional-ized reworking. In the process, another revered Hollywood genre, film noir, received a stylish update. Tragically, five years earlier, Roman Polanski, the director of *Chinatown,* had experienced real L.A. noir, and another kind of criminal "family," when followers of Charles Manson murdered his wife, actress Sharon Tate.

In 1973, twenty-nine-year-old George Lucas celebrated the 1950s, and the car culture of California teenagers, with *American Graffiti.* Four years later, he produced and directed *Star Wars,* resuscitating the action and suspense of movie serials, a Hollywood staple dating from the days of silent pictures. It may have been an old genre, but Lucas's innovative use of state-of-the-art motion pic-

FRANCIS FORD COPPOLA, the bearded director of the Oscar-winning *Godfather* saga, stands with actors Al Pacino, Marlon Brando and James Caan, from right.

CHINATOWN. Jack Nicholson, playing L.A. private investigator Jake (J. J.) Gittes, in the film *Chinatown,* evidently stuck his nose in the wrong place.

ture technology launched an era of special-effects-driven filmmaking. *Star Wars* was the highest-grossing film in 1977 and won seven academy awards. Preferring the San Francisco Bay Area to Los Angeles, Coppola and Lucas were committed to maintaining their independence by keeping the atmosphere and attitudes of Hollywood at arms length, but L.A.'s hold on facilities, financing and distribution was hard to break.

At home in Los Angeles, on the lot of Universal Studios, Steven Spielberg was twenty-nine when he terrified moviegoers in 1975 with *Jaws*. Two years later he vividly portrayed a friendly invasion from outer space in *Close Encounters of the Third Kind.* In 1979, Spielberg directed one of his few movie duds— *1941,* a comedy about the embarrassing World War II false alarm known as "The Battle of Los Angeles."

Hollywood was not only the movie capital of the world; in the 1970s, it also claimed television. In 1972, when Johnny Carson and the *The Tonight Show* left New York for "beautiful downtown Burbank," jokes aside, New York still had Broadway theater, but

GEORGE LUCAS. The USC School of Cinema-Television graduate ponders his next shot. Lucas's epic *Star Wars* series launched a new era of special-effects-driven movies.

STEVEN SPIELBERG poses in front of "Bruce," the mechanical shark used in the director's 1975 movie *Jaws*. Spielberg would become one of the world's wealthiest and most successful filmmakers.

THE EAGLES. Emerging from the L.A. music scene of the 1970s, the Eagles, led by singers/songwriters Don Henley, center, and Glenn Frey, second from left, produced country-influenced rock that expressed the edgy and dark apprehensions of post-'60s America.

SINGER/SONGWRITER/FILM COMPOSER RANDY NEWMAN poked affectionate fun at his hometown in his 1983 anthem "I Love L.A."

Los Angeles was the undisputed home of American popular entertainment.

The music business was also moving west. The Eagles were the most successful home-grown rock band of the 1970s. Their tight, country-folk-inflected sound reflected a changing picture of Los Angeles — easygoing, but with a sharpening edge. In an emerging era of mindless disco, the Mexican-tinged "Hotel California" was a nightmarish remembrance of the dark side of the 1960s, still haunting the decade that followed. "I heard the mission bell," the Eagles sang, "And I was thinking to myself this could be Heaven or this could be Hell."

Sophisticated wit and sharply drawn ironies characterize the work of Los Angeles singer-songwriter and film composer Randy Newman. Member of a well-known family of Hollywood musicians and composers, Newman's idiosyncratic output belies the standard clichés about shallow, witless L.A. In the 1970s, he grimly mocked the historic slave trade in "Sail Away," and his controversial 1974 album *Good Old Boys* contained barbed song portraits of the segregated South. An equal-opportunity offender, in 1977, Newman satirized prejudice with "Short People," and in 1979, he sang an anti-capitalist hymn to greed in "It's Money That I Love." In 1983, he would give

Los Angeles a tongue-in-cheek anthem, "I Love L.A."

If, under it all, Randy Newman really did love L.A., there was no doubt about America's high-tech industry. To a great extent, the technological companies along Route 128 near Boston were being left behind, and Silicon Valley, south of San Francisco, was yet to fully emerge. The action was around Los Angeles — especially at Pasadena's California Institute of Technology (Caltech), and the Jet Propulsion Laboratory (JPL). Caltech had been founded in 1891 as Throop University. In 1907, astronomer George Ellery Hale joined Throop's board of trustees and the school began to grow into a major educational and scientific institution. By 1921, chemist Arthur Noyes and physicist Robert Millikan arrived, and Throop became the California Institute of Technology. In the years to come, Caltech

BIG COMPUTERS using magnetic tape storage systems were increasingly visible in corporations and think tanks. Yet even in high-tech L.A., few foresaw the future impact of personal computers.

would be home to more than thirty Nobel Prize winners and produce major accomplishments in sciences as diverse as molecular chemistry and geology.

The origins of JPL came from the life and work of Hungarian immigrant Theodore von Kármán, considered the father of aeronautics. In 1936, some of von Kármán's enthusiastic Caltech students began testing rockets in the upper Arroyo Seco, west of downtown Pasadena. The work of these pioneering rocketeers, nicknamed "The Suicide Squad," was taken seriously when Germany's V-2 missiles attacked England during World War II. JPL was

THE SUICIDE SQUAD. During the 1930s, Caltech students and faculty tested early rockets in Pasadena's Arroyo Seco.

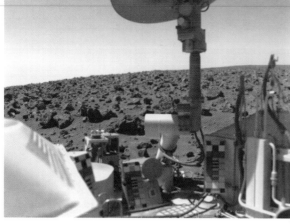

A VIEW FROM MARS. L.A. high-tech expertise played a critical role in the success of the Viking 2 spacecraft, which returned this image of the planet Mars after landing on September 19, 1975.

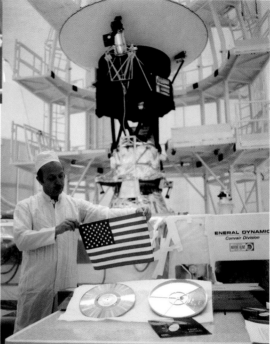

AN OUTER-SPACE CALLING CARD. A Jet Propulsion Laboratory technician examines items sent into space with the Voyager probes. The gold-plated disk contained 115 images as well as spoken messages in fifty-five languages.

officially born in 1944. Five years later, JPL engineers launched a rocket that climbed 244 miles, the first to penetrate outer space.

The Russian satellite Sputnik led to the creation of NASA, the National Aeronautics and Space Administration, which joined Caltech in the management of JPL in 1958. In 1975, JPL launched two Viking explorers, the first "earthlings" to visit another planet when the spacecraft touched down on the surface of Mars. Critics often quipped that Angelenos seemed to belong in outer space. In fact, during the 1960s and '70s, that's exactly where they were taking America and the rest of the world.

Back on earth, sports fans had a lot to love about Los Angeles in the 1970s.

California Angel Nolan Ryan pitched four no-hitters, and in 1973 set a record with 383 strikeouts. But it was the Dodgers' decade. The team won three National League pennants and racked up 910 wins. In 1977, Tommy Lasorda replaced longtime manager Walter Alston, and four of the team's sluggers, Steve Garvey, Reggie Smith, Ron Cey and Dusty Baker, hit thirty or more home runs.

In basketball, the 1972 Lakers, with Wilt Chamberlain, Elgin Baylor and Jerry West, won their first national championship. In 1976, Kareem Abdul-Jabbar joined the team. By 1979, the Lakers were poised to launch a dynasty with the arrival of Earvin "Magic" Johnson.

STEVE GARVEY acknowledges fans during his 1,000th consecutive game, on his way to a 1,207-game National League record. As a Dodger stalwart, Garvey made three World Series appearances between 1973 and 1981.

NOLAN RYAN. On September 27, 1973, the L.A. Angels pitcher pauses after throwing his 383rd single-season strikeout. Until then, Dodger Sandy Koufax held the record.

WILT CHAMBERLAIN. One of the greatest players in the history of the game, Chamberlain gave the Los Angeles Lakers their first NBA championship in 1972.

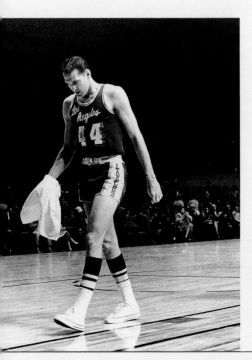

LOS ANGELES LAKER JERRY WEST, an NBA all-star every year of his career, led the team for fourteen seasons, including nine NBA finals. He retired in 1974, but returned to coach the Lakers for three more seasons.

ARTHUR ASHE led his UCLA tennis team to the NCAA title in 1965. As a pro in the 1970s, he was the first African American to win the U.S. Open and Wimbledon tournaments.

During the '70s, a college basketball dynasty was also underway in Westwood. In 1971, the UCLA Bruins began an unprecedented eighty-eight-game winning streak, capping thirteen consecutive Pac Ten titles between 1967 and 1979. Bill Walton led a team that was fast and evenly balanced. Coach John Wooden took UCLA to a record-setting ten NCAA Championships in twelve years, includ-

ing seven wins in a row. During the 1960s, UCLA had also produced the first great African American tennis star, Arthur Ashe. In 1975, Ashe upset fellow Angeleno Jimmy Connors to win the men's finals at Wimbledon and was rated number one in the world.

Not to be outdone, USC was a dominant team in college football. In 1972, the Trojans went 12-0-0 and defeated Ohio State 42-17 in the 1973 Rose Bowl — a game acclaimed as one of the greatest L.A. football moments of the century. The 1974 regular-season final game against Notre Dame was one of the most exciting comebacks in college football history. Late in the second quarter, the Trojans were trailing 24-0. The Irish had the

USC FOOTBALL STAR, ANTHONY DAVIS, second from right, in 1975. The two-time All-American was known for his celebratory end-zone dance.

JERRY BUSS. With a PhD in chemistry, Dr. Jerry Buss made his fortune in real estate, and added fame when he purchased the Los Angeles Lakers, Kings and Great Western Forum in 1979, the biggest sports deal up to that time.

ARNOLD AT GOLD'S. In 1975, body builder and future movie star and California governor Arnold Schwarzenegger, right, takes a breather from pumping iron at the original Gold's Gym near Santa Monica's Muscle Beach.

nation's top-rated defense, but USC's Anthony Davis came back with a 102-yard kick-off return, and in less than seventeen minutes, the Trojans surged ahead to win with fifty-five unanswered points. They went on to win the National Championship that year, and again in 1978.

As for professional football, the Los Angeles Rams had their strongest seasons in 1973 and 1975. They ended the decade with their one-and-only visit to the Super Bowl,

losing 31–19 to the powerful Pittsburgh Steelers. A lot of sports money changed hands in 1979 when Jack Kent Cooke sold the L.A. Kings hockey team, the Lakers and their arena, the Forum, to Dr. Jerry Buss. The price tag was a reported $67.5 million.

During the 1970s, the war in Vietnam continued to pile up its own, far more serious costs—in dollars, social unrest and lives. There seemed to be no end or exit. In one of the most remarkable comebacks in American political history, Richard Nixon was elected president in 1968, and reelected four years later, carrying forty-nine of fifty states. In an unexpected turnaround for a man who was once one of America's staunchest anti-Communists, Nixon met with China's Mao Tse-Tung, and the two countries opened diplomatic relations. The president also promised to find a solution to the war in Vietnam. The beginning of the end came in January 1973, when United States troops began to withdraw.

Despite these successes, Nixon's presidency had already begun to unravel. On June 17, 1972, when burglars broke into the Democratic National Committee Headquarters in the Watergate Building in Washington, D.C., a sequence of events and evidence began that eventually led to the White House. Two years later, the first president from Southern California resigned instead of facing impeachment. The once-bright young man from Whittier returned in disgrace to his former Western White House, on the beach at San Clemente, south of L.A.

Washington politics had its greatest political scandal in recent history, but there's no decade in L.A.'s past without a share of more lurid headlines. The 1970s supplied a string of serial killers. As they had since the 1920s, newspaper editors pictured them with chilling

FORCED TO RESIGN, Richard Nixon, the first American president from Southern California, bids an emotional farewell to his White House staff on August 9, 1974, as daughter Tricia listens.

nicknames: the Hillside Strangler, the Skid Row Slasher, the Trash Bag Murderer, the Freeway Killer and the Sunset Slayer. Judged by the number of victims, William Bonin, the Freeway Killer, topped the grisly list. Working alone, and occasionally with accomplices, Bonin found his victims while cruising L.A. streets and freeways. If he hadn't been caught in 1980, he told police, "I'd still be killing. I couldn't stop killing. It got easier each time." In 1982, a jury convicted the serial killer for the deaths of fourteen young men and boys. He was suspected in the deaths of as many as thirty more.

In an attempt to modernize and become more effective, the Los Angeles Police Department, beginning with Chief Parker in the 1950s, began to adopt a military model of law enforcement. In 1971, one result was the nation's first full-time Special Weapons and Tactics (SWAT) team. The SWAT team got a chance to show its stuff in 1974. A rag-tag organization called the Symbionese Liberation Army (SLA) had kidnapped San Francisco heiress Patty Hearst, the granddaughter of William Randolph Hearst, and apparently coerced her into joining them as a comrade in crime. On May 17, L.A. police were sure they had SLA leadership and Patty Hearst surrounded in an East 54th Street hideout. After surrender demands were ignored, an armed assault quickly turned into a TV news spectacular. Officers fired tear gas and 9,000 rounds of ammunition until the little California bungalow exploded in flames. No one inside survived. But Patty Hearst had never been there. The heiress-turned-bank robber was

arrested one year later and served seven years in prison.

The SLA was only one heavily armed challenge that Los Angeles police had to deal with. Fueled by an increasingly lucrative drug trade, two gangs, the Crips and the Bloods, were turning what were once local "rumbles" into efficient and deadly warfare with automatic weapons. They were predominately African Americans, with roots in the attitudes and activism of the Black Panthers of the 1960s, taken to a criminal extreme. In time, there would be an increase in Latino and Asian gangs as well. Between 1972 and 1978, the number of gangs in Los Angeles County tripled, from eighteen to sixty. During the

THE FREEWAY KILLER. Ending a crime spree that began in 1979, William Bonin was convicted of raping and murdering fourteen young men in L.A. and Orange counties.

AN ESCAPE FROM PARADISE LOST. The Santa Clarita Valley, shown here, and other communities outside L.A. became havens for white families seeking to escape the problems of an increasingly urbanized Los Angeles.

decade there were 355 gang-related murders. It made the days of Bugsy Siegel and Mickey Cohen seem positively tame.

Most gang activity was confined to a thirty-square-mile area in south Los Angeles. As with the perpetrators, most of the victims were African American. But citywide, fear knew no boundaries. In response to the frightening increase in crime, along with a rising cost of living, a faltering economy and opposition to the racial integration of schools, more than a million white Angelenos decided to leave. They moved to more distant towns in the Simi and Santa Clarita valleys, and in San Bernardino and Riverside counties — even out of state. Sociologists and the press called it "white flight." As white Angelenos left, newcomers from Mexico and the rest of Latin America, along with immigrants from Asia and the Middle East, eagerly took their places.

Despite white flight, L.A. didn't stop growing. In 1970, more than one-third of all the people in California lived in Los Angeles County. The City of Angels was becoming America's new Ellis Island— New York's real and symbolic center of immigration and the American Dream. As before, most new arrivals came from south of the border, but important changes in immigration laws also allowed Asians from China, Vietnam, Thailand, Cambodia and Korea to enter the country. The city's Korean community began establishing businesses both east and west along Olympic and Wilshire boulevards, and north and south along Western and Vermont, turning former Anglo and Latino neighborhoods into the heart of a new Koreatown. In the late 1970s, venerable Little Tokyo was rejuvenated with a much-needed senior housing project, a new cultural and community center, and the New Otani, a modern hotel featuring a rooftop Japanese garden.

The largest Asian L.A. community was Filipino. Since arriving in large numbers during the 1960s, they brought their own diverse culture, a melding of Asian and Hispanic heritages. Because of historical ties to the United States Navy, many settled in and around the harbor and shipyards of Long Beach. From there, Filipino Angelenos seemed to disperse and blend more easily than other Asians into the city's growing ethnic mix.

In 1972, when the Mandarin Plaza shopping center was completed in Chinatown, it was the first major development in the area in

IN LINE FOR AMERICA. The '70s saw increasing immigration from Asia. At its peak, Vietnamese immigration averaged 120,000 new arrivals a year. Here, newcomers wait for visas.

WAT THAI. Built in the heart of the San Fernando Valley in 1972, the temple serves an estimated 40,000 Thais, an example of dramatic changes that began transforming the population and culture of 1970s Los Angeles.

twenty years. That same year, Wat Thai temple was built in the heart of the San Fernando Valley, once the archetypical Anglo American suburb. A Thai community settled nearby. Meanwhile, Thais and Armenians had already found homes in East Hollywood, and even before the fall of the Shah in 1979, Iranians, or Persians, as many preferred to be called, began immigrating to Los Angeles. Followers of Christianity, Judaism, Baha'i and Islam settled in Westwood, Beverly Hills, Encino and northern Orange County.

The City of Angels had experienced major transformations before, but the 1970s marked the beginning of something dramatically different. After the Olympic Games of 1932, L.A. had proudly pictured itself as an international capital. Now, to the surprise of many, that boastful image was becoming an unprecedented reality.

MONKS AT WAT THAI in North Hollywood are members of the largest Theraveda Buddhist community in the United States.

A NEW DATSUN arrives at L.A.'s port, evidence of a surging Japanese auto industry, which had already established corporate headquarters in America's car capital.

THE PORT OF LOS ANGELES in the 1970s was already America's most important trading gateway to the Asian economies of the Pacific Rim.

THE WORLD COMES TO STAY

"[Los Angeles is] soon to be a major everything."

ATLANTIC MONTHLY, 1988

On January 21, 1981, the first president of the United States to come from Los Angeles was inaugurated in Washington, D.C. Ronald Reagan was born in Tampico, Illinois, but for most of his life L.A. was home. Reagan showed interest in politics during his years at Eureka College when, as a young New Deal Democrat, he led a student strike to reinstate dismissed professors. After a short stint as a radio sportscaster in the Midwest, a 1937 screen test brought him to Hollywood, where he began a career as a reliable second-tier movie actor, appearing in fifty-three films. In only one did he play the villain. While many future presidents honed their political and public-performance skills as lawyers, Reagan's training was stereotypically Angeleno. He got a first taste of high-stakes politics as president of the Screen Actors Guild, and as an actor, performing for the public was his profession.

During the anti-Communist "Red Scare" years of the 1940s and '50s, the future president turned increasingly conservative. After his marriage to actress Jane Wyman ended in divorce, he found the love of his life, and a political partner, Nancy Davis, a costar in *Hellcats of the Navy*. As the old studio system disappeared during the 1960s, Reagan transitioned to television as

THE OLYMPICS RETURN TO L.A. July 29, 1984, the Los Angeles Memorial Coliseum, built for the 1932 Olympics, is packed again for the opening ceremonies of the 1984 Summer Games.

host of programs such as *Death Valley Days* and *General Electric Theater*. At the same time, he traveled the country as a popular corporate spokesperson and advocate of conservative causes.

During the '70s, political power was shifting to an emerging Republican South, a burgeoning Southwest, and always-influential California. In 1968, the rawhide manner of Arizona's "Mr. Conservative," Barry Goldwater, rubbed voters wrong, and Richard Nixon's deceptive personality eventually engendered distrust. Reagan, in contrast, had an optimistic charm that recalled his political opposite, Franklin Roosevelt.

PRESIDENT RONALD REAGAN AND FIRST LADY NANCY REAGAN, in January 1981. The Reagans brought a casual Hollywood-accented style to the White House.

In 1966, the former movie actor was elected governor of California, his first experience holding public office. The new state leader already had a well-developed and disarming sense of humor. When a reporter asked him what kind of governor he would be, he answered, "I don't know. I've never played a governor." As the leader of America's most populous state, Reagan spent two terms honing political and management skills, confronting the Free Speech protesters at UC Berkeley, and promoting private enterprise and small government, while pragmatically raising taxes and increasing the state budget.

With Ronald Reagan's election as president, the Washington establishment reluctantly accepted an "Out West" style as unavoidably "in." Reagan was belittled and underestimated by some East Coast political pundits, but like the City of Los Angeles, he was both more and less than he appeared to be. He began his administration with a moment of Hollywood-like triumph—the return of fifty-two American hostages held in Iran for 444 days. Equally dramatic, seventy days into his first term he survived an assassination attempt and afterward seemed as steadfast as ever. The president's commitment to reducing the size and influence of government, lowering taxes and supporting for defense and breaks for big business were

called "the Reagan Revolution," but critics believed they led to decidedly mixed results.

In a way, Reagan left the Presidency in 1989 with a very Los Angeles legacy, inspired with feelings of hope, lifted by charisma and charm, highlighted by important achievements, but haunted with a sense that an atmosphere of sunny well-being obscured and ignored darker realities.

In 1981, while Republican Angelenos celebrated Ronald Reagan's inauguration, Los Angeles was observing another historic landmark—the city's Bicentennial. If two hundred years of geographical expansion had complicated the American Bicentennial in 1976, leaving it primarily an East Coast affair, the size, complexity and two centuries of unprecedented growth challenged the City of Los Angeles. Angelenos, like most Americans, preferred to look to the future, and tended to ignore the past. The erasure of nineteenth-century Bunker Hill to make way for the Music Center in the 1960s was one example of this. Despite the dedication and enthusiasm of a Los Angeles 200

Committee, the L.A. Bicentennial effort faced imposing obstacles. How could any single celebration deal with a city whose history was a barely remembered series of explosive changes?

At the first planning meeting, Mayor Tom Bradley warmly welcomed the group, then said, "Please don't hesitate to come to me for anything — except money." As a result, the yearlong two-hundredth birthday party was bare-boned, highlighted by a loose association of events under a Bicentennial banner. On

September 4, 1981, a group of descendants of the *pobladores,* the forty-four founders of the original pueblo, reenacted the walk from Mission San Gabriel to the old plaza. Over time, Spanish names such as Ortega and Lopez had morphed into Northrop and Smith, but there were still Guzmans and Leóns among the group. No news cameras existed to record the founding in 1781, and only a few showed up at the Bicentennial celebration at City Hall.

Despite this, there were already signs that Los Angeles was beginning to appreciate

MULTIFACETED MUSICIAN FRANK ZAPPA joined his daughter Moon Unit in creating the satirical hit song "Valley Girl," reconfirming popular perceptions of air-headed Angelenos.

its long-overlooked or mythologized history. In 1978, there was talk of demolishing the 1926 downtown library for something new and bigger. Although demolition had often been the L.A. way to deal with the past, in response, the Los Angeles Conservancy was born. Not since Charles Lummis fought to save the Spanish missions with the 1895 Landmarks Club, did the City of Angels have such an enthusiastic and ultimately effective advocate for L.A.'s architectural heritage.

Even with signs of positive change, as late as the 1980s, many Americans still considered Los Angeles as essentially an air-headed amalgam of Hollywood, the beach and Disneyland. Seeming to confirm this was the 1982 song "Valley Girl," sung by Moon Unit Zappa, daughter of L.A. avant garde rocker Frank Zappa. With lyrics studded with the latest teenage slang, "Valley Girl" mocked the language of young "la la" Angelenos. Maybe some Valley girls were "grody to the max," but "fer sure," the persistence of such stereotypes left sophisticated L.A. observers eager to "gag me with a spoon."

In the early 1980s, a more worldly L.A. continued to emerge. A new home for the city's Museum of Contemporary Art, designed by Japanese architect Arata Isozaki, reconfirmed L.A.'s prominent place in the international art world. In 1984, a new Aerospace

A MUSEUM TAKES FLIGHT. Built between 1983 and 1984, the California Aerospace Museum in Exposition Park, designed by architect Frank Gehry, features an F-104 Starfighter jet suspended from the exterior.

MOCA. Los Angeles's status as an international art center was made more evident with the completion of the Museum of Contemporary Art on transformed Bunker Hill.

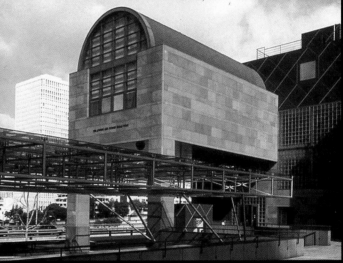

THE LOS ANGELES COUNTY MUSEUM OF ART. During the 1980s, LACMA began a large-scale expansion program, adding the Robert O. Anderson Building for modern and contemporary art, the Pavilion for Japanese Art and a sculpture garden.

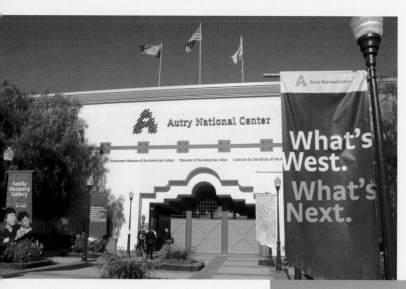

THE AUTRY NATIONAL CENTER opened in 1988 as the Gene Autry Western Heritage Museum. Beginning with a focus on traditional views of the West, the center has become more socially and ethnically inclusive, and now embraces the Southwest Museum and the Institute for the Study of the American West.

PACIFIC DESIGN CENTER. With 1.2 million square feet, the complex, begun by architect Cesar Pelli in 1975, and added to during the '80s, is in stylish West Hollywood.

LOS ANGELES ZOO. During the 1980s, the zoo added facilities for California condors, koalas, meerkats and a new children's zoo called Adventure Island.

THE SPACE SHUTTLE ATLANTIS touches down at Edwards Air Force Base in Palmdale, north of L.A., December 3, 1985. It was one of twenty-five landings at Edwards during the 1980s. The four shuttles—Columbia, Discovery, Atlantis and Challenger—were all built in L.A. County by Rockwell International.

Museum opened, a reminder of L.A.'s leadership in aviation. Featuring a Lockheed F-104 fighter plane suspended over the entrance, the angular structure was designed by architect Frank Gehry. In 1986, the city launched the Music Center Opera Company, soon to be one of the most prominent in the United States. Two years later, the $34 million Autry Museum of Western Heritage opened, dedicated to the study of the history and cultures of the American West.

Making up for a dip in growth rate during the '70s, the population of 1980s L.A. County reversed this temporary trend by adding more than half a million people. In 1984, Los Angeles surpassed Chicago as America's second-largest city. Annexation and growth were as Angeleno as good weather, but there were always communities that insisted on remaining independent. In 1984, the unincorporated community of West Hollywood decided to go its own way.

With a large and active gay population, the new city was soon encouraging a social, cultural and architectural renaissance.

On Melrose Avenue, the "Blue Whale," a geometrically shaped blue building designed by Cesar Pelli, appeared, followed by a green structure in 1988, and a red companion to come. They housed the West Coast's largest center for design and home furnishings. Robertson and Santa Monica boulevards blossomed with galleries, chic shops, cafés and bars. Melrose Avenue had nurtured a funky image since the 1960s, but the street soon looked younger and hipper than ever, a picture of eccentric and freestyle L.A.

Sadly, all this enthusiasm and change took place under a tragic shadow—the international epidemic of AIDS. The first case was identified by a UCLA professor in 1981. America was slow to respond, but Los Angeles became a leader in the fight. In 1985, the city passed the first AIDS antidiscrimination law, and national

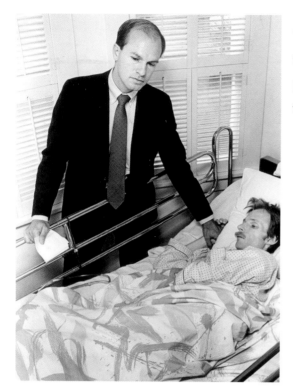

awareness finally increased with the death from AIDS of actor Rock Hudson, and later HIV-positive diagnoses for other well-known Angelenos, including tennis star Arthur Ashe and Laker Magic Johnson. For a moment at least, these personal tragedies seemed to bring a sprawling and divided community a little closer in grief.

Creating a sense of community was a perennial challenge for Los Angeles. During most of the twentieth century, L.A. was redefining the meaning of "city" as a concept and as a place. During the 1980s, Los Angeles experienced a fundamental transformation with profound implications for the future of the city as well as the entire United States.

With a metropolitan area population approaching ten million, Los Angeles became the first metropolis in America, and the world, to have no single ethnic or racial majority. In 1987, 41 percent of Angelenos were white, 36 percent Latino and 17 percent African American. Only a slightly smaller percentage had Asian ancestry. One consequence of this dramatic change was that L.A., with such a prominent Latino population, became home to America's largest Catholic archdiocese. In 1985, the city welcomed Roger Mahoney as L.A.'s first Angeleno-born archbishop.

By the 1980s, Los Angeles was America's leading port of entry for foreign immigrants. The city contained the largest Mexican population outside of Mexico; the second-largest Chinese population outside of China; and the largest Japanese, Korean,

ROGER MAHONEY, raised in the San Fernando Valley, became the leader of America's largest Catholic archdiocese in 1985. In the decades to come, he would struggle with sexual abuse scandals and immigration rights issues.

POPE JOHN PAUL II greets well wishers from his "popemobile" during his September 1985 visit to Los Angeles. To his left is Roger Mahoney, then an archbishop, later a cardinal.

THE CITY OF SAN GABRIEL, the location of L.A.'s first Franciscan mission, is now home to a major Asian population, an example of L.A.'s shifting demographics.

A PROUD ANGELENA and her granddaughter.

LOS ANGELES SKYLINE. During the 1980s, ownership of more than half of L.A.'s downtown buildings passed into the hands of Japanese investors.

Filipino and Vietnamese communities outside their homelands. Immigrant communities built new L.A. landmarks, including the Japanese American Theater that opened in Little Tokyo in 1983.

Of international significance, a booming Japanese economy reached across the Pacific and began investing in the United States— especially in Los Angeles. Japanese automakers, including Honda, Toyota and Nissan, had North American headquarters in the Los Angeles area, and Japanese investment interests acquired large holdings in Los Angeles real estate. By 1988, foreign investors owned 75 percent of L.A.'s downtown skyline, up from 25 percent in 1980. In 1989, Japanese interests purchased Columbia Pictures, the Bel-Air and Biltmore hotels and the Rivera Country Club in Pacific Palisades. Ironically, for much of the city's early history, Asians had been barred from owning land in California.

In 1987, the greater Los Angeles area produced $250 billion worth of goods and services. If the county had been a country, it would have been the eleventh richest in the world. The side-by-side ports of Long Beach and Los Angeles were the busiest in America, and the world's fastest growing. Despite common perceptions, Hollywood movie production played a relatively small role in L.A.'s diverse 1980s economy, accounting for 1.4 percent of local jobs. Los Angeles was primarily a service and entrepreneurial environment. Most companies had well under a hundred employees. And, even with surprisingly few corporate headquarters, L.A. had surpassed San Francisco as the West Coast financial center long before.

In the past, Los Angeles was pictured as a social, political and economic laboratory. With a population as extensive as a country, made up of people from around the world, many of whom came to follow personal destinies, change during the 1980s was transforming and unexpected. The San Gabriel Valley city of Monterey Park is a prime example. Only eight miles from downtown Los Angeles, on formerly Mission San Gabriel land, Monterey Park was first subdivided in 1906 as Ramona Acres, named after Helen Hunt Jackson's influential heroine.

During the 1920s, homes in local Spanish-style real estate developments were mostly owned by white residents. The post–World War II boom brought Monterey Park working-class Mexican Americans, moving up and out of East L.A. barrios. In 1965, a new Immigration Act lifted quotas that had virtually banned Asian migration, and the situation began to change. During the 1970s, immigrants from Taiwan and Hong Kong began arriving in increasing numbers. Some were concerned about their future after

PORT OF LOS ANGELES. In this 1980 photo, stacks of containers line the docks of the 7,500-acre harbor.

President Nixon established relations with the People's Republic of China. Others were drawn by widespread advertisements from Frederick Hsieh, a local developer who promoted Monterey Park as "the Chinese Beverly Hills."

As with previous boomtown sales pitches, Hsieh's ads were alluring and effective. Adding to the appeal, the Asian American entrepreneur noted that Monterey Park's telephone area code was then 818. To many Chinese, eight is a lucky number that bestows prosperity.

Like the "Sick Rush" immigrants of the 1870s, a substantial number of new Chinese arrivals came with previous professional success and money. Commercial land worth $5 a square foot in 1970 was selling for $45 in 1980. In response, many existing, mostly white property owners took the money and ran. One recently sold gas station displayed a sign reading: "Will the last American to leave Monterey Park please bring the flag?" In 1970, 78 percent of the population of Monterey Park was Anglo. By the end of the 1980s, it dropped to 36 percent. Signs in Chinese lined main thoroughfares like Atlantic and Valley boulevards. Nearby, in 1988, the $10 million Taiwanese Buddhist Hsi Lai Temple was built in a community with the incongruous

name of Hacienda Heights. However, not all Monterey Park citizens accepted change without a fight.

An anti-immigration backlash began in Southern California and spread throughout the state. In 1986, citizens passed a statewide proposition declaring English as California's official language. Yet, by the 1990s, as Chinese signs and conversations in Monterey Park continued to proliferate, many began to accept this as unavoidable evidence of L.A.'s new multicultural identity. At the same time, some Chinese were uncomfortable with newspaper articles referring to Monterey Park and other nearby communities as "super Chinatowns," or Asian suburbs. They preferred to see themselves as they were—a large citizen group in an even larger multiethnic community.

Monterey Park and nearby Alhambra are a Chinese food lover's dream come true. In the past, Los Angeles dining had been best known for simple family restaurants, cafeterias and fast food—places like the Pig 'n' Whistle, Clifton's and Philippe's. There had been fancy restaurants, including Perinos and Scandia; upscale hangouts such as the Cocoanut Grove, Ciros, the Trocadero, Mocambo, Romanoff's and Chasens; and earlier favorites such as Al Levy's and Musso and Frank. There also were venerable "foreign" establishments such as the bohemian

WOLFGANG PUCK. Starting in the 1980s, with his restaurants Spago and Chinois on Main, Austrian-born Chef Wolfgang Puck was a major influence in making Los Angeles a capital of creative cuisine.

bargain spot Rene and Jean's, the family-style French food at Les Frére Taix, and El Cholo, serving "Spanish" (read Mexican) food. The 1980s reflected the new Los Angeles with cuisine that established international trends.

The "in" restaurant of the 1970s and early '80s was Ma Maison, featuring "nouvelle" French influences. In 1982, the Austrian-born chef at Ma Maison, Wolfgang Puck, opened Spago. It became an international gourmet destination, featuring innovative new dishes and fresh takes on standards, such as pizza topped with barbecued chicken. At the same time, an influx of immigrants was creating rare opportunities to sample the best cuisine from Japan, Thailand, South and Central America and, as always, Mexico. Again, Los Angeles was a trendsetter. In the 1970s, East Coast gourmets mocked L.A.'s "weird" fascination with raw fish and rice. By the '90s, they were touting sushi as all the rage. Jokes about yogurt- and bean sprout—eating Angelenos turned into a national enthusiasm for health food.

In the summer of 1984, Los Angeles proudly celebrated its new multicultural image with the twenty-third Olympic Games. Mayor Tom Bradley had been instrumental in bringing the Games to Los Angeles, and a new $125 million Bradley International Terminal was ready to receive visitors from around the world. Despite this, in the months before the Games, many Angelenos were concerned that an onslaught of Olympics enthusiasts would create freeway gridlock, and perhaps even attract the kind of terrorist violence that marred the Munich Games in 1972. There were also more recent memories of the 1976 Montreal Games, when the Canadian host city spent $1.5 billion and went deeply in debt.

Fortunately, none of this happened. Although the Soviet Union and Eastern European countries refused to participate, in retaliation for the U.S. boycott of the

Moscow competition in 1980, the Los Angeles Games were considered the most successful in modern Olympic history. Along with record-breaking performances by athletes from around the world, the city was a winner too. Thanks to a coordinated effort by local employers, work schedules were staggered, keeping freeways unusually congestion-free. The weather was sunny and smogless. Instead of terrorist violence, there was the peaceful celebration of a citywide festival of arts.

A record 140 nations participated in the '84 Games, compared to thirty-four in 1932. Among American medalists, Joan Benoit won the first women's Olympic marathon. Runner Carl Lewis took home four gold medals. Diver Greg Louganis was the first man in fifty-six years to win gold medals in both the platform

CARL LEWIS. Longtime member of the Santa Monica Track Club, Lewis won four gold medals (the 100 meters, 200 meters, 4x100-meter relay and long jump), equaling Jesse Owens's record.

MARY DECKER. After her heart-breaking stumble in the Los Angeles Olympic Games, Decker went on to set two world records in 1985. She was the only American runner to hold both the 800- and 10,000-meter records at the same time.

and springboard events. The darling of the Games was petite sixteen-year-old Mary Lou Retton. Competing in the absence of the powerful Eastern Bloc teams, Retton became the first American to win the All-Around Gold Medal in gymnastics. As usual, the Games had moments of tragedy and high drama. Mary Decker, the only runner to hold every American record from 800 to 10,000 meters, was heavily favored to win the women's 3,000-meter race. However, shortly after the halfway mark, she stumbled and fell when South African runner Zola Budd pushed past her.

In contrast to previous government-sponsored competitions, entrepreneurial L.A. turned to private enterprise to foot the bill.

Orange County businessman Peter Ueberroth was chosen to head the United States Olympic Organizing Committee. Some traditionalists complained about increased commercialism, but those with eyes on the bottom line, as well as the finish line, were overjoyed by the results. Los Angeles ended the Games with a $232.5 million surplus. The money was shared with the U.S. Olympic Committee and other national sports-governing bodies, but 40 percent went to Southern California youth and neighborhood community organizations and assistance programs.

Aside from the Olympics, the 1980s was a notable decade for local L.A. sports. Under new coach Pat Riley, and with record-breaking play from stars such as Kareem Abdul-Jabbar, Earvin "Magic" Johnson and James Worthy, the Lakers won five NBA titles. If that wasn't enough for basketball fans, in 1984, L.A. added a second professional team, the Clippers.

In football, in 1980, the L.A. Rams lost to the Pittsburgh Pirates in Super Bowl XIV, then moved to Anaheim in Orange County. It was a sign that L.A.'s neighbor to the south was gaining a metropolitan identity of its own. In 1982, the Oakland Raiders became the Los

CHICK HEARN. Laker announcer Chick Hearn with his wife, Marge, acknowledge cheers from Lakers fans in 1981. Offering his "words-eye-view," Hearn added "slam dunk" and "no harm, no foul," to the American vocabulary.

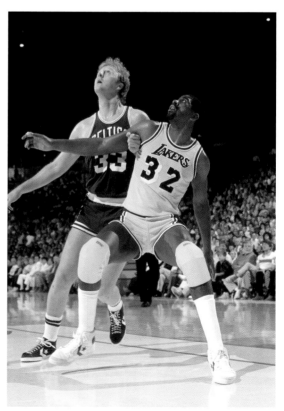

BIRD AND JOHNSON. One of the great basketball match-ups of the 1980s—Laker Magic Johnson and Larry Bird of the Boston Celtics.

THE FIRST LOS ANGELES MARATHON in 1986. Ric Sayre appears to be far out in front on a route that takes runners through L.A.'s diverse neighborhoods.

Angeles Raiders. Two years later they won Super Bowl XVIII. In 1989, Art Shell became the first African American NFL head coach when he accepted the top position for the Raiders. The future of L.A.'s least likely sport, ice hockey, changed in 1988. The Kings acquired one of the greatest players in the game, Wayne Gretzky.

For the Los Angeles Dodgers, the '80s were also a time to celebrate. With manager Tommy Lasorda, the team won 825 games, claiming two World Series championships — in 1981 and 1988 — and four National League Western Division titles. In 1980, pitcher Don Sutton set a team shut-out record. That same year, a rotund rookie left-hander born in Navojoa, Mexico, Fernando Valenzuela, captured the imagination of Dodger supporters, especially the team's enthusiastic Latino fans. As for the Angels, Reggie Jackson hit

FERNANDO VALENZUELA. In 1981, Los Angeles was caught up in "Fernandomania." Pitcher Fernando Valenzuela helped lead the team to a World Series title. The young left-hander also won both Cy Young and Rookie of the Year honors.

WAYNE GRETZKY. On August 9, 1988, the hockey star holds up his new Kings jersey, standing with team owner Bruce McNall.

THE 1982 FILM *BLADE RUNNER,* directed by Ridley Scott, offered a dystopian vision of an environmentally toxic, technology-driven, culturally chaotic Los Angeles.

his 500th home run, but the 1980s were bittersweet times for Halos fans. Behind pitcher Don Sutton's 300th victory, the team came tantalizingly close to a World Series appearance in 1986, but it was not to be.

Sports had stars, and as always, so did the movies. Hollywood had long been a synonym for the motion picture business in America, and the part industry/part art continued to

reflect an image of Los Angeles. The 1982 film *Blade Runner* offered another big-screen update to L.A.'s self-portrait. A cross between film noir and science fiction, it was a detective story set in a futuristic, smog-shrouded, rain-slicked metropolis, with an ethnically mixed citizenry and an atmosphere of high-tech decadence. If the Olympics offered a real-life inspiration of hope for Los Angeles, *Blade Runner* was a fictional antidote to excessive optimism.

While *Blade Runner* was a big-studio film, during the 1980s, the great old production institutions — MGM, Warner Bros., Universal and Columbia — were shuffled and traded like playing cards. Many were acquired by parent companies, including Coca-Cola, Sony and Matsushita Electric, businesses with little or no experience making movies. By the end of the decade only two studios, Paramount and Disney, remained independent. As an era came to an end, the last of the great movie moguls wasn't a filmmaker, he was Lew Wasserman, a master agent and deal maker.

For nearly forty years, Wasserman was considered one of the most powerful people in Hollywood. That made him one of the most influential men in America. Less flamboyant than super-agent Irving "Swifty" Lazar, a contemporary, Wasserman was a major political fund-raiser as well as friend and personal

confidante of U.S. presidents, especially Lyndon Johnson and Ronald Reagan, a former actor-client. Hollywood needed political influence and politicians needed Hollywood money. Lew Wasserman provided a connection.

Wasserman began his career in show business as an usher in a Cleveland movie theater. Later, as a public relations executive at Music Company of America (MCA) in mob-invested Chicago during the 1930s, he was successful as a booker and agent for major bandleaders such as Tommy Dorsey. Rising to president of MCA, founded by show business-minded ophthalmologist Jules Stein, he represented some of Hollywood's greatest talent during the 1940s and '50s.

While others feared television, Wasserman harvested the opportunities. In 1959, he bought Universal Studios and encouraged the production of TV shows. An astute visionary

and tough competitor, during the '60s and '70s he set a precedent when he negotiated profit-share deals for James Stewart and other stars. There were persistent rumors that gang ties from Wasserman's days in Chicago kept peace with the entertainment unions. True or not, his power and influence included all aspects of the business of getting movies and television programs finished and profitable. Finally, during the 1960s, the federal government stepped in to break up MCA's monopolistic stranglehold. But Wasserman's imperial influence continued.

In Los Angeles, his power went far beyond the studio gates. He was an important contributor to the creation of the Los Angeles Music Center in the 1960s, and to the 1984 Olympics. Twelve years before the old mogul's death in 2002, at age eighty-nine, Wasserman sold his Universal Studios holdings to Japan's

Matsushita Electric Company for a profit of $300 million, and afterwards was relegated to the status of shunted-aside elder statesman.

Beyond the power of any single entertainment figure, the motion picture and recording industries were becoming increasingly intertwined. One of the best-selling albums of all time was Michael Jackson's 1982 *Thriller,* but the "Thriller" music video, envisioned by Hollywood director John Landis, was even more influential. With the success of MTV, music videos became powerful sales tools that blended sophisticated cinematic technologies with the latest music. Again, Los Angeles was contributing a new form of entertainment to American culture.

During the '80s, as some things changed in L.A., older trends continued as before. Decades of new freeways and tract developments had overrun much of Southern California's agricultural landscape. But nature hadn't totally left town. Agricultural production remained an

MICHAEL JACKSON'S *THRILLER* has been called the eccentric pop star's greatest performance. This is an image from the "Thriller" music video, a landmark in a new kind of marketing and entertainment.

important component of the local economy. The main crop, however, was no longer citrus, but nursery items cultivated to enhance environments in and around homes and office buildings. And these plants were not only grown on traditional farm acreage, but often on leased undevelopable land such as areas under high-voltage power lines.

While Los Angeles regularly faced natural dangers, the '80s placed a relatively new

THE TINY MEDITERRANEAN FRUIT FLY looks harmless, but it is one of the world's most destructive pests and a major threat to California and American agriculture.

hazard near the top of the list. Beginning in 1975, the Mediterranean fruit fly posed a serious threat to California's fruit and vegetable production and, as a result, to the American agricultural economy. Considered one of the world's most destructive pests, the voracious insect can hitch a ride on a long-distance truck or airline flight and easily cross international borders. During the '80s, Los Angeles was on repeated alert as helicopters sprayed toxic clouds of the insecticide Malathion. In the mid-1990s, when the poison was acknowledged to be a human carcinogen, widespread spraying would come to an end. Afterward, traps and the introduction of sterile flies led the fight, but strict controls and containment, rather than eradication, were the only realistic goals.

In 1987, one of the oldest challenges to the good life in Los Angeles rumbled back. On October 1, at 7:42 in the morning, a previously unknown fault ten miles east of downtown unleashed a 5.9 earthquake, felt up to 200 miles away. The result was three deaths, dozens of injuries and $200 million in damage. Older unreinforced buildings in Whittier, Richard Nixon's hometown, were hit especially hard. A 5.5 aftershock at 3:59 a.m. on October 4 added to the destruction and jangled nerves.

Earthquakes were not the only source of

WHITTIER EARTHQUAKE. The owner of a housewares store in Glendale surveys the damage from the 5.9 magnitude Whittier Narrows earthquake.

NEAR THE CHATEAU MARMONT HOTEL on the Sunset Strip, a billboard is an ironic reminder of John Belushi's death in one of the hotel's bungalows, as a result of "acute heroin and cocaine intoxication."

GANG TRUCE. In 1988, the 88th Street Avalon Crips agree[d] a truce as part of an effort to reduce local violence. It did no[t] hold for long, and turf wars continued within the Crips as w[ell] as with their main adversaries, the Bloods.

DARYL GATES, right, controversial chief of the L.A. Police Department, displays 1,700 pounds of cocaine and $750,000 in cash after an April 1986 drug bust, at the time a West Coast record.

THE NIGHT STALKER. In 1984, petty criminal Richard Ramirez began a series of murders that earned him the nickname "The Night Stalker." After his arrest a year later, Ramirez displayed a pentagram on his palm, a symbol of his devotion to Satanism. "I love to kill people," he said.

GUNS AND CITIZENS. Afraid of being surprised by an intruder such as the notorious Night Stalker, a woman, identified only as Debby, holds her newly acquired pistol in a posed photograph for the *Herald Examiner*.

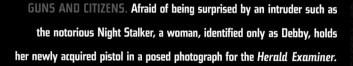

danger in 1980s Los Angeles. The growth of criminal gangs during the 1970s continued during the '80s, funded by a virulent drug trade. In 1989, federal agents seized twenty tons of cocaine and $10 million in cash in an unguarded L.A. warehouse. The City of Angels was declared the nation's leading illegal drug distribution center. The title came as no surprise to local law enforcement. To the rest of America, the drug overdose death of thirty-three-year-old comedian John Belushi in 1982 was a reminder that L.A.'s reputation as an American capital of scandal and excess remained tragically intact.

Twenty-six-year-old Richard Ramirez found his fame through brutality. Always ready with a headline-grabbing nickname, the L.A. press called him "The Night Stalker." A satanic serial killer and rapist, Ramirez had terrorized the San Gabriel and San Fernando valleys since 1978. When police finally compiled a sketch, using testimony of those who survived his attacks, his maniacal appearance disinterred memories of Charles Manson. On the morning of August 31, 1985, only hours after the sketch appeared in newspapers, the Night Stalker was spotted on an East L.A. street. When he tried to steal a car, he was subdued by an angry steel-rod-wielding local resident, helped by three friends. Four years later, Ramirez was finally

PRESCHOOL OWNER VIRGINIA MCMARTIN **prepares to face a series of bizarre, and ultimately unproved, accusations of child abuse.**

convicted and sentenced to death for thirteen murders and thirty assaults.

The power of the press contributed to the capture of L.A.'s Night Stalker, but in 1983, relentless reporting in newspapers and television produced a quite different result. In August, a single parent with a history of mental instability claimed that her two-year-old son had been sexually abused at the McMartin Preschool in the L.A. County coastal community of Manhattan Beach. That September, police arrested twenty-eight-year-old Raymond Buckey, grandson of the preschool's owner, Virginia McMartin. In response to further questioning by child-abuse specialists, some of the children told horrifying stories, including a description of a secret room where acts of sodomy and satanic rituals were performed. Others said they were taken to a cemetery where they watched teachers cut up corpses.

With a firestorm of press coverage, stoked by Walter Satz, an investigative reporter for the local ABC-TV affiliate, newspapers and television stations across America headlined every ghastly accusation. In a time of single parents and families that depended on both parents working, day care and preschools were essential. Terrified mothers and fathers asked: Was my child in a place like McMartin?

In 1987, four years after the initial accusations, a trial finally began with a total of 360 allegations of child abuse. By then the original accuser had died, and the prosecution team was seriously divided about the merits of the case. With virtually continuous press coverage and constant pressures from a frightened public, it wasn't until 1990 that the jury came to a verdict. Jurors were undecided on thirteen counts against Raymond Buckey, and dismissed all charges against Buckey's mother, grandmother, sister and three McMartin teachers.

A second trial ended again in a hung jury and all charges were dropped. Child abuse is a real concern, but the hysteria surrounding the McMartin case was compared to the Salem witch trials of 1692. If anyone underestimated the power of the media in the 1980s, particularly an increasing blend of news and entertainment on television, the McMartin case put doubts to rest. It was the longest, most expensive legal proceeding in American history, and a troubling warning about the uncertainties of law enforcement and the power and responsibility of the press.

As studies showed, most Americans were getting their information from quick and often-unprocessed television reports, while more measured and comprehensive media were losing ground. As local proof, in 1989, the 113-year-old Los Angeles *Herald Examiner* stopped the presses forever. The second-most-populous city in the nation, a city that once boasted five dailies, now had only one— the *Times*.

In the midst of the McMartin case, an outrage of another kind was committed against one of the city's most precious resources. At 11 a.m. on April 28, 1986, fire alarms sounded in the Los Angeles Central Library, a beautifully decorated building designed in the 1920s by architect Bertram Goodhue. Smoke and flames billowed from windows in the Moorish masterpiece as city firemen struggled to fight back. During the next six hours, the blaze devoured more than 375,000 volumes. Of those that survived,

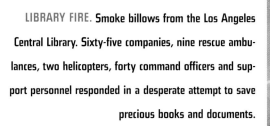
LIBRARY FIRE. Smoke billows from the Los Angeles Central Library. Sixty-five companies, nine rescue ambulances, two helicopters, forty command officers and support personnel responded in a desperate attempt to save precious books and documents.

LIBRARY DAMAGE. After the arson fire at the Central Library, staff and volunteers gather in the library's philosophy and religion section to assess the situation.

750,000 were damaged by water and smoke. It was the most destructive library fire in American history, set by an arsonist who was never apprehended.

The tragedy led to an immediate public and corporate response that astonished L.A.'s cynics and naysayers, and even surprised city enthusiasts. Seventeen hundred volunteers showed up to help clean up and save what remained. The only hope for water-soaked volumes was flash-freezing to prevent mildew, and the volunteers raced against time to get books processed and protected. Using

a donated McDonnell Douglas space simulator to remove moisture and turn it into harmless gas, more than 700,000 volumes were safely processed and stacked in a secret warehouse. Later they would be nursed back to health and returned to library shelves. Southern California corporations and foundations responded with $3.6 million in donations to replace what had been lost.

By 1989, a sleek new seventy-three-story skyscraper loomed beside the squat and delicately decorated Central L.A. Public Library. The new $350 million office building, called

the Library Tower, was the tallest structure west of Chicago, yet there was more to the promise of L.A.'s future than this impressive addition to an East Coast–style skyline. Los Angeles had never been a high-rise city like New York or Chicago, and it was unlikely that it ever would. But if L.A. was on its own urban course, where was it headed?

The Olympics and the unprecedented public response to the Central Library fire were indications that Los Angeles might be capable of finding the pride and imagination needed to create a new kind of urban community from sprawling diversity. But, at the same time, an increasing gap between rich and poor, new challenges to the city's infrastructure and a rapidly changing population were problems that were not about to go away.

LOS ANGELES SKYLINE, 1988. Viewed from Echo Lake, the Library Tower, soon to be L.A.'s tallest building, nears completion. At the end of the 1980s, the city itself remained very much a work in progress.

REMEMBERING THE FUTURE

"Can we all get along?"
RODNEY KING, May 1, 1992

During much of the 1990s, the world's most popular television program was *Baywatch*. The series presented a surf-side picture of Los Angeles, populated by well-tanned lifeguards and their bikini-clad costars. This sunny image was certainly venerable and undeniably appealing, but as the City of Angels felt its way toward the twenty-first century, it couldn't have been less relevant.

As the decade opened, Los Angeles continued to experience a wrenching economic and social reconfiguration. Since the 1920s, the diverse economy of Southern California, which included agriculture, light manufacturing, oil, aviation, high tech and tourism, usually cushioned Angelenos during downturns—even during the Great Depression of the 1930s. In the '90s, this security net threatened to shred.

Only recently Los Angeles was the most productive agricultural county in America, but no more. Farms continued to lose ground to housing, highways and tract homes. Resources of another Southern California staple, oil, had been dwindling for some time. Most importantly, the collapse of the Soviet Union and the end of the Cold War brought $3 billion in defense cuts,

WALT DISNEY CONCERT HALL looks as if it's about to eat L.A.'s linear skyline for lunch, but Frank Gehry's innovative architecture expresses the bold creativity and urban pride that are essential for L.A.'s future success.

HOME SWEET HOME? With an estimated 80,000 people with no place to live in Los Angeles County in 2005, L.A. had the sad distinction of being the homeless capital of the United States.

MULTILINGUAL L.A. The sign outside this church on Wilshire Boulevard suggests the city's multilingual citizenry.

leading to major layoffs and plant closings in L.A.'s military-based aviation and technology industries. During the '90s, nearly half of aerospace workers lost their jobs. If that weren't enough, a confluence of natural disasters, and the worst outbreak of urban unrest in American history, would create a picture of the city as unstable and dangerous. Even tourism suffered.

Despite this, the population of Los Angeles County grew by more than 7 percent as the multicultural metropolis continued to evolve. By the end of the '90s, there were 19 percent fewer non-Hispanic whites and 5 percent fewer African Americans. The Asian population increased by 24 percent and the Latino

population grew by more than 28 percent. A challenging number of the newcomers were undocumented workers, especially from Mexico and Central America. There always were employers willing to skirt the law and take advantage of low-paid workers eager to do anything to escape the poverty or political oppression in their homelands. The result was a growing underclass, providing underappreciated support for the U.S. and California economies as well as adding new strains to city and county services. And protest marches in 2006 showed that new immigrants were no longer passive.

An early warning that the 1990s weren't going to be "a Baywatch day at the beach"

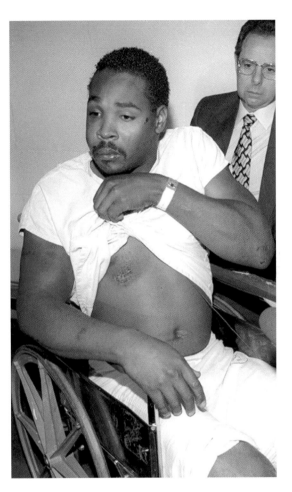

A BATTERED RODNEY KING. Shortly after his arrest, King shows reporters his wounds and bruises from a beating administered by Los Angeles law enforcement officers.

began shortly after midnight on Sunday, March 3, 1991. Rodney King, a tall and muscular twenty-five-year-old African American, brought his 1988 Hyundai to a halt after ignoring repeated commands to pull over by LAPD and State Highway officers. Hitting speeds of 110 miles per hour on the 210 Freeway in the north San Fernando Valley, the chase had been long, frustrating and dangerous.

Suspected of being drunk, or under the influence of drugs, King was yanked from his car and ordered to the ground. When he hesitated, officers closed in with batons, and began beating him on the head, back and shoulders. One policeman held his nightstick with two hands and swung it like a baseball bat. Defenseless, King was finally bludgeoned into submission. For the police, everything seemed to be over. But it had just begun. Unknown to the officers, the violent encounter had been videotaped by a young man in an apartment across the street. After the tape was broadcast on television, Angelenos, and eventually viewers around the world, were shocked and sickened.

Facing growing public concern and outrage,

Mayor Tom Bradley ordered an independent investigation by a commission, headed by local attorney and future U.S. Secretary of State Warren Christopher. The report, issued three months later, was a searing indictment of the LAPD's lack of administrative accountability and unchecked use of excessive force.

In March 1992, the trial of the four police officers who struck Rodney King got underway in Simi Valley, a suburban community in adjoining Ventura County, considered a neutral venue. The all-white jury listened to testimony and repeatedly watched the tape. At 3:15 p.m. on April 29, they announced their verdict: not guilty on all counts. Within hours, a sense of disbelief, frustration and anger surged through L.A.'s black community until it erupted into violence. As with Watts, twenty-seven years before, live television cameras were soon broadcasting pictures of Los Angeles at its worst.

Reginald Denny, a young white truck driver who happened to be in the wrong place at the wrong time, was pulled from his cab and beaten in the street. As night fell, the sound of sirens and hovering helicopters filled the darkness, illuminated by isolated fires. An especially troubling aspect of the violence was evidence of new inter-ethnic antagonisms. Threatened Korean American store owners defended their shops—some with guns.

In response to spreading looting and vandalism, California National Guardsmen and federal troops were called in. Finally, after six days, order was restored. More than fifty people had lost their lives and 2,300 others suffered injuries. As many as 1,000 fires had been reported. Costs would amount to $1 billion.

At the height of the rampage, a bruised Rodney King stood before a crowd of

AFTER THE FIRST RODNEY KING VERDICT, rioting and looting began. Korean-owned liquor stores were targets, but African American—owned businesses were invaded too.

reporters and plaintively asked: "Can we all get along?" Cynics scoffed. Even L.A. enthusiasts realized it was too late to undo the damage to their city's people, places and reputation. Ten months later, King's case was tried again in a federal court. This time the verdict was different. Two of the four LAPD officers were convicted of depriving him of his civil rights and sentenced to thirty-month prison terms, and two were acquitted. In a separate trial, the young man who attacked truck driver Reginald Denny was sentenced to ten years.

The aftermath of the Rodney King beating was another reminder that there were deep and disturbing complexities beneath the picture of L.A.'s sunny surface. Local artists and writers were already probing these deeper realities. During the '90s, Walter Mosely brought an entertaining and insightful historical context to L.A.'s often-overlooked African American history with his novel *Devil in a Blue Dress.* Born and raised in Los Angeles, Mosely knew his city and its past firsthand. His private eye, Easy Rawlins, was immersed in a 1940s African American L.A. that was unknown to most white Angelenos. *Little Scarlet,* published in 2004, set in the aftermath of Watts in 1965, was an exploration of L.A.'s more recent past, mixing injustice, black rage and murder to illuminate the turmoil and violence of that time.

To many, the second verdict in the Rodney King case brought some sense of justice, but the negative impact on Los Angeles was inescapable. Even with a public outcry and the criticisms of the Christopher Commission, the LAPD was slow to change. Admittedly, local law-enforcement efforts were stretched beyond their limit by lack of adequate manpower and the mere scale of the city, but improvements were long overdue. Charged with social insensitivity and failure to respond

UPHEAVAL, 1992. **Predominately African American and Latino south Los Angeles burst into rage after learning that officers charged in the Rodney King beating were declared not guilty.**

effectively to the rioting, Police Chief Daryl Gates, a cop who had championed L.A.'s military-style of law enforcement, was forced to resign. During the '90s, two more chiefs, Willie Williams from Philadelphia and LAPD veteran Bernard Parks, failed to enact meaningful reforms.

To make matters worse, in 1999, the LAPD was hit by its biggest scandal since the days of Chief James "Two Gun" Davis in the 1930s. It began with the 1998 arrest of Rafael Pérez, a member of the Rampart Division's elite anti-gang CRASH (Community Resources Against Street Hoodlums) unit. Accused of selling confiscated cocaine, Pérez cut a deal with investigators and implicated himself and other officers in even more dangerous levels of corruption, including false arrests, station-house beatings, robberies and murder. As a result, more than 100 previous convictions were overturned. Settlements would cost $70 million.

In a stinging humiliation, on September 19, 2000, the Los Angeles City Council voted to accept a federal consent decree that gave the U.S. Justice Department oversight of efforts to reform the Los Angeles Police Department. With hopes that an outsider might help, in 2002, newly elected mayor James Hahn hired William J. Bratton, a veteran of law enforcement in Boston, and recently retired as New York City Police Commissioner. Bratton favored localized policing and a tough approach toward gangs. He had his work laid out for him.

As the 1990s stumbled on, another writer was reminding Angelenos that the Rampart scandal was far from an aberration. James Ellroy had a biography as dark and violent as many of his characters. His stripped-down prose, with echoes of the hard-boiled 1940s, was called "neo-noir." Ellroy's 1990 novel *L.A. Confidential,* and the 1997 film that followed, revisited the police violence and corruption of the 1950s—the era of *Dragnet,* Mickey Cohen and *Confidential Magazine.* In the "city without a history" the past was more alive and more relevant than ever.

Faced with an L.A. that sometimes seemed under siege, some Angelenos decided to retreat to a new profusion of gated communities. But others were even more committed to help their battered hometown recover, rebuild and become stronger. In the days following the violence after the first Rodney King verdict, thousands of volunteers—a "multiethnic brigade," the *Times* called them—showed up with brooms and trash bags to help clean up neighborhoods devastated by the destruction.

Eighteen months after this much-needed excuse for optimism, Los Angeles was tested again. In late October 1993, the mountains

MALIBU FIRE. Seen from the beach, smoke appears to engulf the nearby hills.

L.A. COUNTRY FIREFIGHTERS watch as a water-dropping airplane attempts to hold back an inferno.

seemed to burst into flames. To anyone unfamiliar with the scale of greater L.A., the extent of the inferno was beyond comprehension. Before it was over, fourteen separate wildfires burned from Malibu on the west, to Thousand Oaks in the North, east to Altadena, Sierra Madre and San Bernardino, and south to the wealthy seaside town and art colony of Laguna Beach—locations up to 85 miles apart. In all, more than 137,000 acres were burned, 554 homes were destroyed and three people lost their lives. The total losses were estimated at $950 million.

After the fires were extinguished, Angelenos waited in dread for the rainy season. As always, where flames had stripped hillsides bare, potential floods and mud slides posed a major threat. When the downpours came, it seemed as if they would never end.

HIGH-FLYING FREEWAYS, like this span connecting the Antelope Freeway and I-5, were particularly vulnerable to heavy ground shaking.

NORTHRIDGE EARTHQUAKE. Among the many buildings severely damaged on the California State University Northridge campus was this multistory garage. Fortunately, the quake occurred before dawn when the campus was empty of students.

NORTHRIDGE MEADOWS TRAGEDY. Sixteen people died when underground garage supports gave way, and the three upper floors collapsed.

During the years 1992, 1995 and 1997, Los Angeles experienced the worst flooding since the deluges of 1938.

The great storm of 1995 also highlighted another name in L.A.'s local vocabulary—El Nino. Named by early South American fishermen, who noted that the effect usually occurred shortly after Christmas, El Nino (the Christ child) is caused by warming water temperatures in the Pacific Ocean. Tracked regularly since the 1940s, the result can be intense, short-term changes in the weather. Thanks to El Nino, in 1995, it rained in Los Angeles for the better part of three months, the worst downpour in a century, only topped by the 2004–2005 season, considered an all-time record.

If rain wasn't enough, on January 17, 1994, Angelenos were startled awake at 4:31 a.m. by a 6.7 earthquake centered in the Fernando Valley, which would prove to be one of the costliest natural disasters in American history. A three-story apartment building in Northridge "pancaked," crushing sixteen residents. Across Los Angeles, other apartments, office buildings and parking structures were destroyed or damaged, and numerous homes were shoved off their foundations.

The quake shattered the interchange between the Golden State and Antelope Valley freeways, and brought down a section of the Santa Monica Freeway. In the early morning darkness, one police officer, unaware that a section of the Antelope Valley Freeway had snapped off, raced to join law enforcement and relief efforts. Before he could stop, his motorcycle careened over the edge and he fell hundreds of feet to his death. Fifty-six other lives were lost that morning, 20,000 were left homeless and $20 to $40 billion were added to the total costs from the decade's onslaught of natural and man-made catastrophes.

Adding to the uncertainty, in politics the '90s marked the end of the old L.A. oligarchy. The days were fading when a handful of businessmen and politicians ran things from elite institutions, such as the formerly all-white, all-male California Club. At the turn of the century, power in Los Angeles was becoming decentralized and often elusive. In 2000, the Chandler family relinquished control of the influential *Los Angeles Times* to the Chicago-based, cost-conscious Tribune Company. In 2004, under its new ownership, the *Times* won eight Pulitzer prizes, but that didn't stop cutbacks as newspapers across the country struggled to adapt to challenges from all-news television and the Internet. Before that, corporate institutions such as Arco and Security Pacific Bank had changed hands, were swallowed up or moved away.

National figures from the post–World War II city were passing into history. Former President Richard Nixon died in 1994. A year later, Ronald Reagan announced that he had Alzheimer's, the disease that would take his life in 2004. In 1993, Tom Bradley stepped down as mayor, at age seventy-six. He died five years later. It was time for a new generation of leadership. But where would it come from?

A transition began tentatively. Richard Riordan, Bradley's successor, represented the business-oriented leadership of the past. His opponent was Michael Woo, L.A.'s first Chinese American city councilman and mayoral candidate. In the election, Woo was handily defeated, but his candidacy suggested continuing changes in the L.A. electorate. A political novice and private-enterprise Republican, Riordan's more broad-minded social views

appealed to some liberals and Democrats. His first major challenge was the earthquake, but his long-term interest was education.

The Los Angeles Unified School District, the second-largest in the United States (after New York), was overwhelmed and failing. With students from around the world, language barriers alone were formidable. Four-year high school drop-out rates, especially among African Americans and Latinos, were approaching 53 percent and 60 percent, respectively. Added to a dwindling job market and high unemployment, the result contributed to an increase in local crime.

A temporary truce between the Bloods and Crips, negotiated after the 1992 rioting, helped reduce street crime, but 50 percent of L.A.'s gang members were now Latino, and drugs and gun violence remained major problems. In fact, for a time guns surpassed auto accidents as the number-one killer of young people in California, and military-type weapons were common in criminal arsenals.

Crime, drugs and gang violence infiltrated a lively and influential new form of music. Hip-hop culture can be traced to the 1970s, but it found a national audience in the 1980s and '90s. Along with distinct fashions, art and dance styles, rap music was another African American contribution to American culture. Lyrics were personal, outspoken and sometimes playful, but also often hostile and violent. While rap first surfaced in New York's South Bronx, by the 1990s, it was well established in Los Angeles, especially in Compton, a mostly black community south of downtown. A dominant local style was gangsta rap. With an aggressive attitude and violent imagery, gangsta rap reflected and embraced gang culture.

One of the first Compton rap groups to make it big was N.W.A. (Niggaz With Attitude). N.W.A.'s 1988 album, *Straight Outta Compton,* was raw, tough-talking social commentary set to a relentless beat. In 1991, Death Row

Records was founded by rapper Dr. Dre and Marion "Suge" Knight, a 6'3" ex-football player and Bloods gang member. Death Row was home to the biggest West Coast rappers, including Snoop Dogg and Tupac Shakur.

New York and Los Angeles loyalists had traded barbs for most of the twentieth century, so it was no surprise when an East Coast–West Coast rap rivalry emerged. In a business awash in money and drugs, it was only a matter of time before the creative and financial duel between East and West turned deadly.

It began in 1994 after the Soul Train Awards, a celebration of contemporary black music. Outside a Wilshire Boulevard club, local gang members and the entourages of Sean "Puffy" Combs, head of New York's Bad Boy Records, and Death Row's Suge Knight, got into a fight. When it was over, one man had been beaten to death. Two years later in Las Vegas the violence escalated. After a scuffle outside the MGM Grand Hotel, West Coast rapper Tupac Shakur was shot and killed. There were rumors that the killings had

"BIGGIE" AND TUPAC. The lives of hip-hop artists Notorious B.I.G, left, and Tupac Shakur are remembered for their hard-edged artistry and violent deaths. B.I.G. was gunned down near the corner of Wilshire and Fairfax boulevards in 1997; Shakur in Las Vegas in 1996.

been a $1 million hit ordered by the godfather of East Coast rap, Christopher Wallace, a.k.a. Notorious B.I.G., and executed by the Southside Crips. Despite the allegations, which were never confirmed, the crime remained unsolved when no one claimed to have seen the shooter.

In March 1997, rappers and their entourages from both coasts gathered again for the Soul Train Music Awards. Following an after-party held at the Petersen Automotive Museum on Wilshire Boulevard, Puffy Combs and Notorious B.I.G. were in a black sedan when a dark Impala pulled up beside them. The driver aimed a 9mm handgun and opened fire. B.I.G. was hit several times and died a short time later. Police suspected that the murder was retaliation for the death of Tupac Shakur. There was even talk that corrupt L.A. cops were somehow involved, but as late as 2006, the case remained unsolved.

The killings of Tupac Shakur and Notorious B.I.G. made headlines, but nothing compared to the murders discovered at a Brentwood condo complex on the morning of June 13, 1994. At 12:10 a.m. a barking white Akita, his fur and paws smeared with blood, led a neighbor to a secluded pathway. Barely visible in the shadows were the brutally slashed bodies of Ronald Goldman and Nicole Brown. Nicole was the former wife of USC Heisman Trophy winner, pro-football great and media person-ality Orenthal James Simpson—better known as O. J. Goldman was a waiter at a nearby restaurant. Unaware of what had happened, Nicole and O. J.'s two children were upstairs in the condo, asleep.

When police learned that Simpson had left Los Angeles for Chicago only a short time before the bodies were discovered, they called him back for questioning. Already, there was possible evidence to link the former football star to the murders: blood drops were found on the door of his white Bronco SUV, and on the driveway leading to his gated Brentwood home.

O. J. Simpson had married Nicole Brown in 1985, a union bound to attract attention in race-conscious America. O. J. was a handsome and successful African American, and Brown was the lithe image of a Southern California blond. The couple had two children, a son and a daughter, but the marriage was no Hollywood romance. In 1989, Nicole accused her husband of battery. Simpson pleaded no contest. In 1992, new accusations of physical abuse led to divorce. Two years later, O. J. Simpson was arrested and charged with the murders of his former wife and Ronald Goldman.

Mixing race, sex and celebrity, the case promised to be another L.A. "Trial of the Century," but no one could have predicted the live TV drama that played out on Friday June 17, after Simpson failed to surrender to police as promised. Missing for eight hours, he was finally traced to his white Bronco, heading in the direction of Mexico with his former teammate and long-time friend, Al Cowling, at the wheel. A swarm of TV news helicopters joined the slow-speed pursuit as millions of Americans watched with suspense and disbelief. There was a report that O. J. was suicidal and holding a gun to his head. Finally, Cowling pulled the Bronco into the driveway of his friend's Brentwood estate and Simpson surrendered to police.

The trial began in downtown Los Angeles on January 24, 1995. With live television coverage from the courtroom, for nearly nine months the proceedings were followed with the obsessive fascination usually reserved for a skillfully produced soap opera. As many as 90 percent of Americans watched the trial unfold, all-news CNN and "narrowcasting" cable station Court TV thrived, and obscure reporters were set on the road to stardom.

Much of the prosecution's case turned on detailed DNA evidence police believed linked Simpson to the victims and the crime scene. Facing a jury consisting of nine African Americans, one Latino and two whites, the defense argued that the police

O. J. SIMPSON TRIAL. In another L.A. "trial of the century," Simpson confidently shows jurors that a bloody glove found at the scene of the murders of his former wife, Nicole, and her friend Ron Goldman doesn't fit.

case was essentially a frame-up, built on mishandled or even planted evidence. In response, the prosecution piled detail upon detail, but it seemed to have little effect. At one point, flamboyant defense attorney Johnnie Cochran asked his client to try on blood-stained gloves, one discovered at Simpson's home, the other at the murder scene. After the former football player struggled and failed, Cochran announced triumphantly, "If it doesn't fit, you must acquit!" On October 2, 1995, the jury agreed. O. J. Simpson was declared innocent. Years later, an African American barber from South Los Angeles offered a cynical summation: "The police framed a guilty man."

During the Simpson case, Los Angeles was serving again as a provocative social and political laboratory. American attitudes about race, criminal justice, and the role of media and celebrity were exposed and tested. Although there was no rioting in white middle-class L.A., in a way the Simpson verdict was a mirror image of the first Rodney King trial four years before. Like two of the accused police officers in the King case, Simpson was later found guilty in a civil suit. In that case, a mostly white jury awarded the families of Nicole Brown and Ronald Goldman $8.5 million, to come from liquidation of the former football star's assets. In the end, the families never received the full judgment, and Simpson gained custody of his two children and retired to Florida.

In the world of sports, where O. J. Simpson had once been a hero, the '90s represented another kind of mixed legacy. By 1995, Angelenos were left without a

professional football team. The Rams played their last game on December 24, 1994, and the Raiders announced their return to Oakland six months later. In 1997, however, a new fan base was born when women's pro basketball came to town with the Los Angeles Sparks, featuring local high school and U.S. Olympics star Lisa Leslie.

Five years before, L.A.'s Latino community celebrated another local hero—132-pound boxer Oscar "Golden Boy" de la Hoya. After winning the middleweight gold medal at the 1992 Barcelona Olympics, de la Hoya turned professional and became the first fighter in history to hold world titles in six different weight divisions. His later career was marred by scandal and controversy, but he added successes in entertainment and real estate to his record outside the ring.

OSCAR DE LA HOYA. A product of L.A.'s Latino Eastside, middleweight boxer de la Hoya was a 1992 Olympic gold medalist who went on to win world championships in six different weight divisions.

LISA LESLIE. In high school, Leslie once scored 101 points before the opposition gave up at half-time. She set scoring and rebounding records at USC and won three Olympic gold medals with the U.S. women's basketball teams. In 1996, she signed with the new Los Angeles Sparks of the WNBA.

Born in the East L.A. community of Montebello, de la Hoya was the latest in a series of local boxing heroes. Not all were champions, but their two-fisted careers were a source of pride and inspiration, especially when the Latino community had little else to cheer about.

In baseball, the '90s wasn't a championship decade. Gene Autry transferred operating control of the Angels to the Walt Disney Company in 1995, and the team moved into a new $117 million home, Edison International Field, in 1998. Amenities were lavish, includ-

ing $2.50 peanut butter and jelly sandwiches for the kids and a 27 percent increase in ticket prices for the adults. To some it was fresh evidence that American professional sports were more about money than athletics. When the Angels finally won their first World Series in 2002, Gene Autry, their first and perhaps most ardent fan, wasn't there to celebrate. He had died in 1998, at age ninety-one. In 2003, the Angels changed the record books in a different way when Arizona billboard billionaire Arte Moreno bought the team for $184 million, becoming the first Latino with controlling interest in a major league sports team. In 2005, Moreno stirred up heated territorial passions when he renamed his team the Los Angeles Angels of Anaheim, mixing two geographical heritages. Who said Southern Californians are indifferent to tradition?

As for the Dodgers, the '90s was the first decade since the 1930s that the team didn't make a World Series appearance. But "Dodger Blue" reflected the internationalization of the sport when it signed Korean pitcher Chan Ho Park in 1994 and Japanese right-hander Hideo Nomo a year later. Finally, in 1998, a half-century-long tradition ended when the O'Malley family, who'd brought the team to Los Angeles from Brooklyn in the 1950s, sold the franchise to the FOX Group,

SHAQ ATTACK. At 7'11" and 325 pounds, Shaquille O'Neal was the formidable anchor of the L.A. Lakers between 1996 and 2004. His arrival spurred the team to three straight NBA titles. O'Neal was chosen MVP each time.

owned by seemingly omnipresent media mogul Rupert Murdoch.

In professional basketball the Lakers entered the decade slowly. In 1991, the team said good-bye to Magic Johnson, who resigned after being diagnosed HIV-positive. The 6'9" superstar went on to play on the 1992 U.S. Olympic "Dream Team" and then launched a second career as a philanthropist, entrepreneur and real estate developer. By 1999, the Lakers were back on top. Under coach and former player Phil Jackson, with Shaquille O'Neal and Kobe Bryant leading the way, the team went on to win three consecutive NBA championships. Afterward though, dissention and Shaq's departure to the Miami Heat left the Lakers in a rebuilding mode. Coach Jackson returned from retirement to start the process.

In 1996, Wayne Gretzky decided to leave the L.A. Kings, but not before the franchise had its best season yet, advancing to the 1992 Stanley Cup Finals where they lost to the Montreal Canadiens. Shortly afterward,

KOBE BRYANT. Joining the Lakers at age eighteen, Bryant, center, became the youngest player chosen as an NBA All-Star starter. During his sometimes-contentious relationship with teammate Shaquille O'Neal, lower left, Kobe was the Lakers' scoring leader.

Southern California hockey fans had another team to root for with the arrival of the Mighty Ducks of Anaheim in 1993. Owned by the Walt Disney Company, their new arena was appropriately nicknamed "the Pond."

Sports reflected an increasing consolidation of the worlds of communications and entertainment. The '90s was the decade of the World Wide Web. Warner Bros., a Hollywood mainstay since the 1920s, was swallowed by Time Inc., creating Time-Warner, which in turn was gulped by Internet upstart AOL—a merger that looked good on paper but proved awkward in execution. Even after the "dot-com" bubble burst in 2000–2001, the influence of new technology on entertainment remained evident in such movie visual-effects-driven hits as the *The Matrix* and *Titanic*.

Increasingly, producing a blockbuster Hollywood movie was more like designing a computer program than writing a novel or producing a play. At the same time, profits from the new realm of video games easily eclipsed traditional box-office sales. With proximity to the skill and creativity of the local film community, Los Angeles was a major

TITANIC, directed by James Cameron in 1997, was a combination of full-blown Hollywood romance and new technology.

THE MATRIX. Keanu Reeves takes a gravity-defying ride in the first *Matrix* film, a 1999 visual-effects tour de force, as computer technology continued to transform, and some say, overwhelm movie storytelling.

FIESTA BROADWAY. In celebration of Cinco de Mayo, a Mexican holiday more celebrated in the United States than in Mexico, downtown Los Angeles is home to the largest Latino celebration in the nation.

player in this new entertainment industry, but access to a computer and the Internet could make physical location irrelevant. International projects, such as the immensely successful *The Lord of the Rings* trilogy, maintained links to Hollywood, while much of the actual work was accomplished in other countries where labor and production costs were less.

During the the '90s, more changes in the entertainment world were as close as a car radio. America witnessed an explosion of Latin music, and as before, Los Angeles provided advance notice. In 1990, L.A.'s favorite Eastside rockers, Los Lobos, were honored with a Grammy. On Sunday May 1, 1994, the city celebrated Cinco de Mayo with the fifth-annual Fiesta Broadway. Attracting an audience of 500,000, the Fiesta was the largest Latin event yet in U.S. history. Local radio also exemplified changing demographics. Beginning in 1992, for six straight years one of three Spanish-language radio stations claimed the number-one spot in L.A. listener ratings. It was an era of *rock en español*. Unlike the East L.A. Chicano rockers of the

LOS LOBOS, a band from L.A.'s mostly Latino Eastside, produced music that expressed a changing America, blending traditional Mexican music and North American rock 'n' roll.

'60s and '70s, *rock en español* artists sang in Spanish to a mostly immigrant audience from the Caribbean and Central and South America, as well as Mexican Americans. Recognizing this, a separate Latin Grammy Awards ceremony was initiated in 2000.

During the '90s, while Los Angeles was battered by natural and man-made disasters, through it all, positive changes also were underway. Perhaps the most unlikely was a re-emergence of mass transit. In the 1970s, Mayor Tom Bradley promised the city a subway and light-rail system. Despite opponents and doubters, the first light-rail trains went into service on July 14, 1990, with the inauguration of the Blue Line, connecting downtown L.A. and Long Beach. Ironically, the new trains followed the route of the old Pacific Electric trains, abandoned in 1961.

In October 1992, Southern California got its first heavy-rail commuter line, Metrolink. By 2003, tracks ran east from Union Station to San Bernardino and Riverside, north to Lancaster, south to Oceanside, and west as far as Montalvo in Ventura County. In January 1993, L.A. opened the first four-mile leg of a subway. Featuring individually designed stations with playful public art, new subway, light-rail and high-speed bus systems were ambitious, expensive and controversial. Critics pointed to mismanagement and budget overruns,

BLUE LINE OPENING. On July 14, 1990, the MTA's twenty-two-mile-long light rail between downtown Los Angeles and Long Beach is inaugurated.

GATEWAY CENTER. *City of Dreams/Rivers of History,* an eighty-foot-wide mural and mosaic floor at the MTA Gateway Center, was created by Los Angeles artist Richard Wyatt Jr. It celebrates L.A.'s earliest settlers and the city's multicultural heritage.

MAYOR BRADLEY CELEBRATES THE OPENING OF THE RED LINE, the beginning of a modern subway system for Los Angeles.

THE RED LINE SUBWAY. In 1997, one of two giant drilling machines, nicknamed Thelma and Louise, met to complete the subway tunnel beneath Hollywood Hills.

HOLLYWOOD-HIGHLAND SUBWAY STATION. L.A.'s new transit stations were designed as collaborations between artists and architects. Here, artist Sheila Klein and architects Dworsky Associates claimed inspiration from the movies of Busby Berkeley.

exacerbated when a section of subway tunnel in East Hollywood collapsed during construction. And they asked the obvious question: "Would Angelenos ever abandon their cars?" Mass-transit advocates responded that light rail and the subway were meant to offer long-overdue and essential alternatives. When the Century, or 105, Freeway opened in October 1993, after thirty years and $2.2 billion, it was widely believed to be L.A.'s last.

Recognizing this, some city planners were turning to history to prepare for a twenty-first-century future. Just as trains had allowed the city to connect separated communities in the 1910s and '20s, new plans encouraged the creation of urban "nodes" around transit stations, to bring housing, work and shopping closer together. At the same time, during the first years of the twenty-first century, another unexpected phenomenon promised to reshape the city. Older, long-underutilized commercial buildings were being converted to condominiums and loft apartments. If the trend continued, the future of L.A. would be transformed by a return to a more urban density. Reaching back in time even further, there was the beginning of an ambitious effort to reclaim the Los Angeles River as a natural amenity with the establishment of a "return to nature" policy in some sections, and ambitious plans for riverside walkways and parks.

The vast scale and ever-shifting demographics of Los Angeles had long frustrated attempts to create the same sense of community found in traditional cities such as New York and Chicago. As a result, by the twenty-first century some Angelenos were thinking the unthinkable. Community activists in Hollywood, San Pedro and the San Fernando Valley were considering secession. If the Valley alone were to win independence from Los Angeles, it would overnight become America's sixth most populous city. In addition, the harbor at San Pedro was a major source of revenue, and Hollywood was an international tourist draw. Together, their loss would reduce the size of the City of Los Angeles by a third. "Bigger is better," an L.A. mantra for more than two hundred years, faced a growing challenge.

Partly in response to this, the seventy-five-year-old city charter received a substantial rewrite. A major accomplishment of the Riordan administration, the changes were approved by voters in 1999. The power of the mayor was increased, and community-based neighborhood councils were established to help represent local issues and concerns. Many considered these as steps in the right direction, but secession activists in Hollywood and the Valley persisted, bringing their breakaway plans to a citywide vote in November

UNIVERSAL CITY WALK. Opening shortly after the 1992 riots, Universal Studios City Walk became a place in L.A. where tourists and Angelenos of all ethnicities seemed comfortable together.

HOLLYWOOD AND HIGHLAND COMPLEX. With a central court inspired by the set for D. W. Griffith's 1916 film, *Intolerance,* the shopping complex at Hollywood and Highland was one of the first projects to launch a rebirth of Hollywood after decades of decline.

2002. Although they were defeated, it was clear that Los Angeles needed to reevaluate its structural identity in order to create a more coherent and effective future.

While New Yorkers and Chicagoans, with all their diversity, claimed a clearly defined urban identity, Angelenos seemed to prefer a more dispersed and private perspective. L.A.'s public face often appeared to be haphazard, driven more by real estate economics than urban pride. During the 1990s and early twenty-first century, that attitude seemed to change. After years of wishful thinking and booster hype, Los Angeles

began to show signs of giving more thought to civic architecture and public places, behaving more like the "world class" city it often claimed to be.

As an example, car-culture L.A. rediscovered the pleasures of a leisurely stroll. Old Town Pasadena, a neglected neighborhood known for sex shops and seedy bars during the 1960s and '70s, was reborn as an upscale and family-friendly haven for pedestrians. So were the Venice Boardwalk and Santa Monica Promenade.

In 1993, Universal City opened City Walk. An outdoor entertainment environment originally intended to appeal to tourists, City Walk was quickly adopted by locals as well. The same could be said about the Grove, a cleverly synthetic shopping "village" concocted in 2002 beside the venerable Farmers Market. Even Hollywood Boulevard began reversing a long decline since the 1950s, offering tourists, the late-night club set and even local residents more than the imbedded stars on the Hollywood Walk of Fame. After decades of sprawl, the talk was of returning to old L.A. neighborhoods instead of fleeing from them.

Along with a more intimate L.A., new architectural and cultural landmarks were expressing greater sophistication and urban pride. In 1993, the newly expanded downtown Central Library opened. Preserving the scale and structure of Bertram Goodhue's original 1926 Moorish design, it appended a dramatic new space that extended down instead of up. In the years that followed, imaginatively designed branch libraries also appeared.

After decades with little construction, new schools were rising in local neighborhoods, many with notable architectural appeal. One

THE GROVE. Next to the venerable Farmers Market and the nineteenth-century Gilmore adobe, the Grove features an old-fashioned trolley and prepackaged town square.

THE CENTRAL LIBRARY received a dramatic new addition in 1993, named the Tom Bradley Wing. Large, whimsical chandeliers designed by Thermon Statom hang over escalators connecting five floors that reach down instead of up.

in 2006, not without controversy, replaced the historic 1921 Ambassador Hotel, home of the Cocoanut Grove and the site where Robert Kennedy was assassinated. Preservationists resisted, but the Kennedy family and many Angelenos believed that a new school was a more appropriate memorial than attempting to save and adapt the long-abandoned hotel. A superior court judge agreed.

By the end of the 1990s, the Los Angeles area remained a major center of international trade. The side-by-side container ports at San Pedro and Long Beach were the third busiest in the world, providing a gateway for 40 percent of U.S. imports and exports.

In 1997, L.A. also claimed a prominent place in the world of international art with the completion of the massive $1 billion Getty Center. Commanding panoramic views from 110 acres of a Brentwood hilltop, the new complex was an instant and imposing landmark. Designed by New York–based architect Richard Meier, and named for J. Paul Getty, whose fortune was in part a product of Southern California's oil boom during the 1920s, the new center included museum galleries and institutes for art conservation and research. Since 1974, a second Getty museum, containing 50,000 Greek and Roman antiquities, had been housed in a re-created Roman Villa overlooking the ocean at Malibu. It was refurbished and reopened in 2006. Seven years before, expressing another kind of community pride, the striking new Japanese American National Museum opened in Little Tokyo.

As an entertaining antidote to the problems plaguing L.A. in the 1990s, the $375

THE PORT OF LOS ANGELES, part of the busiest harbor complex in the United States, includes Pier 400, one of the world's largest container facilities. The port handles more than $140 billion a year in trade.

THE GETTY CENTER encourages Angelenos and visitors to explore the arts and enjoy matchless views of the city.

million Staples Center premiered in 1999, offering a new home for the Lakers, Clippers, Kings and Sparks. A multimedia temple for the worship of commercialized sports, it also was a magnet for further development downtown, including the $1.7 billion "L.A. Live" sports-entertainment hub. To the north, the old urban core also received new architectural landmarks. In 2002, America's largest Catholic Archdiocese consecrated a nearly $190 million cathedral designed by Spanish architect José Rafael Moneo. After preservationist protests and a reuse compromise, it replaced the earthquake-damaged St. Vibiana's, built in 1876. While some argued that the church could have spent the money in more pastoral ways, the cathedral was an impressive addition to L.A.'s evolving public image.

STAPLES CENTER. A statue of Erwin "Magic" Johnson stands in front the media-driven sports and entertainment center.

THE CATHEDRAL OF OUR LADY OF THE ANGELS. Completed in 2002, the cathedral was designed by Pritzker Prize—winning Spanish architect José Rafael Moneo. Traditionally, European cathedrals were constructed near rivers. Our Lady of The Angels stands beside the 101 Freeway, which Moneo called L.A.'s "river of transportation."

THE CALTRANS DISTRICT 7 HEADQUARTERS represents a renaissance of provocative architecture in downtown Los Angeles. Designed by Pritzker Prize—winner Thom Mayne of Morphosis in Santa Monica, the building has impressed most architecture critics. Less enthusiastic observers nicknamed it "The Death Star."

In 2003, only one block away, another international cultural and architectural landmark was added to L.A.'s changing portrait. It had been a financial struggle to realize the blossoming shapes of stainless steel that gave form to the new $274 million Walt Disney Concert Hall, designed by iconoclastic L.A. architect Frank Gehry. The end result—inside and out—was declared a triumph. Envisioned as a world-class home for the Los Angeles Philharmonic, led by dynamic young Finnish conductor Esa-Pekka Salonen, the project was initiated with a $50 million gift from Lillian Disney, Walt's widow. Despite this, it took a last-minute fundraising campaign, spurred by billionaire businessman/philanthropist Eli Broad, to save Gehry's vision and L.A.'s pride. In 2005, Broad also initiated a major reimagining of the Los Angeles County Museum of Art by Italian architect Renzo Piano.

At midpoint in the first decade of the twenty-first century, even as outlying counties and communities continued to grow, an

WALT DISNEY CONCERT HALL. Santa Monica architect Frank Gehry envisioned the interior as a "living room" for Los Angeles. A twenty-first-century landmark for L.A., it is one of the most famous new buildings in the world.

ESA-PEKKA SALONEN. In 1991, the thirty-three-year-old Finnish-born conductor and composer became the tenth music director of the Los Angeles Philharmonic. A new concert hall was part of the signing package.

extensive cityscape first defined by Red Cars then expanded by freeways, was being "infilled" as a suburban dream adopted urban forms. As urban "nodes" were taking root, there were plans for an ambitious $1.8 billion downtown development complex, promising to provide Los Angeles with a dramatically renewed city center.

If Los Angeles was becoming truly a world-class city, the world was closer than ever. The September 11, 2001, terrorist attacks on the East Coast may have been thousands of miles from Los Angeles, but modern communications brought them as near as a TV screen. And an earlier foiled scheme to bomb Los Angeles International Airport was a reminder that L.A. wasn't immune from possible terrorism.

Since its infancy, Los Angeles had attracted stereotypes as easily as new arrivals—a city defined from afar. Now the old clichés were falling away. The City of Angels seemed to be proclaiming its own identity. In the process, the city was revisiting its past. As it was in 1850, the latest picture of

California—and especially Los Angeles—was international as well as local. In May 2005, the citizens of Los Angeles elected Antonio Villaraigosa the first Mexican American mayor since 1872. Villaraigosa had risen from L.A.'s Boyle Heights barrio to attend UCLA and become Speaker of the California State Assembly. His victory was a resounding affirmation of growing Latino political influence in Los Angeles and across the United States.

After more than two centuries, many of the challenges for Los Angeles remained the same, including a widening gap between rich and poor, the anxious equation of population growth, environmental quality, and limited resources, especially water. And

ANTONIO VILLARAIGOSA, right. A former speaker of the California state senate, Villaraigosa was elected mayor of Los Angeles in 2005, the first Latino to hold the office since 1872.

JAPANESE AMERICAN VETERANS of the WWII 442nd Regimental Combat Team, the most decorated unit in the United States, participate in the 2005 Nisei Week Parade in Los Angeles's Little Tokyo.

A JAPANESE AMERICAN ANGELENA prepares her traditionally dressed young daughter for the sixty-fifth annual Nisei Week Parade.

SISTER CITIES. L.A.'s status as an international capital is represented by the city's many sister cities. The first, in 1959, was Nagoya, Japan. By 2006, there were twenty-one from six continents.

DOWNTOWN LIVING. Long-ignored office buildings were being recycled into often-pricey loft apartments and condos.

KALEIDOSCOPIC L.A. is suggested by the scrambled letters on this downtown Broadway Street theater marquee, an accidental reminder of L.A.'s long reputation as a home for the off-beat and unexpected.

THE *CALLE DE LA ETERNIDAD* (Street of Eternity), a sixty-four-foot-tall acrylic mural, was painted by Filipino American artist Johanna Poethig and assistants between 1992 and 1993. It overlooks South Broadway Street in downtown L.A.

MARINA DEL REY first opened in 1965, offering an ideal environment for a relaxed and affluent life in sunny Southern California.

VENICE CANALS. Of the original canals dating from the early 1900s, thirty-three were filled after the 1930s. Thanks to preservation and local real estate interests, the remaining six were restored in the 1990s, turning this unique L.A. neighborhood into one of the city's most diverse and stylish communities.

LOS ANGELES ZOO. A new entrance completed in 2005 welcomes visitors to the L.A. Zoo. The city's first menagerie dates to 1885. It moved to Griffith Park in 1912, and was completely rebuilt in 1966.

BEVERLY HILLS' RODEO DRIVE is known for its celebrity clientele and high-end shopping. Even a greater number of less-affluent visitors also enjoy ogling the glitzy storefronts.

somewhere ahead was the inevitability of "the Big One"—the earthquake that could be the city's most terrifying test.

In many ways modern Los Angeles is a product of twentieth-century technology—a self-realized city that used modern tools to will itself into being. The process tamed and remade—some said mangled—the natural environment. Now there was talk of applying twenty-first-century technology to the task of undoing past damage and reclaiming what was lost, like the long-ignored L.A. River. To some that's a crazy, impossible dream, but the best of L.A. often came from outlandish fantasies.

No matter what happens, the future of Los Angeles will depend on creative and effective leadership, something that has often seemed in short supply. Would the old guard, and with them, millions of mostly Anglo citizens resist change, adapt to a new balance of power, or simply move away? Would burgeoning populations from Latin America, Asia and elsewhere produce leaders with the commitment, ingenuity and sometimes ruthless ambition shown by L.A.'s mostly white American

THE CASCADES that first delivered water from the Owens Valley in 1913 still flows. By the twenty-first century, most of L.A.'s water came from the San Joaquin Delta southeast of San Francisco Bay. If growth continues, managing resources will be critical to the city's survival and success.

immigrants of the past? Whatever the case, if the City of Angels is to have a successful future, Angelenos themselves will have to care enough to create it. And as before, what happens in L.A. may well anticipate what happens in America as well.

What historian Kevin Starr wrote about California in his 2004 book, *Coast of Dreams,* seems even truer for Los Angeles: "No longer was California to be found first in its myth and then in reality. California had become, rather, a reality in search of a myth that had once been believed in, had been lost, but never fully repudiated."

If this is true, recalling past futures and reimagining L.A.'s old dreams can be more than an exercise in nostalgia, it can inspire a sense of the city to come. Picturing Los Angeles as it was becomes a contribution to the creation of an image of the city as it can be.

CITY AT NIGHT. Even L.A. critics can't help but be impressed by the carpet of lights seen from the air on a clear night, with the modern skyline jewel-like in the midst of it all.

PHOTO CREDITS

Los Angeles Public Library, Hollywood-Citizen News Collection: 147 right, 203 top, 205 center and bottom, 224 right, 225 right, 236 right, 237 center, 247 right

Los Angeles Public Library, Hollywood-Citizen News/Valley Times Collection: 188 top (Jon Woods), 191–92, 196 bottom, 242 right, 254 top

Los Angeles Public Library, Security Pacific Collection: 11, 20 top right, 22 top, 24 bottom, 26 right, 28 center, 29 top, 30 left, 42, 48, 50 top, 51 top, 51 bottom, 55 top, 58–59, 62–63, 65 top, 70 right, 71, 74, 80, 87 left, 89–90, 91 top, 92, 95 left, 96, 99, 101 left, 102 bottom left, 104 top left, 105 bottom, 107 top right, 109 bottom right, 110–11, 112 bottom left, top and bottom right, 115 top right, 116 top and bottom left, 129 bottom left, 130 left and top right, 132, 142–43, 148 left, 149–50, 151 (Dick Whittington), 152 left, 156 top left and right, 157, 159, 160 bottom (Harry Quillen), 161 left, 162 bottom, 164 top, 171 top right, 181 top, 188 bottom, 202 center, 205 top, 206, 208 bottom, 217 left, 217 right (William Reagh), 241 (Sal Castro), 245 top, 247 left, 287, 294–95 and 300 (Gary Leonard)

Los Angeles Public Library, Shades of L.A. Collection: 52 bottom left, 67, 85 right, 152 right, 154 left and center, 161 bottom, 165 center, 166 bottom, 204 top, 210 bottom

Courtesy of Los Angeles Zoo: 268 bottom

Courtesy of Meeno: 318 top

Courtesy of NASA: 237 bottom

Courtesy of NASA Dryden Flight Research Center Photo Collection: 269

Courtesy of NASA/JPL: 237 top

Courtesy of National Basketball Association: 253 bottom left, 278 bottom, 305–06

Richard Nixon Library: 210 top

Photofest: 168 top, 172 bottom, 202 top, 208 center, 211 bottom, 226 top, 248 left, 249–50, 256, 280, 281–82 right, 301, 304, 307

Courtesy of Port of Los Angeles: 22 bottom, 23 top, 26 left, 81 bottom, 101 right, 261, 273, 314

Courtesy of Wolfgang Puck: 275

Courtesy of Ramona Pageant Association: 107 bottom left

Courtesy of David Reyes: 240 left, 308 bottom

Courtesy of Ernie Reyes: 209

Courtesy of St. Vincent Medical Center Historical Conservancy: 20 top left, 88 left

Southern California Library for Social Studies & Research: 83 left

Courtesy of Tribune Broadcasting: 182 center and bottom, 183 top, 193 top, 201 left

University of Southern California Regional History Collection: 7 left, 14, 15 (second, third and fourth from left), 16–21, 23 bottom, 25 top and bottom, 27 left, 28 top and bottom, 29 center, 30 right, 31, 32 left, 33, 34 right, 35, 37, 39 bottom left and right, 40 top left and right, 43 top, 50 bottom, 51 center, 52 bottom right, 55 center and bottom, 56 top, 57, 60, 64, 66 right, 70 left, 72 left, 75, 78 top, 79 bottom, 86, 87 right, 95 left, 100, 105 top, 106, 107 top left, 108 top, 114 left, 116 right, 169 center, 190 bottom, 195 bottom left

Courtesy of USGS, Golden, Colorado: 298 top (James Dewey), 198 bottom (David Carver)

Courtesy of USGS, Menlo Park, California: 298 center (Michael Rymer)

Courtesy of Arthur Verge: 56 bottom, 136, 137 left, 185 center

Courtesy of Walt Disney Concert Hall: 291 (Federico Zignani)

Courtesy of the Welk Group: 207 bottom

Courtesy of Jon Wilkman, Wilkman Productions: 7 right, 12 left, 239–40 right, 260, 267 top, 268 top and center, 271 bottom right, 292 right, 309 bottom, 312–13, 315, 317 top, 318 center and bottom, 319–21

Courtesy of Wilkman Productions: 15 second from left, 46 right, 61, 81 top, 155 left, 156 top right, 156 bottom right, 173 bottom, 181 center, 189 left, 195 top left, 234 top, 236 left

Index